Language Policies in English-Dominant Countries

THE LANGUAGE AND EDUCATION LIBRARY

Series Editor
Professor David Corson, *The Ontario Institute for Studies in Education,
252 Bloor St West, Toronto, Ontario, Canada M5S 1V6*

Other Books in the Series

The Open University Readers

Please contact us for the latest book information:
Multilingual Matters Ltd, Frankfurt Lodge, Clevedon Hall
Victoria Road, Clevedon, Avon BS21 7SJ, England

THE LANGUAGE AND EDUCATION LIBRARY 10
Series Editor: Professor David J. Corson
The Ontario Institute for Studies in Education

Language Policies in English-Dominant Countries

Six Case Studies

Edited by

Michael Herriman and Barbara Burnaby

MULTILINGUAL MATTERS LTD
Clevedon • Philadelphia • Adelaide

Dedication

*This book is dedicated to all those persons struggling for the
revival and recognition of, or respect for, their mother tongue, and
to those educators, linguists and politicians who support their aims*

Library of Congress Cataloging in Publication Data

Language Policies in English-Dominant Countries: Six Case Studies
Edited by Michael Herriman and Barbara Burnaby
The Language and Education Library: 10
Includes bibliographical references and index
1. Language Policy–English-speaking countries. 2. English languages–Political
aspects. I. Herriman, M.L. (Michael L.). II. Burnaby, Barbara. III. Series.
P119.32.E54L36   1996
306.4'49–dc20   95-42291

British Library Cataloguing in Publication Data

A CIP catalogue record for this book is available from the British Library.

ISBN 1-85359-347-8 (hbk)
ISBN 1-85359-346-X (pbk)

Multilingual Matters Ltd

UK: Frankfurt Lodge, Clevedon Hall, Victoria Road, Clevedon, Avon BS21 7SJ.
USA: 1900 Frost Road, Suite 101, Bristol, PA 19007, USA.
Australia: P.O. Box 6025, 83 Gilles Street, Adelaide, SA 5000, Australia.

Typeset by Wayside Books, Clevedon.
Printed and bound in Great Britain by WBC Book Manufacturers Ltd.

Contents

Acknowledgements

The editors and authors wish to thank all those persons who helped in the preparation of the manuscript in all the critical tasks from copy-editing to critically reviewing the chapters. A special word of gratitude is due to Judith Rochecouste who worked on the manuscript as a whole and made sense out of confused symbols and formatting caused by the use of different computers and wordprocessing packages.

Notes on Contributors

Richard Benton is Honorary Lecturer in Linguistics at The Victoria University of Wellington. He graduated in History from the University of Auckland and completed his MA and PhD degrees in Linguistics at the University of Hawaii. Since 1972 he has headed the programme on Maori language and education of the New Zealand Council for Educational Research. He has conducted research and lectured on bilingual education, language policy, and the maintenance and revitalisation of indigenous and minority languages in New Zealand, the Pacific Islands, the Philippines, Ireland, Spain, Singapore, the United Kingdom and the United States, and has written extensively on these topics. He is also actively involved in researching and developing the potential of information technology in language revitalisation.

Barbara Burnaby is Chair of the Department of Adult Education at the Ontario Institute for Studies in Education. Her research areas include language in Aboriginal education (mostly in Canada) with a special interest in literacy in Canadian Aboriginal languages. As well she works in the field of English as a second language for adult immigrants to Canada and adult literacy. She has taught in Japan and done evaluation work in China.

Michael Byram was educated at a grammar school and then read Modern and Medieval Languages at King's College, Cambridge. After completing a PhD on Danish literature, he taught foreign languages in secondary education. Since 1980, he has worked in the School of Education, University of Durham, training teachers of French and German and researching in two areas, the education of linguistic minorities, and the cultural dimension of foreign language teaching.

Michael Fleming is Lecturer in English and Drama at the School of Education, University of Durham. He is Director of the Secondary Post Graduate Certificate in Education Course and is responsible for INSET and MA course in English and Drama for practising teachers. Before joining the University, he spent 15 years teaching in secondary schools.

Michael Herriman is Senior Lecturer in Education at the University of Western Australia and Director of the Centre for English as a Second Language in the University. He has undertaken several major research projects related to language issues in Australia and has been a member of state and commonwealth committees inquiring into language policy issues especially in ESL and foreign languages. He has published widely in the areas of literacy, language awareness and English language testing.

Thomas Ricento is Associate Professor in the Division of Bicultural–Bilingual Studies, The University of Texas at San Antonio. He received his PhD in Applied Linguistics from UCLA in 1987. He was a senior Fulbright Lecturer in Colombia, SA in 1989. He served as Director of English Language Programs at the Japan Center in Hikone, Japan from 1989–91, and has served as a consultant for ESP programmes in Mexico and the US. He has published articles and reviews in *TESOL Quarterly* and the *Journal of Pragmatics*, among other publications. He is co-editor of a special topic issue of *TESOL Quarterly* on Language Planning and Policy and the ELT profession to appear in 1996. Other research interests include written discourse analysis across languages, and genre analysis.

Stanley Ridge was born in Durban, South Africa, and studied at the Universities of Natal, York (England), British Columbia, and Stellenbosch. He taught at Kearsney College in Natal, and at the University of Stellenbosch before taking up the chair of English at the University of Western Cape. He has been Dean of Arts and is now Director of Development and Public Affairs for the University. Recent academic work has included participation in language committees of the National Education Policy Investigation, the reports from which have been published by Oxford University Press.

Linda Thompson has taught English to bilingual children in nursery and primary schools in the UK and to trainee teachers at Universities in Sweden and the Netherlands. She is currently Co-ordinator for the primary English Language and Literacy courses for teachers and Director for Research Degrees at Durham University, England. Research interests include the enculturation of bilingual children into mainstream schooling, and child language development.

1 Introduction

MICHAEL HERRIMAN and BARBARA BURNABY

This book presents descriptions and analyses of language policy in Britain, Canada, USA, New Zealand, Australia and South Africa. In these countries, English is the dominant language in terms of its social and political influence and (with the exception of South Africa) has the largest number of speakers. Except for Britain, all share a similar colonial heritage in which the English language was a prominent instrument in the colonising process. All involved conquest of indigenous populations and denial, suppression or neglect of the languages spoken by them in favour of English. The governing systems in these countries are also similar, being based on the Westminster system. Though USA and South Africa are now republics and completely separated from Britain, the others have ties of an affiliational or legal kind. The significant point is that their histories are not dissimilar, nor is their current situation inasmuch as each has, in the past and present, experienced waves of immigration and, as a part of this, a resurgence of claims for language recognition and related rights by recent immigrants, by their original indigenous peoples and by other language and ethnic groups which represent significant proportions of their populations. For this reason it is interesting to compare responses to the language demands generated by recent cultural and political changes they have undergone. In most cases governments have responded to these demands with policies on languages, as well as on political, social and welfare rights, which implicate language.

In this introduction, we first outline the purpose of the book. In several sections that follow, central concepts relating to language policy are discussed to orient the reader to the scope and focus of each concept for the purposes of the book. Thus, policy, language, reasons for language policy, and places where policies are situated are all considered. Next, we make some general observations on central themes. Finally, we describe the structure of the rest of the volume.

1

The Purpose of This Book

Our intention in collecting the material for this book was to provide contemporary data on language policies in some of the world's largest and most powerful countries. During the second half of this century, English has consolidated its power as the major lingua franca in the world at least for business, science, communications and technology, and for other purposes as well. It has had a strong impact on many countries where relatively few inhabitants are of British descent, not only in former British colonies for historic reasons but also, increasingly, elsewhere for economic reasons. But how does English operate within large countries where English is the dominant language, where people of Anglo-Saxon or Celtic descent form a large proportion of the population (South Africa excepted), and where the culture of these people has controlled the culture of political and social relations (only until recently, we hope, in the case of South Africa)? How is the power of English within these countries played out in terms of official status of the language and in internal relations with groups and individuals who use other languages? What aspects of personal and civic life come into focus, and what systems in society are identified as parts of any problems and/or solutions that develop?

The data described in this book can be useful as source material for those scholars and students interested in language status issues in any one of the countries or in comparative language policy. Those of us who work in such fields in our respective countries often despair of getting a comprehensive picture of language policies even within our own countries. As the chapters in this book clearly indicate, language policy in large modern states is almost inevitably complex, mostly contestable and involves various issues and solutions at many levels of government and in many regions. Therefore, these overviews are intended, at one level, to supply information to readers about their own domestic situation. However, the point of collecting these chapters into one book is to provide interested parties with the opportunity to look beyond their own situations, to see if their issues have parallels elsewhere, and to learn of other ways of handling issues. If it is difficult to get a clear idea of one's local situation, it is even more challenging to get comparable information from elsewhere. Finally, in putting these descriptions together it is intended to facilitate not only readers' understanding of and means of improvement of language policies in their respective countries, particularly where that concerns planning issues in relation to language in education, but also their access to comparable information for the creation of new theory about the operation of languages in their social and political contexts.

Perspectives on Policy

The concept of policy is in itself difficult. For a start, the term 'policy' is not monolithic nor has it a clear denotation. By using the term there is a danger of assuming that we are talking about one thing or kind, or that each of the countries considered below has developed a set of pronouncements that have at least a similar status. The fact is that the kind or form of policy in each country is sufficiently different as to make one question the appropriateness of the term 'policy' itself. 'Policy' therefore seems to have a range of referents. Though originally more associated with the notion of prudent conduct or practices, it has come to have the connotation of a principled *policy* approach or plan in some matter affecting public or individual interest. This captures the distinction between policy that has some basis in precedents for plans or actions undertaken by governments or civil associations (or is in accord with established practices or even laws) and policy that is decided on a whim or on the basis of confrontation with a single, one-time problem (often called policy-on-the-run). Some reluctance to think of the latter kind as 'policy' seems to come from the lack of consistency or appeal to established ways of doing things whereas 'policy' suggests at least a planned course of action. The notion of consistency is important because, in situations where there is no enunciated policy on a matter of some kind, there is an implicit recognition that the way things are done is indeed a policy, in the absence of competing or consistently applied alternatives. For example, it will be seen that language policy in Britain is of the unstated kind and in this respect is consistent with the constitution which is based on precedent rather than statute. From the perspective of the context of a policy then, one might understand it as either being deliberate and planned, the result of crisis management, or not a consequence of planning but rather of accepting things as they are.

From the perspective of this book, it is appropriate that a broad range of principles and plans, along with their effects, is discussed. The range includes statutes at various levels of government, government promulgated statements that imply bureaucratic action or support, and regular action taken by smaller institutions (especially schools) or by less formally constituted groups in the community. Most of these are consciously planned with some degree of effort at integration with policies at higher levels, but some are not. Some are stated and deliberately implemented while others are tacit or even disguised in the actions of government, employers, business, the media, and community groups. For our purposes, the latter are not the less policies for being unarticulated, although they are harder to identify.

To the extent that policies are deliberately and consciously created, they usually involve some form of planning. Language planning has been described by Weinstein (1980) as '. . . a government authorised, long term, sustained and conscious effort to alter a language function in society for the purpose of solving communication problems'. Policy and planning with respect to language falls generally into two areas called corpus planning and status planning, terms originally used by Kloss (1969). Status planning involves decisions which affect the relative status of one or more languages in respect of that of others. An obvious status planning issue would be a declaration of a language as an official one, such as was the case with French in Canada in The Official Languages Act (1969).

An interesting contemporary aspect of status planning, which is seen in this volume, is the focus it has given to planning issues as they involve language in the classroom and language in education. This focus not only comes from the now-obvious fact that, in any multilingual or multi-dialectal country, decisions are needed on the language or dialect of instruction and on other languages to be taught. This is a contestable and hotly debated area. It also betrays a more subtle aspect of language, this being its implicit connection to educational theories, values and goals. At a practical level, an education through a given language will normally mean that that language is acquired in addition to the language spoken in the home. That is, the language of instruction will become a major linguistic resource of the person or even the dominant one, as often it will supplant the home language, at least outside of the immediate home or community. This process has often brought about the decline of community and indigenous languages more effectively than any form of deliberate linguistic proscription would have. The issue of language in education gives support to Cooper's (1989) claim for a third aspect of language planning to be called acquisition planning. By planning a role for a language in education, one is planning for its acquisition and its place and status in society.

Hence the reader will find that the principal arena of language status policy and planning in the countries covered in this book is the educational one. This may support a general claim that the most effective means of changing the status of any language is to involve it in changes implemented within education, either as a practice or a policy. In this case education refers not only to school education, but also to adult and continuing education (including programmes for adult literacy). Changes to status will occur in these cases not only as a result of competition for funding, but perhaps more because a declaration in favour of a particular language will mean that it is *ipso facto* seen as more valued. This serves to emphasise Cobarrubias's (1983) claim that issues of status planning are not ethically neutral.

By contrast with status planning, the issue of corpus planning is not as politically or ethically contentious. Corpus planning concerns the development and regulation of the forms of the language itself. In virtually all societies with many speakers of a given language, there is a massive amount of corpus definition occurring by means of the publication of dictionaries and style manuals, school curricula, standards for broadcasting, and the like. In the following chapters, corpus work in English is not mentioned (although it represents a huge industry), but some mention is made of explicit and planned corpus work for other languages. For example, the development of French as it is spoken and written in Canada has received support in government, the academy, business and the arts since the heightening of attention to the French presence three decades ago. Also, indigenous languages in a number of the countries described below have been supported in developing and describing the forms of the languages. However, when asked to write about language policies in their countries, the authors in this book wrote almost exclusively about status planning, that is, about the ways in which societies recognise, accept, and sanction the use of languages in their communities and institutions as opposed to the forms those languages take. Thus readers interested in corpus planning will have to resort to other sources.

Perspectives on Language

The unifying factor in the studies in this book is the English language. However, because it is so dominant in all the countries, it is the unmarked case. Thus, the authors devote most of their discussion to the relationships of other languages to English. In effect, there are at least three groups of languages, other than English, that are considered in this volume. One group is the indigenous languages whose speakers were in the respective countries before English 'arrived' and gained the ascendancy. These include Welsh and Gaelic in Great Britain, the Amerindian languages and Inuktitut in the USA and Canada, Maori in New Zealand, the Aboriginal and Torres Strait Islands languages in Australia, and the indigenous languages of South Africa. On the whole, they have been largely ignored or repressed over several centuries, but, in the past few decades, have gained political visibility and some measure of support by policy. Yet this is ironic because, except in South Africa, most of these languages are greatly endangered on account of previous policies and practices and the effects of English as the language of power. Some have become extinct. Happily, the South African case is different and the major groups of indigenous languages, which are numerically superior in the country, have recently been made official languages.

The second group of languages considered in the chapters below is the European languages that were brought to the respective colonised countries at around the time when English speakers were attempting to take control (from about 1500 to the turn of the 20th century). The most obvious examples are French in Canada and Dutch (developed as Afrikaans) in South Africa. Both are official languages in the respective countries. In addition, struggles in the USA, particularly over German, are reported in the 19th and early 20th centuries.

The third group is the languages brought to the countries by more recent immigrants. All of these countries experienced waves, mainly of European migrants, after World War II. Though this statement applies to Britain as well, the immediate post-war migrants there came more from its former colonial possessions in Asia and Africa and from the West Indies. These groups have been largely assimilated to the use of English, but this to the detriment of preservation of the home languages. However, since then all the countries, with the possible exception of South Africa, have continued to receive high levels of immigration. The recent difference has been the diversity of the backgrounds of the new immigrants and of their languages, most remarkably those from Asia. The accommodation and integration of these linguistically and racially varied groups is a matter for current debate, as will be seen below.

Of further note on language groups is the fact that several countries have large racial minorities, such as the blacks in the USA and Indians in South Africa. Their language issues have not been much raised in the discussion below. This in part has been because race more than language has been the focus of their relations with the rest of the population, and also because of the dominance of the major languages during the period of settlement of these groups as well as the subservient position imposed on them. Language issues related to the rights of Hindi-Urdu and Dravidian group speakers in Britain have emerged owing to their more recent arrival there.

With the proviso that linguists have no single way of separating what are called languages from what are called dialects, the material in this book focuses more on relations between languages than it does on those between dialects. This has occurred because the authors were creating overviews of very large and complex sets of activities. Despite there being virtually no official standards for English (excepting perhaps the tacit recognition given to the Received Pronunciation – RP – in Britain), there is, in most countries, an implicit understanding of the forms that represent a standard dialect. This in the broadest sense might be said to represent a policy on dialect (in the absence of an official policy). It has very important consequences for the issue of people's access to this standard dialect, especially when it becomes the language standard for the formal transactions of education, the law, and the bureaucracy. It is usually the case that the further the dialect is from the

standard one, the more remote is the group which speaks it from access to
political power and influence. This can be seen in the studies presented here.
Dialects of English resulting from linguistic interactions between indigenous
peoples (Indian English in the USA) or other oppressed minorities (Black
English Vernacular in the USA) and native speakers of English have been
matters of comment in most of the countries discussed below. A process of
creolisation is still occurring in Australia and is seen by many as detrimental
to the survival of many threatened Aboriginal languages since it has come
to be used as a lingua franca among Aboriginal people. In Britain, where
historically many dialects of English have evolved over time, explicit concern
seems to be more about the English varieties of immigrants (such as those
from the Caribbean) than local ones.

In sum, for the purposes of this book, languages are treated not in a
linguistically technical way but more from a common sense perspective. It is
how they are used and perceived to be used that is important because that is
largely the way that they are responded to in explicit and tacit policy. Policy
almost exclusively takes languages and standard English at their face value.
In census questions, respondents give their own perceptions of the languages
they speak and how well they speak them. When decisions have to be made
about the language rights of individuals (Do they have the right to vote for
a Francophone school trustee? Are they eligible for English as a second
language training?) they are rarely tested for their actual proficiency in the
relevant language(s). Linguistic tests are expensive, and salient political
facts are not constituted by the actual language skills of individuals or groups
but by public perceptions of language by voters, clients, the media, bureaucrats and the like.

Why Language Policy?

To the person unfamiliar with language issues, the question of why we
should have language policy at all, is probably intriguing. After all, language
seems to be a very personal attribute and something that in everyday life is
quite uncontroversial. Many people may not confront language situations
that would seem problematic because they mostly have contact with people
in their immediate social group. On the other hand, some people may see
their accent, dialect, or mother tongue as a daily issue that they personalise
as their own problem. This is a political as well as a sociolinguistic reality. To
the extent that people might see language as problematic, it is often as a
result of communication breakdown, owing either to simple misunderstanding,
dialect or language difference. Many might also associate language problems
only with meanings or intentions (insofar as intention relates to meaning),
that is, in short-term, situation-specific problems. Indeed, many jokes turn

on just such situations, especially when they involve native speakers of different languages.

Problems of miscommunication, as trivial or serious as they might be, are not the focus of a need for language policy except in the broadest sense. It is, instead, where rights, freedoms and power are associated with language that policies become important. The most obvious case is where languages are proscribed. The main examples in this book are the deliberate (whether implicit or muted) suppression of indigenous languages such as took place in North America in the 19th and 20th centuries. Another obvious case is the situation where persons do not have access to either immediate or long-term social rights or benefits as a result of the language they speak or do not speak. This has been a common problem for indigenous peoples, for recent immigrants and for speakers of European languages in competition with English, as illustrated in the examples in this book. The extent to which language was an issue in the access of repressed groups, such as East Indians in South Africa and Afro-Americans in the USA, is only briefly outlined. In the short term we can think of persons without access to satisfactory legal and medical treatment. In the longer term, the obvious cases concern access to education, literacy and even careers. Access to social goods depends to some extent on the person's pleading his or her rights in that one is expected to know one's rights (in much the same way as one is expected to know the law). This presents a conundrum when access to knowledge about those rights is couched only in the official/standard language. The lack of access to the language of the civil service, the media, business and so on is, therefore, a barrier to participation in civic life defended by a circular argument. Remedies to redress such denial of access to people's rights can focus on individual or group rights or both; but this distinction alone can create civil and social divisions as seen in the Canadian case.

The question: 'Why have language policies?' must be answered by pointing out that even if there is not something officially called a policy, a policy exists anyway inasmuch as the linguistic status quo becomes policy implicitly. The arbitrariness of this situation indeed provides grounds for the argument that policy should be specified. In the discussion so far, it is apparent that problems are caused by the existence of a dominant language, a language of state and bureaucracy, a language that confronts the abilities of those not born into the community of its speakers. The policy (status planning) issue concerns the consequences of developing an explicit policy to replace that which is implicit in practice. A central policy act is to declare one or more languages as official language(s). The case of Canada at the present time is interesting in this regard since the declaration of two official languages has led not only to the continuance of vital issues being contested between the two language groups (i.e. it did not solve the problem), but has generated also renewed and new claims for similar status rights for other languages. Thus, the Canadian move has implicated language in the greater question of struggles for political rights.

The official language of a country, whether declared or not, can also engender fears about access to the standard language among speakers of community and indigenous languages and even dialects, such that a need for policy can arise. The initial problem stems from the fact that the official or dominant language becomes the standard language with inherent rights. This causes status problems for competing community languages, and inequalities resulting from differential access to the standard language. In the classroom, for example, the interactional and interpersonal language might well be a vernacular, but the forms of expression required from students are a standard expository oral and written language of academic discourse and examinations, these forms being quite remote from the vernacular. Extreme examples are found where the students are first language speakers of another language altogether. In the USA in the past few decades, federal funding programmes and the implications of court cases have created policies that address language issues for students who do not speak English – or at least standard English. However, resentment of minorities generally and of public support of minority linguistic groups particularly, has led to a further push to declare English as the official language in some states (already accomplished in a few) and nationally as well. In other words, there is resistance in the mainstream to accommodation of non-(standard)-English speakers' needs. Since English clearly is the dominant language in the USA, declaring it official can only serve to repress minorities' rights. The more-than-linguistic issues entailed have been made clearer by the 1994 vote in California to deny schooling and social services altogether to illegal immigrants.

Explicit or implicit policies regarding the status of the official or standard language, by their mere existence, affect the viability and stability of other languages used in the community. In all the New World countries covered in this book, there is a complex of community languages which, in various ways, compete for recognition. In all of these countries there are also languages that were spoken by indigenous peoples prior to European colonisation. Those languages, which are mostly at risk of extinction, are important cultural repositories in addition to being a critical means of communication for their speakers. A central factor is that if these languages die out in their respective communities or countries, there is no other source from which they can be revitalised. Languages brought to the countries by recent immigrants are not under that particular pressure since they have speakers in the countries of origins. Yet, a similar concern for their viability in the adoptive

Good on meaning of Lit. to people

country is realistic, not just for those of minorities with relatively few speakers but also for all languages used in the community. For each language there is a set of traditions and practices that are coded in the language. Any threat to or diminution of the language is a threat to the culture it encodes. In all declared multicultural societies, language is therefore a part of a cultural resource to be protected. That this idea is now contentious, as will be seen in the case studies, demands that there be some policy for protection of minority language rights. The protection of Maori in New Zealand is a case in point, as is the inclusion of indigenous languages as well as English and Afrikaans in the new constitution of South Africa.

Underlying the issues addressed above is the peculiar role that language has in not only giving expression to the self, but also in effecting one's participation and sharing in the community, social, and ethnic group or in the nation. The peculiarity comes from the fact that self-identity is not only self-constructed, but is derived in large part by perception of group membership. Language represents the individual's most powerful lien on the group. Language, as much as anything, can capture the essence of group membership. If belonging to a group means sharing its culture, then language is a primary means by which the culture is articulated, whether the culture is an oral one or has access to written forms. Language is therefore the principle medium for expressing civility, communality and shared values. Equally important is the fact that the concepts that mediate the forms of life which make the culture distinct are crystallised linguistically. One need not subscribe to a completely deterministic point of view to recognise this connection. The connection of language to culture and personal identity has been the focus of much of the theory of self-identity and cultural identity and has been demonstrated in recent political and ethnic conflict on most continents. Along similar lines, indigenous peoples in the Americas have argued that linguistic genocide involves more than language.

These arguments for having explicit, planned and inclusive language policies appear convincing, but the reality, if judged by the cases described here, is not so convincing. There is no obvious form of policy that can solve all the problems discussed. A strict legal set of policies may create more problems than a tacit policy, or at least different problems (for example, the real Canadian and potential USA policies on official languages). It might be argued that policy is always a consequence of initial difficulties and that the shape of the policy is determined by the difficult situation out of which it arose (as in the New Zealand situation). Policy formation is, on this account, a dynamic but responsive reaction (as in Australia especially). Thus, policy might normally or always been seen as a form of corrective feedback. The most that can be said is perhaps that language is important enough in everyday life to require an explicit policy on the basis of which decisions can be made that affect people's rights and obligations. This demands much of policy, and not least that we should be clear on what a policy is.

The Locus of Language Policy

The most interesting aspect of the cases presented in this volume might be the the wide range of possibilities indicated for the expression of policy concerning language. This leads to the question of whether there is an ideal locus of policy. There are numerous possible sites for it. In liberal democratic societies with several layers of government there is opportunity for policy determination at central, regional, and local levels. Language policy is often developed even at the level of local schools or community groups. Though desirable in many ways, there is a danger in localising policy in the absence of protective or over-arching policies to guard rights that might otherwise be threatened by narrow or sectarian local interests. A similar threat can arise at the state, regional or provincial level. The case of policy determination in Canada is interesting in that it contains issues involving all three levels. Policy planning should be carefully exercised to involve local and national interests. Too often political considerations overtake general or communal interests in these matters.

A related issue is the one of determining the form of expression of the policy. Should policy be cemented in law and should it be stated as the policy of the government on which citizens have the right to vote? In the USA, as will be seen, a series of state referenda on language policy in relation to English precedence has shown that this is perhaps not the best way to formulate policy in regards to issues of language. Apart from possible inequitable outcomes, the other problem it masks is the fact that language issues such as these cannot be adequately expressed in terms of a simple proposition.

Another alternative is for governments to set up an independent commission of inquiry into language which should recommend on formulation of policy (as in Canada in the 1960s and Australia in the 1980s). This still leaves open the prerogative of government to act upon or ignore the inquiry's recommendations. Such a commission would need to ensure its impartiality and that it represented and canvassed the interests of all concerned parties and individuals. At the head of government there are two possibilities for determining policy. One is the prevailing legislature, the elected Parliament, which can be presumed to have the interests of the whole nation in view (except perhaps in Canada currently where the official opposition and the next largest party have explicitly and implicitly separatist agendas for their respective regions). Policy of these origins can clearly reflect sectoral views, be they of region, class, race, or other.

The judiciary is the other body that might formulate policy given its experience with the law. The governmental structures in the USA give the judiciary major powers that have strongly affected language in that country. Language policy can even be enshrined in the constitution of a country as it is in South Africa and Canada. In the case of language policy, it could be argued that the need for expertise in language should be given precedence over general political expertise, and that, therefore, policy might best be determined by an independent commission taking expert evidence.

Once policy is determined, the issue becomes one of how it should be expressed. Legislation is an obvious choice. But the question of the usefulness and significance of language legislation must be confronted. It might seem that where there is legislation on language there is less likelihood of problems arising. This is often not the case, however. Where broad and general laws exist, issues arise concerning their interpretation. Where there are specific laws, their very specificity leads to expectations of careful delineations in contestable situations. Such delineations may not be acceptable or possible. Where there are laws there can also be contests between central and regional governments over powers of jurisdiction. This is notably the case in Canada and the USA. Overall, legislation is the least flexible response to language problems because it is so difficult to change.

The case studies show the dependence of policy on context. The context of each of the countries surveyed here is unique, and though all are multilingual the similarity ends there. What is clear is that there is no ideal means of expressing policy and that, even though there are problems raised by language matters in each country and many of them seem to be barely resolvable, the situations are unique to the country in each case because of the special set of social, linguistics and political issues raised, and thus the solutions may not be generalisable. In some countries and situations, policy has been devised to solve language issues; in others, policies on other matters have created language issues; in yet others, language issues arise because of the lack of policy governing particular social and linguistic situations. In Canada, the most extreme case is found where the issue of political rights is almost entirely expressed in linguistic terms or along language lines.

General Comments

While it is not at all clear that explicit language policy, especially language policy of any particular sort, is an uncontestably good thing, it is much more certain that language planning has a definite value. Since language policies, explicitly or by default, always exist in any given situation, it is important for these to be articulated, reviewed, and coordinated regularly. This need for review arises because languages themselves and languages in relationships are constantly changing. Old policies create new problems; a change in one part of the network provokes shifts in other parts; choices made by individuals affect the group as a whole. The political systems in the countries represented in this book all show a tendency to attend to political hot-spots. Resulting policies may therefore apply to specific problems without anticipating what the consequences will be in other segments of the communities. However, there are examples, as well, of broad spectrum studies of the needs of all language groups. It is particularly to be hoped that the new South African language policies will serve as an example of studied, coordinated language administration.

One reason for the importance of studying and renewing language policy comprehensively is to deal with the unfortunate fact that governments, individuals and groups seem to view language status, rights and resources as win–lose relationships. If one group is given a status in policy, others are seen to have lost status; rights given to some individuals are perceived as diminishing the rights of all the rest; if resources are provided for an activity, even the most patently needy one, other groups demand the same. Without a vision of the whole, including a balanced view of all the country's communications needs and linguistic resources, this win–lose stance cannot be overcome. If comprehensive study could result in a rationalised policy that protected language rights of all groups appropriately according to their situations, and if clear explanations could be provided for unequal provision of resources according to need, then it might be possible to persuade a larger proportion of the population that everyone is winning through the measures. However, to accomplish such an overview may be a challenge that is beyond the capacity of human intellect and collective cooperation. It is, nonetheless, a goal to be worked for.

Language is a symbol for group solidarity. It is used, rightly or wrongly, as a measure of the success of one group in relation to that of another. It is manipulated by groups and individuals to gain advantage in power struggles. Therefore, a great deal of language policy is not about language at all. A first step in working towards the goal of creating language policy that does not produce a win-lose response from the stakeholders would be to try, in every instance, to disentangle what really relates to language in a policy and what is actually based in some other issue. If more light could be shed on language and the heat diverted to where it belongs, then some supposed language problems might not seem so intractable. This is not to say that there are not genuinely heated language issues, but rather that not all contemporary language problems are of necessity as hot as they seem.

Structure of this Book

Each chapter in this book presents a description of language policies in one country where English is dominant: South Africa, Australia, New Zealand, Britain, USA and Canada. They all begin with a summary of the political/governmental context of the country and some demographic information on the population and its languages. Then an overview is given of general policies on language. This is followed by discussion of some issues that arise from the policies.

We would like to thank the authors who have cooperated with us in producing this volume. They have been most helpful and generous in researching and writing to suit the aims and format of the collection.

2 Language Policy in a Democratic South Africa

STANLEY G.M. RIDGE

Contexts and Statistics

Voting in South Africa's first democratic elections concluded on 27 April 1994, bringing to power a government of national unity under a Constitution[1] with a strong and explicit basis in a rights culture. The Constitution has a life of five years, during which period a final constitution must be developed. A body of constitutional principles, defining the framework within which the final constitution must be developed, is set out in Schedule 7 of the Constitution.

For all the appearance of gradualism in these transitional arrangements, there have been profound changes. Apartheid and any legal basis for its defence or continuance are now alien to the statute book. The 'sovereign court of Parliament' has yielded to the primacy of the Constitution. All the homelands and self-governing states created for apartheid purposes have been reintegrated into South Africa. To bring government closer to the people and allow for regional diversity, the four provinces of the old South Africa have been subdivided into nine. Education has been brought under one national ministry, instead of the legion of apartheid fragments. And the reconstruction and development of the country will proceed subject to a Constitution which enshrines the major rights, including language rights.

These structural changes clear the way for building a more just society: but there are huge problems to be overcome. The economy, damaged both by apartheid priorities and international isolation, has to provide opportunities and resources for change. The effects of apartheid education are felt in a gravely under-skilled working population, and widespread illiteracy. There are massive housing shortages, caused at least partly by an unwillingness on the part of successive white National Party governments up to the early

15

1980s to acknowledge the flow to the cities because it belied the ruralising, decentralising, master plan of apartheid. Health care is extraordinarily inaccessible to major parts of the population. And even planning the changes which are now necessary is hampered by the absence of reliable data. Previous governments were singularly incurious about some aspects of the national life. Demographic data, for example, is impressionistic for the majority African part of the population, with the last census (1991) working on aerial photographs for estimates in many cases, rather than on a more conventional survey.

South Africa's languages

It is estimated that there are approximately 40 million citizens of the new South Africa. Eleven languages account for the home language of more than 98% of this population. Under apartheid, each of them had official status in some part of what is once again unequivocally South Africa. These 11 languages are listed below. The estimated proportion of the population using a language as a home language, along with the approximate number of millions of speakers, is given in each case.[2]

Zulu	21.96%	8.8 million
Xhosa	17.3%	6.8 million
Afrikaans	15.3%	6.0 million
Northern Sotho	9.64%	3.8 million
English	9.01%	3.6 million
Tswana	8.59%	3.4 million
Southern Sotho	6.73%	2.7 million
Tsonga	4.35%	1.8 million
Swati	2.57%	1.0 million
Venda	2.22%	0.9 million
Ndebele	1.55%	0.6 million

The remaining 1.32% is needed to bring the total to 100%. This is made up of languages from many parts of the world, often referred to as modern 'heritage languages'. Most of the population of Indian origin use English as a home language, though there are attempts to keep languages such as Tamil, Hindi and Gujerati alive. Arabic, both classical and modern, is taught in Muslim contexts and in some schools and several universities. It may become more important as South Africa resumes its place in the world community. Of the modern European languages, Portuguese figures prominently. This is hardly surprising when one considers the proximity of Angola and Moçambique, two countries once colonised by Portugal. There is also a well-established German-speaking community, with strong links to Namibia, which was once a German colony. What is surprising is that French, the official language of a major part of Africa, is little used. Like Arabic, French may grow in significance as South Africa is able once again to celebrate being part of Africa and the international community. South Africa was largely isolated from the rest of Africa from the 1950s until the early 1990s and this has left its mark. African languages from other parts of Africa are represented largely through migrant workers, and Swahili, the lingua franca of East Africa has excited almost no interest to date.

The African languages of South Africa have both oral and written literatures. The oral literatures are rich, but the very limited written literatures have been affected by publishing conditions under apartheid. There are newspapers and magazines of fairly wide readership in these languages. Afrikaans developed from Dutch under a variety of influences in South Africa over two centuries, and has been an official language (replacing Dutch) since 1925. It has a substantial literature, and has been developed for scientific and public purposes. Something more than half of all L1 speakers of Afrikaans are black. English is also spoken as a first language by significant numbers of black South Africans.

It is testimony to the ravages of South Africa's successive black and white colonisations that there is only a tiny cluster of speakers of San languages in the Northern Cape province, and that they have generally abandoned their hunter-gatherer lifestyle. Other members of these speech communities live in remote areas of Botswana and Namibia. There is only archaeological and documentary evidence that they were once a presence through much of Southern African. The related Khoi have vanished altogether.

Several of the 11 official languages are used in communities in extending beyond South Africa's borders. Lesotho, a mountain kingdom entirely surrounded by South Africa, has Southern Sotho as its main language.[3] Swati is the main language of Swaziland, Tswana is the main language of Botswana, and there is a large Ndebele-speaking population in southern Zimbabwe. There is also a significant Afrikaans-speaking population in Namibia. In all these countries, English is the official language and the primary language of education.

Literacy

Literacy levels are low. One measure gives 8.3 million or about 20% of the population as 'lacking the reading and writing skills necessary to live and work' in their communities (SAIRR, 1992: 212). Other measures suggest higher figures. Clearly, literacy must be a large consideration in language policy in an emerging democracy.

The major pressures are for literacy in English and Afrikaans, as these are the common languages of the industrial workplace. Literacy in African languages gives access to a small printed literature, some newspapers and magazines, and state notices and documents, particularly in the areas which were governed as apartheid homelands. The effects of literacy on the rich oral traditions, both literary and communicative, in the African languages is cause for concern. The half-articulated sense among city people that print literacy is a marker of sophistication and oral literacy a slightly shameful and primitive practice, is a real threat to a vital cultural resource in a country which needs to rebuild community.

Access to English

At this point it is apposite to note that a significant proportion of the total population of South Africa cannot understand English: exactly what proportion cannot be accurately determined, but it is so high by all measures that it cannot and must not be disregarded in developing policy. The Department of National Education (1994: 7) suggests that as much as 58% of the population cannot understand English, and using work by Schuring as its source contends that just under half South Africa's citizens (48%) have access to neither English nor Afrikaans, hitherto the official languages. However, the intelligibility survey used in planning by the South African Broadcasting Corporation (SABC) in 1994 makes English the most widely understood language (69%), ahead of Zulu (65%) and Afrikaans (59%) (MRA, 1994). This still means that 31% of the population cannot even understand English, let alone speak, read or write it. Any language policy concerned with equity and the ability of citizens to participate fully in the national life has to take these facts into account.

The difficulties of language planning become evident when one notes the strong tendency among both urban and rural Africans to opt for English as the preferred official language. In a multi-optional survey conducted among African men and women towards the end of 1993 in both urban and rural areas, 'English was the preferred language in all categories of respondents' for use as the official language. It received 67% support from the least favourable category (those aged 50+, and an average of more than 80% overall. Zulu attracted about 33%, Sotho and Tswana together about 33%, and Afrikaans less than 10% support overall (Kellas, 1994).

Language Policy in the Constitution

The new Constitution of the Republic of South Africa (Act No. 200 of 1993), which came into effect in May 1994, embodies an explicit language policy. All 11 languages listed above have official status nationally, and each provincial legislature has the statutory right to determine, on a two-thirds majority vote, which of the national official languages will be official for provincial purposes. In the Western Cape province, for example, Afrikaans, English and Xhosa are the official provincial languages. These are clearly the home languages of the overwhelming majority of citizens. The situation is not as simple in the province of Gauteng. It is South Africa's great urban-industrial melting pot, centred on Johannesburg, and most of the 11 languages are spoken there by significant groups of citizens.

The policy is rooted in a culture of rights, and is anticipated in the phrase from the 1993 Constitution which declares that: 'all citizens shall be able to enjoy and exercise their fundamental rights and freedoms'. The policy also grows out of an espousal of multilingualism and multiculturalism as a national asset. Constitutional Principle XI, the force of which must be reflected in the 1999 Constitution, proclaims somewhat elliptically and ungrammatically, 'The diversity of language and culture shall be acknow-ledged and protected, and conditions for their promotion shall be encouraged.' All other sections of the Constitution with a bearing on language have to be interpreted against a background of this concern for rights and for multi-culturalism.

Section 31 of the Constitution specifies that: 'Every person shall have the right to use the language of his or her choice.' But that is a safeguard against proscription of the use of any language in or outside official contexts. Lest it be thought that such a clause is unnecessary, there have recurrently been such proscriptions in the country's varied political history since the 17th century.[4]

With regard to official contexts, Section 3 of the Constitution establishes the right of each person to insist that the state or provincial administration communicate with him or her in whichever of the applicable official languages he or she chooses. This right, like several others, is subject to practicability, so must be seen as a statement of direction rather than a right in a stricter sense of the word. What might this mean in practice? Given the low level of multilingual competence of most civil servants, there is little chance of this right's being realised for most African languages over the counter or the telephone. But a correspondent might more reasonably expect a reply in his or her language of choice. There is an even greater chance that, having regis-tered a language preference, a citizen might receive all official notices regarding income tax, for example, in that language.[5]

Section 8 of the Constitution establishes the right to equality before the law. This includes a provision that no one shall be unfairly discriminated against, directly or indirectly, because of the language he or she uses. The indirect discrimination envisaged would most probably arise from inadequacy of translation by court interpreters. Raising the professional level of interpretation services must be a major priority for the Department of Justice. In fact, as Trew (1991) pointed out in a National Education Policy Investigation (NEPI) working paper: 'To give full rights to the linguistically disenfranchised, would be to ensure that reliable interpretation is available at all points of contact between the public and the state. . . . If the voice that is provided through interpretation is audibly stumbling and uncertain, citizens will hardly feel that they have acquired a voice at all.' The complexity of the task is suggested in research on specific trials by Reichman (1993a & b), an advocate who has compared courtroom transcripts which reflect the interpreter's version with what the witness actually 'said'.

Education is a crucial area for the language policy, in terms both of rights and of the furtherance of multiculturalism. The key constitutional clause relating to language and education is Section 32, which grants each person the right 'to instruction in the language of his or her choice where this is reasonably practicable'. Two aspects of this warrant comment. First, we should note that it is the individual's right, and that in exercising it he or she has to make a personal choice. What this will mean in practice is difficult to ascertain. Such choices, where they have existed, will have been the prerogative of the parents, and it is not clear whether parents no longer have any rights in this area. The second aspect concerns the problematic notion of reasonable practicability. This issue is both politically sensitive if it vitiates the policy's declared intentions, and practically fraught, given the low level of development of some of the languages for academic purposes, the lack of adequate teaching materials, the shortage of well-trained teachers, and the stringencies induced by an economy much damaged by apartheid. Some room for relief, whether publicly or privately funded, is intended by the provision in Section 32(c) which permits the establishment of educational institutions based on a common culture, language or religion.

Under Sections 3(1) and 3(9)(a) of the Constitution, the state incurs an obligation to create conditions for the development of all official languages and for promoting their equal use. Conversely, in Section 3(9)(c), it is obliged to prevent the use of any language to dominate, divide, or exploit. The policy direction intended by the legislature would seem clear enough.

The desire to extend the rights and status pertinent to each language rather than reduce them is laudable. It also makes sense in some contexts. Yet status is a relative concept, and it is hard to imagine the status of one language being enhanced in a particular community without the status of another language at least being changed, if not correspondingly reduced. Sections 3(2) and 3(5) of the Constitution establish the requirement that the rights and status of a language may not be diminished. In a country which previously gave paramount status to English and Afrikaans, the languages of the main players in the economy, appeals to the constitution to protest against perceived diminution or retention of that status can be expected.

On the other hand, use of the newly official languages is usually subject to a practicability clause. Parliament and any provincial legislature may give content to the notion of practicability by legislation. Section 3(8) provides for legislative decisions on use of official languages in government, taking account of usage, practicality and expense. Institutional inertia will still continue to favour Afrikaans and English, and language rights in communications with government departments would have to be exceptionally important for the newly enfranchised speakers of other languages to be asserted above the claims of housing, health care, education, training and the need to keep the economy growing. The new government's Reconstruction and Development Programme (RDP) has gained widespread acceptance for its focus on these latter concerns.

However, there is some structural provision for language. To deal with the many issues raised by these clauses, Section 3.10 of the Constitution requires the establishment by the Senate of a Pan-South African Language Board. It is present in the Constitution as a concept to be fleshed out, but the concept includes giving attention to issues of language development, promotion of respect for other languages, promotion of equal use and enjoyment of official languages, provision of translation facilities, and recommending changes in legislation. As Titlestad (1994a) points out, the concept of the Board is vague and the issues it will have to deal with are very complex. Clarity is necessary soon if it is going to be a significant body.

Lenses

The policy enshrined in the Constitution is a product of negotiation, and bears the marks of the compromises which are essential to that process. This places a particular burden on those who elaborate it in practice, not least the yet-to-be-established Pan-South African Language Board. Disjunctive statements have to be reconciled, gaps have to be closed, and unanticipated issues addressed in ways which prepare for the formulation of the 1999 Constitution. In the absence of a clearly consolidated national position, I shall attempt to describe the main strands of thinking and preparatory work which informed the negotiations and will undoubtedly have a bearing on further elaboration of the policy.

Pressure for Afrikaans

At its best, Afrikaner nationalist thinking has had a heightened regard for linguistic and cultural identity, born of a struggle to maintain them. At its worst it has aimed at domination. For more than a century, significant groups of white Afrikaners have been concerned to assert their right to Afrikaans, a language which developed from Dutch. This movement ensured that Afrikaans replaced Dutch as an official language in 1925, and fostered an aggressive policy for the establishment of Afrikaans once the National Party came to power in 1948. Apartheid – or separate development – was originally defended as a means of preserving the linguistic and cultural identity of each group. But this rationale yielded to a fevered anti-communism, a growing paranoia, and the exigencies of maintaining a position of dominance. 'Bilingualism' in terms of the double official language policy increasingly became a euphemism for the predominance of Afrikaans. And, by 1976, the government was attempting to make Afrikaans a compulsory medium at schools for Africans. This precipitated the 1976 student revolts, which were a symptom of a much deeper malaise, and obtained for English some kind of absolution for the oppressive parts of its own history. Since then, the Afrikaner nationalist movement has split several times. For the Conservative Party and its allies, Afrikaans remains 'the first and primary language' in South Africa, with English as a second language, and no room at all for African languages (NEPI, 1992a: 98). However, for those Afrikaner nationalist groups which committed themselves to negotiating a new order, the concern for preserving linguistic and cultural identity has regained compelling force as a non-sectarian rationale for protecting the language. The Constitution is informed by it, at least in part.

Backing the Afrikaner nationalist movement's desire for the affirmation of Afrikaans has been the *Suid-Afrikaanse Akademie vir Wetenskap en Kuns*, a powerful, and all-white, cultural academy.[6] It has been the main arbiter of standards in Afrikaans language use. The five Afrikaans medium universities (Potchefstroom University for Christian Higher Education, the University of Pretoria, the University of Stellenbosch, the University of the Orange Free State, and the Rand Afrikaans University) have also made significant contributions to the debate as concerning an issue of vital importance to them. From another perspective, black Afrikaans academics at the University of the Western Cape have made distinctive contributions. They have claimed the language as the property of a much larger constituency, revived an interest in subordinated varieties of Afrikaans, and pointed out that more than half the mother tongue speakers of Afrikaans are not white. This inclusive view has increasingly been adopted by those concerned for the future of Afrikaans, whether white or black.

The African National Congress

The African National Congress (ANC) also entered negotiations with extensive language policy debate in the background. The Freedom Charter, adopted by the Congress of the People in 1955, was and continues to be a major point of reference for ANC policy. It has little to say about language, except that 'All people shall have equal rights to use their own language'. However, some sentences articulate an inclusiveness and respect for diversity which has informed ANC thinking on linguistic and cultural matters. The ANC Language Commission, with the example of Namibia on South Africa's doorstep, and with the work of scholars like Robert Phillipson and James W. Tollefson fresh in their minds, opted for having no official language (ANC, 1992a). Rather, the Commission proposed according all 11 languages 'full recognition' and spoke of the need to treat 'affirmatively' the languages which have suffered under the 'massive predominance' of English and Afrikaans. The ANC's *Policy Guidelines* document (ANC, 1992b), published a few months later, undertakes to 'recognise, protect and develop all languages' (Clause N3.1), but sets the more practical goal for education of providing all individuals with access 'through their mother tongue and a language of wider communication to all avenues of social, political, economic and educational life' (Clause J4.1). It also recognises that it may be necessary 'to designate a single common language to be used for record purposes or for other special use, either at the national level or in the regions' (Clause N3.2). Key terms which may influence practice under the constitution are 'language of wider communication' and 'common language . . . for record purposes'.

The National Education Policy Investigation

The National Education Policy Investigation (NEPI) was set up in December 1990 by the National Education Coordinating Committee (NECC) 'to interrogate policy options in all areas of education with a value framework derived from the ideals of the broad democratic movement'[8] (NEPI, 1992a: vi). Its report, in 13 small volumes published jointly with Oxford University Press, is the most comprehensive critical survey of the issues and options in education. The NEPI *Language* report is primarily concerned with language issues in education, but it makes some general points about language in South Africa as background to the discussion. These include treating the multilingualism of the country as a resource rather than a problem, recognising the changing contexts of language use in a rapidly changing country, taking account of dialect, and understanding affective issues as often distorting the linguistic realities and needs of the country. Nevertheless, the *Framework Report* (NEPI, 1992b: 182) recognises the need for every South African 'to have access to English'.

The English Academy of Southern Africa

Another major contributor to the debates has been the English Academy of Southern Africa. On matters of language policy it has advised on preferred forms and practices, and has encouraged discussion of a range of issues. Since its 1986 conference, it has been consciously concerned to see English in South Africa as one language among others, and to assert the rights of the other languages alongside English. However, it is also concerned that the *de facto* status of English as the main language of wider communication and of record in South Africa be recognised, pointing out that the constitutional negotiations were all in English (English Academy, 1994: 1). This double emphasis is clear in its own submission to the constitutional negotiation forum, CODESA (English Academy, 1992, reissued 1993). It argues first for research-based planning, using accurate information on demography and people's attitudes. Secondly, for flexibility to allow for future changes. Then it urges, on pragmatic grounds, that English be the main official language of South Africa, with the other 10 languages enjoying 'official status at various levels of public life, in various circumstances, and possibly on a geographical basis', such details to be spelled out in legislation. In the absence of any standard regional variety it further proposes that the official standard should be 'standard British English'. It is at pains to add that it is not concerned with accent here, nor to exclude regional enrichment of the standard language. Rather, it wishes to ensure that fairness is possible in law and administration, and that teaching is not made impossibly difficult. In the circumstances, this is not an unreasonable concern. Titlestad (1994b) deals with a number of issues suggested here, pointing out that any rationale for English as a language of wider access implicitly supports 'the international standard or a variety close to it'.

What emerges from both the NEPI reports and from the English Academy documents is the need to make distinctions between various functions which a language may be called upon to serve. Desai and Trew (1992) argue that while English is inescapably necessary for certain purposes and in certain contexts, a changing spectrum of functions may best be served, for a specific person, in his or her first language. They call for the recognition of 'the dignity and value of all South African linguistic traditions', and the protection 'of citizens from linguistic disenfranchisement'.

The National Language Project

Another major contributor has been the National Language Project, based in Cape Town. It has, since 1986, explored language issues and provided a forum for discussion both through conferences and through its publications.[9]

It also has a substantial research programme. Characteristic of the lateral thinking which it has encouraged has been the proposal of Alexander (1989, 1991) that the languages in each of two large African language families in South Africa, Nguni and Sotho, be 'reconciled' with one another, thus making their promotion and development more likely in practical terms. The languages in each family were originally dialects within a continuum until they were reduced to writing. Written forms created standard languages. Reconciling the Nguni languages would mean having one standard written form of Common Nguni without destroying the variety which their separate traditions represent. The same would happen to the Sotho group. The proposal may not be practicable for political reasons, with Zulu and Xhosa speakers, like Shaw's English and Americans, 'divided by a common language'. There are too many shibboleths. But it does helpfully deflect thinking about language issues from a linear path.

The trade unions

Finally, in a country with a high illiteracy rate, it is not surprising that the organised trade union movement is a force in developing language policy. The largest of the groups of unions, COSATU, formulated proposals for a national worker literacy campaign in 1991. Community organisations have expanded this to a call for a major Adult Basic Education (ABE) programme. And the government's education policy is based on a philosophy of lifelong learning. Fine-tuning its proposals, COSATU has called for ABE programmes 'to develop a flexible modular system of ABE with appropriate core modules constituting national standards to balance considerations of equity, portability and differing educational needs' (Steinberg, 1992: 21).

Early Pressures on Policy

There can be no coherent assessment of the effectiveness and implications of the new South African language policy because so little of it has been put into practice, and so much must be done within the next years. My account is rather a series of suggestive news flashes dated November 1994.

National and provincial parliaments

The first reported public celebration of the new multilinguality was in the national parliament, with one white MP from Kwa-Zulu-Natal addressing the house in impeccable Zulu, and a black MP picking up the debate in equally impeccable English. It was an auspicious start, and must have presented an immediate challenge to the fledgling simultaneous translation service. Most debate has, however, been in English. This has raised other language issues.

One white, National Party MP created a furore in parliament early in August, 1994 by criticising the 'bad English' spoken by black ANC MPs (West, 1994). The ANC responded that it would be within its rights to instruct its members to address the house in their home languages, resulting in a 'Tower of Babel' if all 11 were used. In mid-September, a parliamentary committee without a translation service was thrown into disarray when a conservative member insisted on speaking Afrikaans as his constitutional right, and had other members resorting to Zulu and Venda in reaction (*Argus*, 1994). And in the Western Cape provincial parliament the premier was forced to intervene after a provincial minister returned an Afrikaans letter with the request that it be submitted in English 'for meaningful attention' (West, 1994).

Parliament might debate in English without most citizens being adversely affected, provided that they had access to reports of the debates which interested them in a language they could understand. These reports could be in newspapers or on television or radio. However, the role of public media goes beyond providing such information. They must give access to the national life and to the wider world. Similarly, education must give the ordinary citizen access to learning, and the courts must afford access to justice. These activities have a direct role in language development and promotion.

Broadcasting

The South African Broadcasting Corporation (SABC), the main radio and television broadcaster, is a statutory body,[10] funded partly by state-collected licence fees and partly by advertising revenue. It had a history of conforming to National Party policy under the apartheid government. With a view to its wider accountability for independence, all candidates for the new Board were interviewed in public by a panel headed by a judge. The new Board has been controversial since its inception, and the issue of independence has by no means been laid to rest. Perhaps the most controversial issue so far has been a draft policy options document which proposed, as one of 15 scenarios, making the flagship television channel English only, and putting Afrikaans programmes in a channel which would be shared by the other 10 languages (McNeill, 1994).

The document was leaked to the press, and there was an immediate challenge to the constitutionality of the proposal. The Constitution, after all, stipulates that the status of each language may not be diminished. The SABC has sought legal advice on the interpretation of Sections 3(1) and 3(2) of the Constitution, and has, perhaps significantly, referred to 'equit-able' rather than 'equal' treatment of languages in public statements since.

The first argument for its being equitable to give English priority in broadcasting is that, according to the MRA survey discussed above, more South Africans understand English (69%) than understand any other language. This is a crucial consideration for a language policy which aims to assist the participation of all in society. However, other, less principled arguments may weigh more heavily. English is the language of the major news networks. English is the language of international communications and technology. And English programmes are readily available internationally at low cost and can be used without adaptation or dubbing. The average imported English programme costs R350 per minute. Imported programmes in other languages, which have to be dubbed, cost R850 per minute. Local talk shows cost between R1000 and R2000 per minute. Local drama shows cost R4000 per minute. And 'prestige' local productions cost R9000 per minute, or 26 times as much as imported English programmes (McNeill, 1994).

Publishing

The strong Afrikaans lobby is alert to any suggestion of slippage. Ton Vosloo, executive chairman of the newspaper and publishing group, *Nasionale Pers*, warned in mid-August 1994 that 'Peace would be seriously damaged if Afrikaans was marginalised for political reasons' (Dasnois, 1994). This was not a threat, but a reading of the political situation. *Nasionale Pers*'s policy response to this situation was two-pronged. The group's newspapers 'would play a watchdog role against any devaluation of the language [Afrikaans]'. However, the group would publish books in English and other languages, as well as Afrikaans, as a service to education.

Education

The challenge of English is everywhere, not least in education. Stellenbosch, the oldest of the traditionally Afrikaans-medium universities, had its constituting Act of Parliament changed in the early 1990s to entrench Afrikaans as its official language. This was a controversial move, probably aimed at staking a claim for the future of the institution in a country which may not be able to sustain as many Afrikaans universities as in the past. All other Afrikaans universities are now offering significant numbers of courses in English, as the language of educational access for the overwhelming majority of black South Africans.[11]

At the other end of the educational spectrum, when offered a choice, significant numbers of black parents have opted for English as the language of instruction for their children, even from the first year of primary school (NEPI, 1992a: 13f). *Edusource Data News* (August 1993) reported that it was already so in 43% of schools, and that 86% of the teachers in those schools were satisfied with the policy. Only 66% of teachers in schools switching to English after four years were satisfied. This low level of satisfaction may have been because of problems like those observed in 1985 by MacDonald (1991) in Bophuthatswana: 'English lessons prior to Std 3 did not equip pupils with the necessary language skills to learn their content subjects' once they switched to English as a medium in Std 3. Offering a more complete picture, Heugh (1993) reports that in 1992 the Department of Education and Training (responsible for African school education until the introduction of the new integrated system) gave parents the choice of several options on language medium for the primary schools their children were attending. Two-thirds of the schools voted, and of these 54% voted for a gradual transfer to English, 22% for English from Grade 1, 13.4% for a sudden transfer to English after four years of schooling, 7.5% voted to retain the status quo, and only 1.545% voted to have Afrikaans as a language medium at any stage.

The drive for English is far from unproblematic: 79% of all pupils in South African schools in 1990 were African (SAIRR, 1992: 183). Almost all of these would have had a home language (or home languages) other than English. Nearly half of them would have been in the first four years of school, and at that stage would have been taught in an African language. The remainder would have been in higher standards and taught through the medium of English by teachers for whom English was not a home language. White Afrikaners and the majority of 'Coloured' people, together constituting more than half of the non-African 21%, would have had Afrikaans as a home language. However, most of them would have been taught through the medium of Afrikaans. NEPI (1992a: 38) reports that the National Party government of the day and the ANC agreed that: 'English . . . should be studied by all children. The reasons are that it is a language of access to a vast range of resources nationally and internationally, to higher education, to technology, to economic opportunities, [and is] the mother tongue of a sizeable number of South Africans, and lingua franca both within the country and beyond its borders.' However, giving this position to English does not imply a drift away from multilingualism. NEPI (1992a: 44) is representative of majority political and academic opinion in warning against the common idea that monolingualism is to be striven for as a precondition for really satisfactory development.

As the editor of the National Language Policy journal, *Bua!* (1994: 9,1) points out, there is a real danger, in debating the role of English in education, 'that we will get caught in a circular mode of reasoning, seeking justification for the domination of English because English has already become dominant in the eyes of the population'. However, there is an equally troubling danger that levels of competence achieved in English will not deliver the envisaged

benefits to the majority of South Africans. South Africans thus face the far
from unique task of both strengthening the teaching of English and seeking
to promote and develop the other national languages.

Justice

Access to justice is another area occupying the attention of linguists. The
established languages of the courtroom are Afrikaans and English. Use has
been made of interpreters down the years when dealing with evidence
presented by someone who could not speak either language, and the courts
have sometimes distinguished themselves by not taking translations at face
value. But courts have not always been alert to the difficulties. In general,
there are major inadequacies in current practice. As is to be expected in a
country with more than three-quarters of its population black, most people
standing trial and giving evidence are black. Yet most magistrates, judges
and public prosecutors are white, and few have any command of an African
language or any intimate understanding of South Africa's range of cultural
conventions. Almost all interpreters working in African languages, and
many working in other languages, have not had a professional training which
would make them alert to the ethics of their role, to cultural nuance in translation and the exigencies of discourse (Crawford, 1993).

Language in public life

Regardless of the official status of languages, the situation in practice is
often of more importance to users, and is more effective as a 'site of struggle'.
Overwhelmingly the most vocal participants in the language debate are
Afrikaners, fearing the future of their language. Organisations like *Vriende
van Afrikaans* (Friends of Afrikaans) have launched a nation-wide campaign,
designed to transcend the racial barriers of the past, while asserting the
rights of Afrikaans speakers, black and white. One favoured strategy is to
insist on being served in Afrikaans, and to write to the manager or someone
in a position of influence if not given satisfaction.

There have clearly been other pressures on South African Airways. The
cabin controller used to make announcements to passengers on internal flights
in Afrikaans and English in that order. Then the order changed, with English
being used first. On one flight in April 1994, passengers were greeted in English, Xhosa and Afrikaans, instructions were given in English and Afrikaans,
and then an additional announcement was made that passengers who wished to
be served in French or German could speak to a cabin attendant. By early
November 1994, this had changed, with no mention of French or German,
but an offer made to anyone who wished to use one of the nine other official

languages to attempt to assist them. All this was handled with great politeness. There may, of course, be a measure of latitude allowed to cabin controllers, but the shifts recorded mark a broadly significant pattern.

Some Items on the Agenda

However the existing policy framework is elaborated after late 1994, it will involve tackling huge tasks. Some of these have been suggested already and must be discussed in more detail here. Others are sketched for the first time.

Translation and interpretation

In public life, excellent translation and interpretation services are required. By mid 1994, the central government language office, the State Language Services, was developing a capacity to offer translation services from and into all South Africa's official languages. It was also forming a pool of interpreters for the state meetings and conferences. Provincial and local governments have similar if less complex needs, and will have to develop or expand their own language services. They will be in competition with the private sector for a very small pool of people qualified to translate from and into the African languages. There are professional bodies which are actively concerned to improve the situation. The South African Translators' Institute has been examining the implications of the changes in the language order at its conferences for several years. There is also a Translators' and Interpreters' Association of South Africa, and an Association of Court Interpreters, both of which have taken steps to establish training opportunities.

Language medium in schools

Any decision about the language medium in schools must have major implications. Currently, English is the major language medium at higher primary and secondary level, yet most of the teachers do not have a command of the language adequate for them to enable their pupils to make nuanced distinctions. The problem is not as great in schools with Afrikaans as a language medium, as it is also a language which has been developed for academic purposes, and most teachers in Afrikaans medium schools speak the language as their mother tongue. But if there were a decision to expand the use of the other languages, currently underdeveloped for that purpose, there would be major difficulties. Whatever happens, the need to improve the quality of education generally will require some national professional campaign of language enrichment and professional development.

The medium issue is, in any case, very complex. There is a common practice in classrooms where the language medium is other than L1 for the teacher to use the first language (or languages) of the class in apposition to the main language medium (usually English). Even the concept of L1 has to be qualified severely. Makoni (1993: 18) points out that most urban African children speak some kind of creolised argot which is far removed from the standard version of their mother tongue. Teaching such children through the medium of their standard L1 may have the same affective and psychological arguments adduced against it as against using English. African teachers in Gauteng province are divided on the use of the argot in apposition to English, but it may well be a major means of creating space for another voice and making English more responsive to local realities.

Promoting African languages

The African languages have been both promoted and neglected during the apartheid years. They have been promoted insofar as there is a published literature in each of them, and they were developed after a fashion as school subjects. They have been neglected in that they have been dealt with as though at a remove. Publishing in the African languages has been constrained both by ideology and by economics, often working together. The voices of protest in the African languages were largely silenced by banning. Very much more African protest writing has been published in English (which was presumably more accessible to the politicians and so less to be feared) than in all the African languages put together. But the economic factor was equally potent. With a relatively small reading public in each of the African languages, the major market was the schools. Publishers could not afford to issue works which were not going to be prescribed. And nothing with a critical edge was going to be prescribed. Relatively bland reading, removed from the life experience of the pupils and other readers, was the result.

A similar pattern of distancing has been evident in the way the languages are taught. They have been treated in most cases as if they are classical (or remote foreign) languages. Degenaar (1994: 20) has said: 'One breathes through language.' Few L1 African pupils could feel that. And few L2 pupils or students reach the end of their courses able to sustain an ordinary conversation. There clearly has to be a major revision of syllabuses and teaching methods, with a major emphasis on access to the living language. There must also be a major thrust to improve teachers' command of the language. As the apartheid barriers are dismantled, there will also be more natural access to the living language. For example, it is not possible to scan the radio and television channels at any stage without coming upon a programme in one of the African languages, and there is increasingly a tendency in news and topicality programmes to present people speaking their own languages rather than providing some kind of overriding translation or dubbing. The demand for courses has also increased, Making ingenious use of existing resources, Rhodes University employs selected Xhosa-speaking service staff, including gardeners, to teach a Basic Xhosa Communication Course to students, academics, and business and professional people (Smith, 1993: 10).

Basic adult education

Using the resources right before our eyes will obviously be necessary when it comes to adult basic education. In 1990, there were 108 private sector bodies involved in literacy work in South Africa (SAIRR, 1992: 213). Their number has grown. They are largely concerned with developing a literate workforce. COSATU's demand for worker literacy training reflects a matching interest from the employee side. Within the private sector, then, reasonably rapid progress is possible. Other organisations, largely churches, civics and NGOs are attempting to meet needs in the wider community.

There is less congruence when it comes to an understanding of what literacy is. Conventional, utilitarian notions of reading compete with Paolo Freire's broader concepts of empowerment. But this debate is not being conducted at a theoretical level. The pressure to deliver competence in the 3 Rs is in useful tension with the pressure to be able to read the world.

A major practical need is the development of suitable materials and curricula. SACHED (The South African Committee for Higher Education), a major progressive institution, has produced a workable curriculum in 1994, and groups such as the English Literacy Project, Genmin (The General Mining Corporation), and the Molteno Project, along with SACHED, have been developing course materials (Steinberg, 1992). There is a good deal of informal coordination, but some national pattern must be established. There is also a need for large quantities of suitable reading matter to be produced.

Promotion and constraint

In terms both of policy and political necessity, the 11 languages, and especially nine of them, must be promoted. A National Terminology Service is being expanded to help with lexical matters in these languages. It is less clear who will give guidance on establishing standards of use: probably the Pan-South African Language Board. The third main aspect of promotion is publication. In this regard both the state and the private sector should preferably take action in encouraging writing and offering subventions.

The way policy is implemented will inevitably be shaped by a variety of factors. There must be a tension between the insistent pull of cost, and a desire to build a multilingual, multicultural society in which difference is an asset. There is also a dynamic emanating from the notion of language rights: political pressure to secure what is promised by the constitution is legitimate, and likely to be resorted to when groups feel their language under threat.

A third factor is English. It has manifest utility. It is a popular choice. It is probably the major shared language. And yet, so insidious is 'linguistic imperialism', that English could, in a kind of innocence, eclipse other languages. Language activists in South Africa, many of them English speaking, warn against this danger in strong terms, even stridently. It is worth noting, though, that a campaign against English would also be pernicious in its effects. It would infringe on the rights of those for whom English is a home language, and it would squander a valuable national resource. However, its most serious consequence would be to reduce our understanding of complex language phenomena and needs to what can be described in binary terms of approval or disapproval, friendship or enmity.

Desai and Trew (1992) have spoken of large numbers of South Africans facing 'the realities of linguistic exclusion' from the public life of the country. That situation is intolerable for democracy. There are also more intimate kinds of linguistic exclusion in a rapidly urbanising society recovering from a sustained and systematic assault on community. The language policy in the South African Constitution creates civil space for these matters to be addressed. In practice, the challenge will be to understand the actual and changing roles of languages in our society, determining how and for what purposes they are needed, and then, in appropriate ways, to build up both the languages themselves and people's ability to use them.

Notes

1. 'Constitution' with a capital C refers to the current constitution of the Republic of South Africa, Act 200 of 1993.
2. The problems with demographic information have already been mentioned. They are compounded by the inclusion of the former independent homeland states in the new South Africa. The percentages given here were agreed by the multi-party team working on the language policy, and represent the best guess available. They are reproduced in Department of National Education (1994).
3. I use the term 'main language' to describe the majority language of the country. In these cases it is the overwhelming majority language.
4. The Dutch East India Company administration proscribed the use of French by Huguenot immigrants in the late 17th century and saw their rapid assimilation. In the early 19th century, a policy of Anglicisation was followed, ostensibly in the interests of orderly administration. Early this century, in the period after the Anglo–Boer War, English was the compulsory language of schooling. Any use of Dutch or Afrikaans by pupils during school (except during Dutch classes) was proscribed. Offenders in many schools were treated as dunces and made to walk the playgrounds bearing humiliating sandwich boards. The tacit proscription of

the use of African languages in certain kinds of public gatherings – an unconsciously self-imposed constraint – was just as powerful until political resistance to apartheid became more articulated.

5. In *South Africa's New Language Policy: The Facts*, the Department of National Education points to the role of the State Language Services in providing translation and interpretation services. It is 'currently developing a capacity to deal with the nine African languages', and is 'forming a pool of interpreters' (p. 9). However, the minimum commitment would be to publish important notices in all languages, and have forms and a letterhead available in all languages (p. 8).

6. After an abortive attempt to open its doors in 1974, the Suid-Afrikaanse Akademie vir Wetenskap en Kuns admitted its first black full members in 1995.

7. 'Black' is used in this chapter to refer to all people who are not white. Most black speakers of Afrikaans are 'Coloured' – that is, of racially mixed heritage. Other black people are 'Indian' – of West Asian Extraction – or African, the overall majority group in the population.

8. The 'broad democratic movement' was a consensual, informal cluster of political groupings representing the overwhelming majority of South Africans. Parties to it had worked within and outside the country before 1990 for political liberation. Once the election process was under way in 1994, politics gained more sharply defined edges, and the broad democratic movement receded as an identifiable political force. However, the term is still used to describe the broad thrust of the parties concerned.

9. In September 1991, the National Language Project organised a three-day international conference on 'Democratic Approaches to Language Planning and Standardisation'. This has had a major impact on the debates. The NLP has also published *Language Projects Review* (now *Bua!*) since 1987, and a variety of volumes of essays on language policy and planning and of materials for teaching.

10. The South African Broadcasting Corporation was established in terms of Act 22 of 1936.

11. The Rector of the Rand Afrikaans University, Professor Cas Crouse, announced to students late in 1993 that the university, alone in having Afrikaans as part of its name, was contemplating a dual medium policy. There was, he said, 'a struggle between heart and intellect. The heart says we must maintain RAU unchanged, as a home for the Afrikaans-speaking student. The intellect says that in the light of shrinking state subsidies we must move to a larger client base by extending our services to accommodate non-Afrikaners as well' (Webster, 1993). The Potchefstroom University for Christian Higher Education delivers many of its courses in English on its Vanderbijl Park campus, although the Potchefstroom campus is still thoroughly Afrikaans. And other Afrikaans universities offer certain courses in English.

3 Language Policy in Australia

MICHAEL HERRIMAN

Australia's language policy cannot be characterised simply or easily. However, we can begin to understand its nature and evolution by first of all clarifying the role of government in the nation. For a country of only 18 million inhabitants, the governmental structure of Australia is complex, with three layers of bureaucracy. Being a federal system, it has a central national government which administers the most important areas of national interests and welfare. Legally it does this by means of its constitutional prerogatives, and practically it does so through its powers of taxation. At the next level of government are the states, which existed as legal entities before the proclamation of a national government in 1901. As a consequence they had significant powers, some of which (including the power to levy taxes) were assumed by the federal government; but many, particularly in the areas of social services, have been retained in some measure. It is in these latter areas that certain federal prerogatives are contested by the states. Language policy developed as part of the federal government's concerns in regard to immigration issues, but during the development of the policy it became tied more to educational matters and hence came to involve the states. Australia is not quite comparable to most other countries covered in this book, except inasmuch as it has, in common with most others, devolved the responsibility for education to state, provincial or local authorities.

In Australia, the states have the role of educational providers and control the curriculum of primary and high schools. The federal government (called 'the Commonwealth') has few stated powers in education, but by virtue of its taxation powers and subsequent grants to states, and its commitments as a signatory to international covenants (its 'external affairs powers'), it has nonetheless been able to exercise considerable and indeed increasing control over educational matters. Not the least affected is the area of language policy. In fact, language policy can be said to have evolved most prominently in the area of language rights (in the sense of access) in schools, although, as already suggested, this was not its original focus.

Language Policy

In any discussions of language policy there might be a tendency to think of a language policy as if it were something fixed in statutes, clearly specified, immutable and all encompassing. None of these attributes really applies to Australia, however, as the policy has never been codified in law and has changed significantly in emphasis over its short history. Furthermore, the policy could be challenged at its edges by policies of the state governments which in turn have developed policies for language, though these all apply most directly to the status and teaching of languages other than English in schools. For that reason this chapter will be concerned only with policy at a national level in Australia.

The most interesting and most daunting aspect of language policy in Australia is the changes that it has seen over the years since 1984, the first year of a stated policy. Despite the fact that the same political party has been in power nationally (from 1983 to 1996), the policy has been subject to considerable change, to the extent that it is difficult to use the term 'policy', at least in the sense in which it connotes a degree of consistency. At best, the policy is a loose set of guidelines that can guide priority areas of spending by the Commonwealth government, on languages and language teaching. Its somewhat precarious position, subject to changes in political winds, does not make it completely meaningless. In fact, the policy can be said to have an inner core of issues that are fixed as the issues around which discussion and debate occur, and an outer layer of programmes derived from the core, that seem to be open to interpretation and subject to re-assessment in terms of their funding. In this sense there is no comparison with language policy in Canada, the core of which is enshrined in the constitution as part of the Canadian Charter of Rights and Freedoms, or with policy in South Africa, or at the other extreme with England where no policy exists *de jure* (though, as noted elsewhere, this opens the claim for a policy operating *de facto*).

Perhaps the least promising aspect of the policy is that it has been seen to be subject to a set of economic concerns that might override the claims of language rights in education, notably more ephemeral and insubstantial claims for certain educational, productivity and employment outcomes. Some areas of social concern in Australia (immigration policy, for example) have gained bi-partisan political support, but language policy, which in 1984 was developed by both the government and the opposition parties, has devolved to become part of one party's broader agenda. The recent history of the manipulation of language policy for other than intrinsic purposes does not strengthen the claim for the importance of a policy. Nor does it secure the rights of persons to preserve or protect their language, or gain another – a set of rights that can be claimed in Canada for example. It is against this strained background that language policy in Australia must be seen.

The Language Background of Australia

The lack of a stated policy does not mean that there is no policy: it signals instead a commitment to existing arrangements as a policy, inasmuch as it sanctions the status quo. English has been the main language of Australian civil life for more than 200 years. To have declared it an official language would have implied that there was a situation which required a decision on its relative status. Such a demand might have arisen during the 19th century when there were many non-English speaking immigrant groups and communities. For example, there were significant numbers of German and other European settlers who were joined later by many non-English speakers from Eastern Asia and the Pacific who had come to settle, engage in commerce, farm, seek gold and pearls, or were brought indentured. Yet despite the languages they introduced into the community, it would be difficult to imagine a challenge to the dominance of the English language which was well established and entrenched by its use in the law, the press, the liturgy, the bureaucracy and the classroom. Hence a policy on a national language was probably never at issue, not in the least because a nation did not exist until 1901.

That in Australia there were already more than 200 languages and many more dialects at the time of the first English settlement, was of no more concern to the colonists than was the land tenure of the speakers of those languages, the Aboriginal and Torres Strait Islands' peoples. Yet the period of great dominance of English came to be in the first half of the present century when, following declaration of nationhood (in 1901) the English majority had established an Australian identity distinguished not in the least by its language and reinforced in its popular literature. This nationalism, joined to unionism, culminated in the White Australia Policy; a policy regarding immigration restriction (putatively based on skin colour, but preferring a Northern European version of that), which might better be seen as the country's first language policy since a criterion for immigrant entry was often the passing of a language test. It is only in the last 50 years that the picture has changed, and more so in the last 30, with the abandonment of the White Australia policy. This has allowed for migration of persons from anywhere in the world provided that they met seemingly non-discriminatory criteria or were refugees from warfare, oppression or disasters.

The rapid evolution of a language policy in Australia is surprising given the recent growth of a numerically significant non-English speaking population, when compared with other countries where historically long-standing language divisions are found. Nevertheless, it could be argued that the very recency of the change in language situation caused a shock that was reflected in the development of a policy for language recognition and planning, and the educational use of language resources. The resulting policy probably reflects the unique set of conditions that emerged in Australia in the post World War II period.

Establishing the causes of the evolution of Australia's language policy is not easy, just as predicting outcomes of the 10 years of moves that preceded it would not have been easy either. This chapter will attempt to chart the developments leading to the present policy and assess the effectiveness of that policy for the educational and social issues it is meant to address. In the next section the language resources of Australia will be described. This will be followed by an account of the development of language policy over the last 20 years and the factors that gave shape to policy. The first official policy, the National Policy on Languages (1987) will be examined together with details of its implementation. Four years after this policy statement, a government White Paper ('Australia's Language: The Australian Language and Literacy Policy') was released. This brought significant revision to the National Policy with a different social and linguistic focus. Finally, an account of the present and possible future state of policy in Australia will be given.

The Language Resources of Australia

Australia is often said to be one of the most monolingual countries in the world. This claim is usually made in order to shock Australians out of their seeming low regard for the learning of languages other than the one they first acquired, or to emphasise the need for the learning of certain languages for political purposes; the latest being for trade with countries in the Asian region, justified in order to promote an economically sustainable future. Taken literally, it may be close to the truth; but the claim of monolingualism does mask the fact that Australia is a linguistically diverse nation. Though this diversity tends to be overstated sometimes (for example when it is also claimed that it is one of the most linguistically diverse nations in the world), there is an aspect to it that is critical to the consideration of a language policy. This aspect is the recency of arrival in Australia of many migrants from non-English speaking countries and its impact on existing linguistic resources and those made available for access to education and social services generally.

The common conception of Australia as an English-speaking country is accurate according to the most recent census data (1991). It is reported that 82.6% of the population speaks only English at home, and of persons speaking the next 29 identified languages (with 0.1% or greater percentage representation each), it is probable that many are bilingual (the other language being English) or use English to some degree, as is probably the case with the remaining persons (the 1.3% claiming to speak a language other than the 29 identified languages).

Unlike the situation in most other countries covered in this volume, there is no clearly identifiable other major language spoken in Australia, this in itself reinforcing the dominance of English. In fact the only other major languages reported as spoken at home (if taken as represented by more than 1.0% of speakers) are Italian (2.6%), German (1.8%) and Cantonese (1.0%). The 29 languages or language groups identified in the census of 1991, and their numbers of speakers, can be seen in Table 3.1. The various groupings also reveal a bureaucratic rather than a cultural conception of languages: for example, Yugoslav languages are grouped as one language (said to comprise 'Yugoslav' and 'Serbo-Croatian', though 'Croatian' appears separately) as are Aboriginal languages. Chinese languages presented greater difficulty, as both Cantonese and Mandarin are mentioned along with 'Chinese as stated' and 'Chinese other'. The anomalies may have as much to do with reporting by respondents as with the language typology used by the Bureau of Statistics.

These figures notwithstanding, it is difficult to determine the extent of other-than-English language *use* at present, and as Lo Bianco (1987: 14) notes, the extent of multilingualism in Australia. The census of 1991 identifies Australia as the birthplace of 75.5% of the population and another 'main English speaking country' as that of a further 9.3%. Of the remaining 13% (omitting 2.2% not responding) only 39 countries are identified (for having more than 0.1% representation), but many of these are polylingual (e.g. the former Yugoslavia). Clyne (1982) has noted the problem of using place of birth as an indicator of language(s) spoken, so these data must be seen as broadly indicative only. Lo Bianco (1987) identified at least 88 languages spoken in the community and it is generally accepted that between 120 to 150 languages might be spoken in the major cities. Clyne (1991a) states that about a hundred community languages are used regularly in Australia. Overall, the census figures are inadequate for predicting language use because they take no account of persons born in Australia living in non-English speaking households. And, as noted, the figures on languages spoken at home in the published census data only identify the 29 languages seen in Table 3.1.

It must also be noted that 41,039 persons identified themselves in the census as speaking an Aboriginal language in the home (against 265,459 persons identifying themselves as Aboriginal – a notable contrast with the 1986 census figures showing 36,000 and 189,000 respectively).

Table 3.1   Language spoken at home: 1991 census (persons aged 5 years or more)

Language spoken at home	Persons	(%)
Speaks English only	12,877,197	82.6
Speaks other language:		
Aboriginal languages	41,039	0.3
Arabic including Lebanese	147,322	0.9
Chinese languages:		
Cantonese	155,934	1.0
Mandarin	52,861	0.3
Chinese as stated	27,930	0.2
Chinese other	14,531	0.1
Total	251,256	1.6
Croatian	60,731	0.4
Czech	9,178	0.1
Dutch	47,543	0.3
Filipino languages	56,614	0.4
French	45,741	0.3
German	115,315	0.7
Greek	274,975	1.8
Hindi	21,585	0.1
Hungarian	29,128	0.2
Indonesian/Malay	28,900	0.2
Italian	409,480	2.6
Japanese	26,670	0.2
Khmer	13,598	0.1
Korean	18,798	0.1
Latvian	7,528	0.0
Macedonian	61,410	0.4
Maltese	52,031	0.3
Polish	64,924	0.4
Portuguese	24,249	0.2
Russian	23,673	0.2
Serbian	23,264	0.1
Spanish	86,169	0.6
Turkish	38,090	0.2
Ukrainian	12,327	0.1
Vietnamese	102,101	0.7
Yugoslav n.e.i.[a]	42,000	0.3
Other[b]	203,480	1.3
Not stated	371,185	2.4
Total	15,587,501	100.0

[a] Comprises 'Yugoslav n.e.i.' and 'Serbo-Croatian'.
[b] Includes 'other language indicated but not stated' and 'inadequately described'.

The census data, however, do not identify the languages in question. Lo Bianco cites data that identify 36 Aboriginal languages with more than 200 speakers as well as two creoles (Kriol and Torres Strait creole). The creoles are of interest because in contrast to the other languages their numbers of speakers are growing and the variants becoming more widespread. There are 50 Aboriginal languages in all said to be viable including a number of dialects. Of other Aboriginal languages and dialects there are diminishing numbers of speakers and some languages are disappearing altogether. It is currently estimated that one language is disappearing each year (Lo Bianco, 1987) and that 500 may have disappeared since European colonisation. The lack of any government support for or interest in Aboriginal languages prior to the development of a language policy, together with a general suppression of Aboriginal culture has largely caused this regrettable situation, although the situation has since been eased.

Development of the Policy

This brief account of the diverse language resources in Australia can help in our understanding the causes of development of a language policy; but linguistic diversity alone cannot be seen as the principal factor determining that a policy would develop, or that it would have the particular focus it has. Policy developed rather as a result of several pressures, the initial one being the growth of an awareness of ethnic identity and the move to introduce a multicultural awareness and curriculum focus in Australian schools. Another pressure was the concern of linguists and teachers over the decline of language study in schools. The term 'ethnic' came to have particular connotations, and these are discussed further on in this chapter.

The policy developed also as part of a concern for preserving and promoting ethnic identity and culture in Australia in the 1970s against an earlier response to immigration which had initially been assimilationist and later became integrationist. These earlier responses were not governed by any well-considered analysis of the social or psychological needs of the newly arriving people, but more by a concern to subsume their culture within the mainstream Anglo-Australian. It is difficult to chart exactly the move towards the multicultural policy that evolved in the 1970s; there was gradual change brought about by the sheer weight of numbers of newly arrived persons, their hard-won accession to positions of some authority in the community and perhaps a realisation that they might be a political constituency. There was also an almost cataclysmic change in Australian life in 1972, when a national election brought a very reformist, centralist and socially conscious Labour government to power, which fostered a sense of equality of opportunity that had been missing from official national life.

As part of its new social agenda, two major policy developments occurred after 1972. One was a focus on immigration matters both from the perspective of services and facilities available to migrants and their cultural impact on the Australian community. An active and articulate Minister for Immigration (Mr Al Grassby) became spokesperson for a broader public perception of Australia as a culturally diverse country. He not only advocated a pluralistic cultural perspective, but claimed rights for migrants to use their home language and to have it recognised in schools. His thinking also included the notion of language as a resource. The new government set up Migrant Task Forces in the states to examine access and needs of migrants for a broad range of social services. These moves set in train the forces that were to culminate in a broad non-partisan policy on multiculturalism.

The other significant move of the new government in its three-year term was to assume wide-ranging control of education by means of setting up a commission for schools (The Australian Schools Commission). The aim of the Commission was to assess the whole system of schooling in Australia and to provide opportunities for all students to succeed in school, by minimising state and sectoral differences in quality and funding. This was effected by taking over responsibility for funding of public schools from the states and assuming funding of all independent schools (at various levels of support depending on a calculated category of need). The Commission went further in providing additional large grants to states and individual schools and school systems for specifically targeted programmes to remove social and educational disadvantage. The moves to counter disadvantage did not include initially the disadvantage of language suffered by those whose first language was not English, the language of instruction in schools. The Schools Commission marked the beginning of the incursion of the national government into education policy and curriculum, a move that has become strengthened with time. Restructured as a key Commonwealth Department, it eventually came to take over, and has now a major impact on, formulation and implementation of language policy.

Unlike the government's egalitarian social reform agenda in education, the recognition of a need for the reforming of attitudes to 'ethnic' matters came from a broader concern expressed through the Ethnic Communities Councils. The expression of ethnic consciousness and rights was not principally heard in education, but rather in demands for social services related to social welfare, employment, medical, legal, educational and interpreter services, as well as for language rights in the home language. Education as an institution had been very conservative and assimilationist in thinking to this time. For example, since 1970, the funding for special English language support in schools came from the Commonwealth Immigration Department and not from the states' education ministries. The Immigration Department had also funded special English language programmes for adults since 1950.

The government which succeeded the short-lived Labour administration at the end of 1975 was even more responsive to the growing multicultural mood. This was greatly owing to the personal interest of the then Prime Minister (Mr Malcolm Fraser) in immigration and ethnic affairs. Amongst other moves and to some extent pushed by an opposition party which had by now a strong policy in these matters, it commissioned an inquiry in 1977 to be headed by a prominent lawyer (Mr Frank Galbally) to report on post-arrival services and needs of migrants. The 'Report of the Review of Post-arrival Programs and Services for Migrants' (The 'Galbally Report', 1978) probably had as its most important impact, the establishment of an official policy on multiculturalism. In tabling the report in parliament, the Prime Minister (Mr Malcolm Fraser) declared that:

> Further steps to encourage multiculturalism are needed . . . [the Government] will foster the retention of the cultural heritage of different ethnic groups and promote intercultural understanding. [Schools] are the key element in achieving such a goal and we will allocate $5m. over the next three years to develop multicultural and community language programs. (Fraser in *Hansard*, 1978: 2728, 2791)

The report was well received by the various ethnic groups, which by this time had gained official status in the form of Ethnic Communities Councils (ECCs) in the states and were represented by a national body, the Federation of Ethnic Communities Councils of Australia (FECCA). It placed much emphasis on the disadvantage faced by students who fail to gain an adequate standard of English language, and advocated greater support for ESL in schools. Its general spirit was adopted by the other major parties in parliament to the extent that the report could be said to represent the high point of multiculturalism. In the following year (1979) the Ministry of Education produced a discussion paper entitled 'Education in a Multicultural Australia'. This canvassed the important issues of teaching English as a second language and the maintenance and teaching of community languages. One of the responses to the Galbally report was the setting up of an advisory body on multiculturalism funded by the Commonwealth government, the Australian Institute of Multicultural Affairs (AIMA) in 1979. This new body undertook as its first project a review of multiculturalism in education. In the review, multicultural education referred to 'studies encompassing three broad strands – the teaching of English, the teaching of languages other than English used in the Australian community, and the study of ethnic and cultural diversity in Australia' (p.*v*). In its report (the *Review of Multicultural and Migrant Education in Australia*, 1980) the 'teaching of English' is identified solely as 'teaching of English as a second language' because lack of English is seen as 'the major barrier to effective participation in Australian society' (p. 13).

At this point education itself became principally identified in the delivery of multiculturalism. The multicultural agenda was still seen as one mainly to do with immigration matters, but a subtle shift was evident towards education as the agent. An unfortunate consequence of the political discourse of this time was the use of the term 'ethnic' to refer to persons in the population who were not from what was held to be the predominant Anglo-Celtic mainstream. Though its use was well-intentioned and did give recognition to the cultural diversity of Australia, it also bred some cynicism and the claim that all residents were ethnic.

The heightened interest in the multicultural character of Australia did generate a re-assessment of its languages, especially in the light of the language teaching available in schools. The decline in the study of the traditional languages became juxtaposed against the fact that there was a large language resource in the community which was untapped and unrepresented in schools (with a few exceptions). State governments had been giving some support to Saturday morning ('Ethnic') schools teaching some of the main languages (in some cities up to 30 languages) of the community, but this was not deemed to be part of the curriculum of regular schools. Aside from German, Italian, Modern Greek and Spanish, the widespread teaching of other community languages was virtually overlooked. Of the Asian languages, Japanese and Indonesian had begun to be offered in schools, but at this time they were by no means significantly represented by native speakers in the community (though this would change in the ensuing years). Even less was the case of Aboriginal languages being studied. The AIMA report had recommended major changes to the content of teacher education courses and the curriculum of the classroom in order to generate a greater focus on the teaching of community languages as well as a sensitivity to multiculturalism.

The focus on languages had been a part of the Ethnic Communities Councils concerns also, and was expressed in the realisation that there had to be greater awareness of the linguistic needs of persons with limited access to English. This included proposals for provision of language support and interpretation services in bureaucracies and social services, the training in the professions of persons from the major language groups and access to radio programmes in the community languages. Clyne indicates the following as some of the language-related demands arising from the Ethnic Communities Councils' pressures:

- Availability of interpreters in hospitals, law courts, prisons and schools.
- Improved facilities for the teaching of English as a second language.
- Maintenance programmes for community languages at all levels of education.
- Bilingual education (where required).
- An ethnic radio station.
- Films in community languages on television.
- Teaching of community languages as an integral part of the education of all Australian schoolchildren. (Clyne, 1991a: 8)

Support for the under-recognised and under-utilised language resources of the country also came from professional associations of linguists and language teachers, which at various of their professional meetings, passed resolutions urging the government to reconsider the language situation in Australia. The concern of professional linguists related as much to the decline in numbers of students studying the traditional 'foreign languages' in schools and universities as it did to their concern for community languages. In response to the growing pressures, including as well representations from the Aboriginal community and the societies for the deaf, the Commonwealth Department of Education released a document 'Towards a National Language Policy', in 1982. Its intention was to 'stimulate public debate on language policy' and its rationale was expressed in the following statement:

> The existence of . . . diverse languages within Australia gives rise to a range of issues concerning the roles which each should play and the steps which should be taken to enable the best management of our linguistic resources. (p. 1)

There is no broad social concern expressed here, but rather the language as resource argument that would continue to be expressed by language advocates. To the extent that a social concern is expressed in the document it is towards acknowledging the need for access to English for all and a recognition of the need for multilingual television and radio. The agenda for social equality through other languages as well as English was still very much the agenda of the ethnic groups.

It is likely, however, that by this time federal politicians would have been well alerted to issues raised by the ethnic groups in their constituencies, although these too would have been related to language mainly in as much as it impinged on broader issues of multiculturalism, recognition of language rights, and access via translation and interpretation in the community language, as well as through English, to social services and social goods. The 1982 document identified language in the narrower setting of the following issues: English as the national language; English as a second language; English as a mother tongue; the role of non-standard English; literacy; language and cognitive development; the role, retention and learning of languages other than English; bilingual education and mother tongue maintenance; and issues relating to Aboriginal languages.

A shape for the policy

On 25 May 1982, the national parliament acknowledged the need for a language policy, a move that had been mooted by the Commonwealth Department of Education a year earlier. The Senate, the Upper House of the parliament, proposed the first inquiry into languages from a national perspective, to be conducted by one of its standing committees. This committee, The Senate Standing Committee on Education and the Arts, comprised six senators equally representing the government and opposition. Halfway through its inquiries the membership changed when the government was defeated at the polls in March 1983, and a Labour government came to power. Two of the original senators were retained.

The next important move in the formulation of a policy came with the release of a report, A National Language Policy for Australia (ANLPA), by a distinguished panel of linguists from six of the professional associations with a declared interest in the language policy issue. This group (the PLANLangPol Committee), which as noted already, must take credit for getting the policy issue on the national parliamentary agenda, had been set up in August 1981, and its report in January 1983 covered in much greater detail most of the issues in the 1982 paper (TANLP). It provided a succinct and perceptive documentation of the state of English, Aboriginal and community languages in Australia, and projected strong directions for a policy. As might have been expected, it had a scholarly focus on languages *per se*, rather than on their role in expressing ethnic identity and the multicultural heritage of Australia.

It could also be said that by 1983 some of the more community based concerns related to multiculturalism had been addressed. A strong influence of the programmes for schools recommended by Galbally in 1978 was felt in schools, especially those with larger ethnic populations. A heightened awareness of the need for community language teaching and an increasing awareness among teachers of language and cultural issues ensued. Ethnic schools (teaching languages outside of the mainstream schools) had flourished with federal government support, and despite debate over their performance (Ozolins, 1993) they appeared as another emblem of multicultural recognition. By this time also the agenda of the language policy gave less emphasis to ethnic radio and television because of the successful introduction of the

Special Broadcasting Services television channel further supporting the ethnic radio stations earlier set up.

The Senate Standing Committee reported its findings in December 1984. It had received 241 submissions and 179 documents and had taken evidence from 94 witnesses. It was the most comprehensive statement on the language situation in Australia to that time, reflecting the diverse and extensive evidence provided and maintaining a broad cultural and educational perspective. Its focal point was the language needs of the whole country rather than the defence of community languages against an English dominance. Though clearly stating the scope for policy, the report did not see itself as setting down the policy. Its first recommendation states:

> The Committee recommends that language policies should be developed and coordinated at the national level on the basis of the four principles:
>
> - Competence in English.
> - Maintenance and development of languages other than English.
> - Provision of services in languages other than English.
> - Opportunities for learning second languages.
>
> (Recomm. 1: 1.16)

These principles it acknowledges as having been taken from a National Language Policy Conference convened by the Federation of Ethnic Communities Councils in 1982. Given what must have been a large number of claims on behalf of sectional and special interest language groups (for a full account, see Ozolins, 1993) the committee had maintained a balanced and consensual view.

The report is difficult to summarise. It touched on almost every aspect of language in the public life of Australia in its discussion and subsequent 117 recommendations. The main headings it used were: towards a national language policy; language use in Australia; Australia's national language; teaching English as a first language; teaching English as a second language; adult illiteracy; teaching English as a foreign language; Australian Aboriginal languages; language needs of persons with communication handicaps; languages and Australia's international relationships; teaching languages other than English; translating and interpreting services; libraries; and, languages and the media. It adopted the view that English 'is, and will remain, Australia's national language'. It gave official recognition to 'Australian English' as a dialect or set of dialects. It also suggested paths for status planning for English. The report has a somewhat detached and academic focus with a strong sense of simply laying out the issues that need to be taken up in subsequent policy decisions.

On matters of implementation there were suggestions for various forms of public institutions to monitor the issues raised and decide on policy. The submission of the Federation of Ethnic Communities Councils had proposed that a National Language Act be promulgated to guarantee language rights and access to information. This path was rejected by the Committee on the grounds that formulating enforceable legislation would narrow the scope and specifications of the policy. This suggestion was not unreasonable in view of the massive set of issues raised in the recommendations. It suggested instead a national advisory council on language policy to advise state and Commonwealth governments on language matters.

A problematic language issue addressed by the report was the educational status of languages spoken in the community versus the languages traditionally taught in schools. Those hoping for a clear resolution of this tension would have been disappointed by the recommendation that determining 'languages of major relevance to the majority of schools' be the prerogative of educational authorities. Funds were to be 'directed mainly to such languages although a substantial portion should also be reserved for other languages' (Recomm. 87: 11.92). As to prioritising languages, the report suggested 'two or three languages of ethnic groups within the Australian community – not necessarily the largest groups, and not necessarily all of European origin'. The Asian languages cited as 'of major importance to Australia' were Japanese, Indonesian and Chinese. The committee seemingly avoided identifying European 'languages of major importance for Australia' (it would have been too controversial), and simply identified French, German, Spanish, Arabic and 'perhaps Russian' as 'major world languages'. 'Two or three Aboriginal languages' would also be identified 'after consultation with Aboriginal groups'. The report further absolved itself by adding that 'this is an indicative listing only'. The surprise was the failure to give recognition to significant community languages generally and the omission of some obvious ones.

Some of the impact of this direction was softened by moves which had taken place in most of the states to establish policies on languages in schools via commissioned reports, conferences and workshops. These were generated in some part out of concerns for state autonomy in educational matters, but also out of genuine concern for providing equal opportunity for participation in the educational process. In acknowledging the ethnic diversity in schools, these policies mainly reflected ethnic and multicultural issues in schooling. Most gave significant attention to the teaching of languages other than English as well as the relative status of instruction in English as a second language.

Since neither legislation nor an official response were generated by the Senate's report, and it was suggested that policy directions should follow, the next move in the evolution of policy was the commissioning of a specific national policy statement on languages. The task was given to Joseph Lo Bianco, a consultant in the area of language and culture who had previously completed a major language report for the Victorian government: 'The Place of Languages other than English in Victorian Schools'. Lo Bianco worked on the national policy from July 1986. The advance copy of the report was released in December and the final report in 1987. When adopted by the federal Cabinet in June 1987, the 'National Policy on Languages' (NPL) became the official and definitive statement on language policy in Australia.

The National Policy on Languages

The Lo Bianco report, as it is usually referred to, covered all the issues addressed in the Senate report, but did so in a more detailed and researched way. It can be seen as being based on four principles (Lo Bianco, AACLAME Report, 1990: vi.). The first and primary principle is the availability of English and English literacy for all. Next comes support for Aboriginal and Torres Strait languages; a language other than English for all; and access for all to widespread and equitable language services. In the NPL, these are defined in more detail as a set of general and specific principles (covering three pages and too extensive to quote here).

Its most notable general feature is a more generous outlook on the linguistic and cultural resources of the ethnic community, a focus on multiculturalism, a broader concern for Aboriginal languages and culture, and support for the teaching of languages other than English. On the latter issue it cemented an agenda that had been strongly supported in all state policies, not the least because of wide public concern with the lack of opportunities for second language learning (it was estimated for example that less than 12% of children studied another language at the final year of schooling at that time as against 25% 20 years previously – it is not insignificant that a much larger proportion of the age cohort were completing year 12 by the time of the report). The report is less conservative in general on educational matters and supports bilingualism much more confidently than did the Senate report. It endorses language learning and maintenance on well argued psychological, socio-logical, economic, equalitarian, internationalistic and pedagogic grounds.

A major step taken in the report was the identification of a set of languages for wider teaching in the community which as a consequence were to be the ones targeted for special funding in education. These were: Arabic; Chinese; French; German; Greek; Indonesian/Malay; Italian; Japanese; and Spanish. The argument in support of these is somewhat circular in that it states:

> . . . these languages warrant promotion over and above specific support for other languages since it is expected that more students will take these than other languages and relatively more schools will teach these languages than other languages. (Lo Bianco, AACLAME Report, 1990: 125)

As an hypothesis it is also a self-fulfilling. It was not intended that this identification preclude others (classical and minor community languages) being taught, however.

Two major developments suggested were concerned with implementation and funding. For implementing the policy it had proposed an advisory council be set up from the community of interests together with a national institute for research, documentation and development of languages. Detailed roles were described for these bodies. The recommendations came to fruition in the Australian Advisory Council on Languages and Multicultural Education (AACLAME) and the National Languages Institute of Australia (NLIA), the latter located in various universities throughout the country. ACCLAME was to have four standing committees covering English language learning, Aboriginal languages, languages other than English (LOTEs), and language services to the communication disabled, as well as two temporary committees.

The Lo Bianco Report went much further than the Senate in that it gave estimates of the cost of funding the various programmes it endorsed. This gave the impression of a carefully planned policy with clear targets. Indeed, though the report is complete in itself, it clearly saw the need for ongoing language planning. It recognised the tensions between state and federal government and was reconciliatory in tone. The report not surprisingly received widespread public and political support. It appeared to mark a sense of maturity in regard to languages in a plural national culture. It also attracted considerable notice overseas for its breadth and scope.

Implementation of the national policy

In being tied to funding, the NPL was able to proceed with assurances of government support for specific programmes. To this extent it suited the government well because it did not require the establishment of a large bureaucracy. Instead, it was mainly to be funded through existing national channels and administered by existing institutions in the states. One of the existing programmes (the ESL schools programme for new arrivals) was gathered under the umbrella of the policy and a set of new ones was derived. These new programmes were: the Australian second language learning programme; the adult literacy action campaign; the multicultural and cross-cultural supplementation programme; the Aboriginal languages programme; and the Asian studies programme. Funding was also granted to the council on language and multicultural education (AACLAME), the advisory body which was to monitor policy development.

The first major review of action following the NPL was released in May 1990, three years after its inception. It was prepared by the Advisory Council (AACLAME) for the Minister for Employment, Education and Training and was entitled 'The National Policy on Language' (TNPL). It reaffirmed the direction of the policy and provided detailed reports on programmes and activities of the council. It also listed the allocation and spending of funds granted to the programmes, reported on commissioned research, evaluations and reviews of three of the programmes, and on the setting up of the National Languages Institute of Australia. It provided directions and priorities for the future and made 17 recommendations to the government including requests for increased funding. It contains an impressive account of the way in which the NPL had generated activities in all the areas targeted. That the activities described could have taken place in the absence of the NPL is possible, but the impact of the policy was to ensure a coordinated approach to language issues. It also likely prepared the national consciousness for an acceptance of the need for continued assessment and organisation of the language resources of the country.

Another policy

Several other events were taking place at the time that the follow-up report to the NPL was released. The year (1990) was International Literacy Year (ILY) and the attention of Australian educators was focused on the event with widespread local participation. The Commonwealth Department of Employment, Education and Training had also commenced work on a discussion paper on literacy and language policies – a preparatory exercise to generate community consideration of what would become a major policy statement on 'an Australian Literacy and Language Policy for the 90s'. In line with parliamentary tradition the first of the papers was to be called a 'Green Paper' and the final document a 'White Paper'. The announcement of a new policy document outside of the established mechanism of ACCLAME was surprising. The direction signalled in the title, giving precedence to 'literacy' over language, was also a sign of a major shift in direction. The focus was consistent with the prevailing interest in literacy as part of ILY activities, but it was also announced that the Green Paper would be released with a report on post-secondary English language training, confirming the shift in focus.

In general and in its specifics, the Green Paper was criticised from the moment of its release and was unfavourably received in the professional community of languages/linguistics. Matters were not aided by its title: 'The Language of Australia; Discussion Paper on an Australian Literacy and Language Policy for the 1990s'. Its critics saw not the generic use of the term 'language', but a deliberate signal that one language in particular, English, was the focus of the policy, confirming the earlier fears engendered by the apparent focus on literacy. Its main departure from the NPL was in a narrow-ness of focus and a construing of the goals of a policy in terms of clear economic and employment ends rather than ends of social justice, educational access and personal satisfaction. The literacy focus outweighed any other concern, with an ominous hint towards a user-pays system for participation in lan-guage and literacy programmes. Though Aboriginal languages and LOTEs were still emphasised in the new policy, their relative status was diminished in view of the greater emphasis on English language literacy. The original NPL emphasis on equitable and widespread language services was signifi-cantly diminished.

The Green Paper appeared to have taken no notice of the AACLAME document released six months earlier, giving a signal that a major shift in policy was intended. At a meeting shortly after the release of the Green Paper, the Minister for Employment, Education and Training stated that the NPL 'had got us nowhere'. The controversy aroused by the report prevented consideration of some of its merits, notably the concern that semi-literacy was a barrier to participation in the workforce. It, perhaps rightly, expressed concern over the outcomes of some programmes in adult literacy, and it expressed the mood of many educators in supporting Asian languages more strongly. Grave concerns were expressed over its suggestion that private delivery by competitive bidding might improve some adult programmes. Though it should be recalled that the Green Paper was meant only for discus-sion, it did signal that a change of direction in language policy was intended. It also ensured that there would be an active response to the paper as input to the final policy document.

Readers of the other report noted in the Green Paper, that of the Working Party on Post-secondary English Language Training, would have read the signals more easily. The opening sentence of that report emphasises the potential human capital value of migration, not its cultural or linguistic benefit:

> . . . as a result of inadequate English language training Australia has failed to take full advantage of the massive infusion of skills that immi-gration has brought to the country since World War II. (p. 1)

If the figures it cited are correct, there is indication of a massive wastage of potential and, at least in this respect, the report is justified in raising this as an issue of importance. It was not given importance in the NPL.

However, it could be argued that this concern should have been addressed to ACCLAME and added to the scope of the NPL to treat within its programmes. The problems identified in the report concern both inadequate levels of English proficiency at exit from courses and failure of adults to participate in the programmes. A problem with lack of English skills was not found only in recently arrived migrants; at least 360,000 longer-term residents were estimated to be in the category of having language difficulties. The government's concern with these issues in a time of high unemployment and diminishing jobs at lower-skill levels is perhaps understandable, but it is regrettable that it came to overshadow and alter the focus of the NPL. It is appropriate to point out that the former federal Department of Education (which was previously the Department of Education and Youth Affairs) had been recently re-organised to become the Department of Employment, Education and Training. This change and the precedence given to 'Employment' in the title could be said to have signalled a change in thinking about the aims of education, from intrinsic to extrinsic goals.

It is necessary at this point to describe some changes that were occurring in Australian education around the time of these language policy developments. These mainly concerned the locus of control of schools and education. The Commonwealth government, which had been in power since 1983, had continued its involvement in educational planning on the grounds of providing uniformity in the system. To its disbursement to the states of specially targeted funds (in addition to recurrent grants and capital grants) it attached accountability criteria that to some extent made the states answerable for their spending. The Commonwealth had also embarked on an optimistic campaign to provide uniformity of educational standards and outcomes in the systems and had also sought to break down differences between states with the chief purpose of making it easier for students to move from one state to another. The main tool in this arrangement was to be a set of nationally agreed upon curricula derived from agreed outcome statements, and at the time it had support of the states' Ministers of Education. The goal was not achieved however.

The 'White Paper'

The White Paper was released in August 1991. Its title was 'Australia's Language: The Australian Language and Literacy Policy'. The title, significantly, reversed 'literacy' and 'language'. Critics of the Green Paper's title would have preferred to see 'language' pluralised, as in the earlier suggested title 'The Languages of Australia'. This is also not insignificant as the new policy declared that English is the official language of Australia. The Minister's foreword to the White Paper is brief, direct and clearly focused in the direction more than hinted at in the Green Paper (though in most respects the White Paper is much more moderate than the former document). The paper claims to 'deliver the Prime Minister's promise to maintain and develop the National Policy on Languages, incorporating the principles of the NPL into a new language and literacy policy (ALLP)'. It is significant already that this is a ministerial document. Although AACLAME was meant to be the body responsible for developing and reviewing language policy, its role in the generation of the White Paper appears to have been minor.

A general utilitarian and economic rationalist spirit motivates the White Paper; it seems an age removed from the academic, social justice and multicultural concerns that drove the NPL. Its political rhetoric can be judged in the following passages:

> Language and literacy issues are central to the reshaping and the improved performance of our education and training systems. . . . Global economic forces are demanding changes in the structure of Australian industry, in our ability to compete in world markets, and in our readiness to adapt to new jobs, new career structures, and new technologies.

The language-related activities preceding the White Paper are characterised as being of 'analysis and review'. The paper then states (seemingly by way of contrast) that 'The case for action is clear and compelling.' The ALLP claims to be:

> . . . a statement of national needs, priorities, goals, objectives, targets and strategies for developing programs that will address three specific goals.

In other parts of the report, e.g. see below, four goals are identified.

The principal focus of the White Paper is on literacy. Even though it adopts as 'key goals of a national language and literacy policy' the four-principles notion that had guided the Senate and the Lo Bianco Reports, a close look at the expanded versions of those principles makes it clear that they coalesce in the literacy concern rather than remaining the four areas of broader concern of the two previous reports. The goals of the White Paper's Australian Language and Literacy Policy (ALLP) are the following:

1. All Australian residents should develop and maintain a level of spoken and written English which is appropriate for a range of contexts, with the support of education and training programs addressing their diverse learning needs.
2. The learning of languages other than English must be substantially expanded and improved to enhance educational outcomes and communication both within the Australian and international community.

3. Aboriginal and Torres Strait Islander languages should be maintained and developed where they are still transmitted. Other languages should be assisted in an appropriate way, for example, through recording. These activities should only occur where the speakers so desire and in consultation with their community, for the benefit of the descendants of their speakers and for the nation's heritage.

4. Language services provided through interpreting and translating, print and electronic media and libraries should be expanded and improved. (ALLP, Comp. Vol.: xiii)

The comparison of the scope of these goals with the principles of the NPL is stark. There is some difficulty in places in deciding just what the focus of the new policy is. This derives from inconsistency between the new policy as stated in the key goals and the substance given to them in the expanded version (the report was released in two volumes, though not for reasons of size as both are quite slim). The general goals lead the reader to expect extensive discussion of the range of issues they implicate, but the extended discussion is often more direct. Unlike the NPL, it is reflective rather than argumentative. The goals also devolve more to specific programmes for allocation of funding rather than acting as principles upon which language planning can take place. The notion of a country's languages as a cultural resource is missing. Thus the broad, comprehensive and detailed sweep of the Lo Bianco (NPL) document is lost. In its place is a shorter-term rationale for the funding of particular programmes, a situation that seems to leave policy to the whim of political parties, ephemeral issues and sudden changes. It also creates a precedent for future political overriding of an area that ideally should be part of a national consensus, as it had appeared to be following the Lo Bianco document. To this extent the claim can be made that Australia's language policy has lost the force it had in preceding years.

There is an extensive discussion of literacy, indicating that the evidence submitted by witnesses was considered and that a broad definition of literacy was entertained for some time (ALLP, Companion Volume: 34–9). When the programmes are set down, however, the view of literacy is significantly contracted to a concern with establishing quantifiable measures of literacy achievement. It would have been helpful to planners to have had a clearer indication of the kind or level of literacy targeted beyond the mere term 'active literacy' or the broad descriptors of the ASLPR (an Australian adaptation of an American rating scale for foreign languages). Literacy, furthermore, is identified only as literacy in English. When the heading 'Aboriginal and Torres Strait Islander literacy' appears, one is entitled to think that the discussion may be about literacy in the home languages or even bi-literacy. It is therefore a shock to find it meaning that 'Aboriginal and Torres Strait Islander people have a particular need for more English language and literacy assistance'. The 'particular need' refers to lower than normal standards of literacy in some communities. On the issue of the population in need, the estimate given is that one million adults have literacy difficulties. Of these, 72% are from English-speaking backgrounds. The figure is disputed, however, being an extrapolation from a study of a much smaller population. The author of that study had advised caution in making a general interpretation out of responses to a specific set of embedded numerical items on part of a test. Even if approximately accurate, the figure indicates reason for a concern about English literacy. But no consideration is given to the possibility that the literacy needs of persons from non-English speaking backgrounds (NESB) may be qualitatively different from those of English speakers, particularly in the area of acquisition of discourse structures. As well as English literacy, ESL provision was to be increased under the policy and some innovative approaches were suggested.

There is strong support for other languages and a clear intention that the learning of LOTEs be increased, but the motives have changed. The maintaining and developing of LOTEs for intercultural and multicultural purposes is lost to the notion of learning LOTEs principally for economic reasons. A target of note is the more than doubling of the number of students studying a language in the final year of schooling and the guarantee that all children will have an opportunity to study a language 'appropriate to their needs' by the year 2000. There is an extensive canvassing of the educational and pedagogic issues to be addressed in providing opportunities for a wider and longer study of languages. A wider set of priority languages is suggested. It is proposed that the Commonwealth government focus on and fund eight core languages in each state, to be chosen from the following list:

> Aboriginal languages;
> Arabic;
> Chinese;
> French;
> German;
> Indonesian;
> Italian;
> Japanese;
> Korean;
> Modern Greek;
> Russian;
> Spanish;
> Thai; and
> Vietnamese.

Special funding is to be given to schools to encourage the study of these languages on a per capita basis ($300 per student) calculated on the number of students studying the language in Year 12 of schooling. States wishing to choose other languages would have to fund them internally.

A special priority had already existed for the funding of developments in Asian languages teaching and Asian studies and this grant was to be continued. Asian languages are established as priority languages in the policy and are to be given special developmental funds for related teacher training. The former Ethnic Languages Program is to be known as the Community Languages Program and is to be taken from its after-hours and Saturday morning time-tabling to be made part of language teaching in schools. Increased funding is made available for this. By contrast, there is minimal regard for bilingual education except as a possible aid to literacy in transitional programmes.

The report shows sensitivity to other major issues implicated in increasing language study in schools. One is teacher education and the need for support for the priority languages in tertiary (university and higher technical) education. Another is the need for more language study for vocational purposes. A significant need identified in earlier reports and taken up here is the place of language study in primary schooling, an area which with some exceptions has been greatly overlooked in the past. The paper missed the opportunity to discuss language more thoroughly in the context of community languages and bilingualism, where some of the most innovative programmes and experiments in second language learning have taken place.

The most generous view of the new policy sees it as directing attention to an important issue that was not as clearly identified in the past (literacy). Moreover it is directed much more clearly at adults with literacy difficulties. It also allocates significant amounts of funding to the programmes identified in its priorities. The importance of Asian languages (though still debated) is also emphasised. It retains the emphasis on services (access to interpreting, training of interpreters, library services for literacy and literacy through the media) thought to have been lost when the Green Paper was released. The policy also provides for competitive bidding by agencies for certain of the literacy and ESL programmes previously delivered in public institutions. This may well have beneficial outcomes. The identifying of language with broad educational goals related to national interests is also important, but that this appears to diminish and preclude other language concerns is unfortunate. As might be expected from a ministry involved with employment, education and training, the identification of language issues with job training and unemployment programmes is strong. In fact some of the funding announced for the language programmes is proposed to be shared with job training initiatives.

The most serious defect in the new policy is a structural one. With the NPL, the Commonwealth government had set up an integrated structure for a national policy on languages with a broad set of principles to govern existing language resources, to integrate programmes of all kinds related to language, to suggest funding and research and further policy developments and to subsume and guide future language issues and developments. It might have been expected that any further developments in policy would have derived from the existing policy and its mechanisms. The White Paper (ALLP) instead has taken an independent line and effectively by-passed the NPL, while using some of the previous rhetoric to disguise the move. By declaring itself the new policy it has superseded the NPL. The new policy cannot be said to have a comprehensive philosophical and linguistic basis. This is nowhere better seen than in the lack of a clear operational definition of literacy, a concept right at its centre. The policy is rather a set of issues that have some contemporary importance, as much as anything, for being implicated in the government's plans for more basic structural and economic reforms. Its very existence in the present form provides a precedent for language policy and planning that is *ad hoc* and governed by political expediency rather than a long-term commitment to principles of the kind that are usually suggested in the use of the term 'policy'.

The only structural resemblance the ALLP has to the previous policy is in its dependence upon cooperation with the states for programme delivery. The policy was formulated at a time of a seeming consensus over a national curriculum for schools. This was proposed in the form of common goals statements for seven major areas of learning. The likelihood of agreement on this curriculum is remote now, which must affect the outcomes of some programmes. As for delivery structures, the present policy is dependent on educational institutions; to this extent language policy has become more linked to educational policies and has drifted away from language concerns. It was seen already that this is the case with language policy in the states of Australia. However, in the major states the language policies are expressed as part of broader social justice policies in schooling and incorporate such matters as rights and prerogatives to do with ethnicity, gender and disadvantage.

Despite the supplanting of the NPL by the ALLP, many of the programmes and mechanisms set in train by the NPL still exist. The National Languages Institute of Australia was changed to the National Language *and Literacy* Institute of Australia. It has continued and expanded since the implementation of the new policy, but mainly as an agency advising, coordinating and funding research. It is sad to reflect on its decline from the original role envisaged by Lo Bianco, of becoming the 'policy-maker in language to sustain the research and teaching to effect permanent improvement in the cultivation of Australia's language resources' (1991: 27) and in this respect taking over from the Commonwealth government whose role was to be a coordinating one. As part of the funding arrangement in its original constitution, it was to become self-supporting eventually. That it is not, will leave it potentially prey to any cost-cutting administration, and lacking in autonomy.

The advisory body AACLAME was a casualty of the new policy, however. A new body, the Australian Language and Literacy Council, has been set up to incorporate AACLAME and two other advisory bodies, the Asian Studies Council and the National Consultative Council for International Literacy Year. The new body is answerable to the National Board of Employment Education and Training, a statutory authority reviewing education at all levels. Thus an important and relatively independent advisory voice on language matters was lost.

Language policy at present

The states of Australia now have language policies built in to statements of their educational goals. The Commonwealth government has a policy established as a set of programmes for delivering priority languages services and addressing language needs including research into teaching and learning of languages. The programmes are delivered at the state level by; the state departments of (school) education, other schools' systems, universities and equivalent institutes of higher education, institutions of Technical and Further Education (TAFE), adult education agencies and by private providers. The main programmes with current expenditures (1994) are as follows: Children's literacy ($5.1 m), Adult literacy ($52.63 m), Children's ESL ($117.76 m), Adult ESL ($120.35 m), Children's LOTE ($17.45 m), Adult LOTE ($5.35 m), Aboriginal literacy and language ($8.25 m), Advisory councils and research ($6.44 m). The dominance of ESL and adult literacy in terms of funding can be clearly seen.

One of the chief delivery problems involves LOTEs. The policy recognises the lack of well trained and native speakers to teach, and schools equipped to provide languages other than English. Some shared arrangements and teaching at a distance is proposed, but it is unlikely that there will be a recognisable improvement in the immediate years. This is as much due to years of neglect of the area by governments and educational authorities.

The best adapted area for positive outcomes is the child ESL programme. It has benefited from years of hard politicking and professional development by its advocates. It is too early to judge the likely success of the programmes for Aboriginal languages and literacy. The major part of these programmes are administered outside of the Employment, Education and Training ministry with the purpose of involving representative Aboriginal groups more directly in matters close to them. These programmes are still largely being determined. The task of preserving and maintaining languages will probably require much more support than the funds presently allocated provide.

Conclusion

In the 12 years during which Australia has had an articulated policy on language, the most obvious feature of the policy has been its changing character. As a broad generalisation, it is possible to discern two major policy phases characterised by the two reports of the NPL and the ALLP. The NPL was a policy driven by a large set of concerns involving ethnic identity, cultural and language preservation, language rights, equal opportunity and access to education and other social benefits, and a view of the nation's language resources as an economic asset as well as a broad humanising and internationalising influence. It emphasised language diversity and multi-lingualism.

The ALLP took a more narrow perspective, focusing on access to the English language and what it called 'active literacy' in English. It was motivated by educational and training concerns rather than by the broad social goals of a perceived multicultural society. Its emphasis on learning languages other than English was driven by economic imperatives as much as by an urge to preserve community languages.

Although both policies claimed to be driven by principles, it is in assessing the level of generality and of applicability of these principles that the differences become clear. The principles of the NPL defined language in relation to Australian cultural life and had set out essential prerequisites for consequent action and further developments. They have a universalistic quality. The ALLP principles are rather a set of goals for action around the narrower concerns. In supplanting the NPL the ALLP has no comparable view of language or languages in the Australian culture. There is none of the NPL's sense of continuity or provision of norms for making future judgements about language needs.

Australia's present language policy is a set of programmes, mainly funded by the Commonwealth government, which address quite specific language needs and prioritise these needs. Most of the programmes were in place before the ALLP, but some were directly instituted by it. There are funding commitments made to the programmes each year, but being governed not by principled commitments, the programmes could be easily adjusted or eliminated at any time. Rather than related to a national language policy, their existence could be said to be tied to much more general policies elaborated as part of the general political platform of the party in power. Australia's language policy may soon be tested however. The political party which had formed the government since 1983 was defeated at the polls (March 1996) and its successor is a government devoted to micro-economic reform, 'downsizing' of the Commonwealth public service (especially in areas of health, education and welfare), and privatisation where feasible. Of great concern is the fact that the outgoing government had made language policy an instrument of party political platform and not a matter of broad national concensus as it had previously been.

What was lost with the advent of the ALLP was a semi-independent advisory body (AACLAME) that had gained respect for its relative autonomy. In its place is a government instrumentality answering not to a broad constituency but to a ministry which controls the ultimate power over policy via its control of funding. It is interesting to speculate on possible consequences of the push from the Ethnic Communities Councils (in 1983) to have had national legislation supporting language policy. At the time, given the general national consensus, it did not appear necessary. Any attempt to have set even the broadest principles in law would have been contentious and possibly self-defeating. The compromise was not really successful, however, if measured by the control the Commonwealth government bureaucracy has been able to gain over policy. Australia has no statutes of Rights or Freedoms and legislation relating to personal freedom has been always regarded suspiciously. If legislation were ever introduced that addressed language rights of individuals or groups it would be conceivably of the most general application. The contestability of language legislation in Canada and the United States as seen in this volume, emphasises the difficulty of drawing up laws that reflect true public sentiment. Nor do laws always ensure the purpose for which they are promulgated. In Australia any such legislation would also be challenged by the states, the prime instrumentality for delivery of language services in most cases. In any case, the future of language policy in Australia must now be unclear.

4 Language Policy in New Zealand: Defining the Ineffable

RICHARD A. BENTON

New Zealand is an almost exclusively English-speaking country, yet has another language, Maori, as the only official language so designated by statute. Nonetheless, as the Court of Appeal pointed out in 1979, in relation to an attempt to test a previous law (Section 77A of the Maori Affairs Amendment Act 1974) recognising Maori as an 'ancestral' rather than an official language:

> English has been the customary language of the Courts of New Zealand from the earliest colonial days. It is the only language of most of our people. (Richardson, 1979: 6)

Two things at least have changed since that judgement, which held that Maori-speakers could not demand as of right that documents be translated into Maori or that interpreters be employed in cases where they were involved – they had first to prove that they were 'not proficient in the English language'. The first is the passage of the Maori Language Act of 1987, granting official status to the Maori language, including the right of any Maori speaker to use the language in courts of law, and the second is a significant increase in the proportion of the New Zealand population from non-English linguistic and ethnic backgrounds.

Although until 1996 no language question had been included in a New Zealand census, statistics are regularly gathered on both ethnicity and country of origin. Information about Maori is based mainly on a comprehensive survey undertaken in the 1970s (Benton, 1991b); the Maori Language Commission is planning a new survey in 1995. Recent studies of localised ethnic communities (e.g. Aipolo & Holmes, 1990; Adlam, 1987; Holmes *et al.*, 1993; Meanger, 1989; Roberts, 1990; Stoffel, 1982; Surus, 1985)

have indicated that knowledge and use of the ethnic language declines in the
New Zealand-born generations among all non-English-speaking immigrant
communities, although the rate and degree to which English takes over all
the functions of the other language varies considerably. Taking into account
both ethnicity and country of origin (cf. Department of Statistics, 1992;
1993), the approximate number of speakers of languages other than English
among the main ethno-linguistic groupings in New Zealand at the time of the
1991 census (out of a total population of 3.4 million) would appear to have
been:

Samoan	50,000+
Maori	45,000+
Chinese languages	30,000+
Indian languages	25,000+
Dutch	25,000
Cook Island Maori	20,000
Tongan	15,000

Other groups with relatively substantial numbers of ethnic mother-tongue
speakers would have been:

5000–10,000 speakers: German, Niuean;

3000–5000 speakers: Fijian, Philippine languages, Khmer, Vietnamese,
Japanese;

2000–3000 speakers: Tokelauan, Serbo-Croatian, French, Italian,
Polish, Greek, Spanish;

Fewer than 2000 speakers: Danish, Arabic, Thai, Farsi, Hungarian,
Irish, Norwegian, Russian, Swedish, Welsh.

Three of these languages (German, Japanese and French), as well as Maori,
would also have had a considerable number of non-native speakers from
their own and other ethnic groups, with various degrees of fluency, as they
are widely taught in New Zealand schools.

Although in the five years from 1986 to 1991, the Chinese (traditionally
mainly Cantonese, but with an increasing Mandarin-speaking element) and
Indian (mostly Gujerati) populations of New Zealand had risen proportionately from 0.6 and 0.4% of the total population to 1.1 and 0.8% respectively,
93% of New Zealand residents were still of either Maori or European descent
in 1991, and 93.4% had been born in an English-speaking country (84.2% in
New Zealand, 1.5% in Australia, 7.2% in the British Isles, and 0.5% in
Canada, the US or South Africa). Although Samoan may have overtaken
Maori as the second most widely spoken first or dominant language, the

Samoan ethnic group comprised only 2% of the population (up from 1.6%), compared with 12.9% identifying as Maori (12.6% in 1986). The 1% decline (between censuses) in both the English-speaking and Maori/European groups, however, indicated an increasing diversity in both ethnic and linguistic background in many parts of the country, and especially in the major cities where immigrants tend to concentrate. Added to this have been the resurgence of interest in the Maori language, as a core element in both Maori and New Zealand national identity, and a realisation that multilingual proficiency may be an important factor in expanding international trade. The response has been a corresponding increase in the attention being given in government and educational circles to the formulation of explicit language policies.

A key factor in New Zealand educational and linguistic planning is the status and role of the Maori language, with its dual functions of the core cultural artefact and symbol of the indigenous ethnic minority, on the one hand, and a symbol of an emerging national and Pacific identity on the other. Almost all government and many non-government agencies and enterprises have official Maori designations in addition to their English names. Indeed, the names of many national organisations, ranging from the Sociological Association to the National Council of Churches, have been changed to reflect an emerging bicultural ideology, by replacing 'New Zealand' with 'Aotearoa/New Zealand' in their English appellations. A major focus of attention in this chapter will therefore be the question of 'ownership' of the Maori language in the context of language planning and policy.

After a brief historical overview, this chapter will look in turn at some general issues in New Zealand language policy, particularly those identified in the public discussion document *Aoteareo: Speaking for Ourselves* (Waite, 1992a,b). These include various aspects of language teaching and learning: languages of wider communication, heritage languages, classical languages, sign language, English as a second language, as well as considerations of language rights, access to services, tourism and trade. The main focus in this and subsequent sections will, however, be on policy in relation to languages and language groups, rather than on the detail of how such languages should be used or spoken. After looking at *Aoteareo*, attention will be turned to consideration of a specific question: Who owns the Maori language? Some of the disparate threads from these two sections will be gathered together in a discussion of current trends and possible future directions in overt and covert language policy in Aotearoa/New Zealand, forming the final sections of the chapter.

Historical Context

In 1840, when Britain took over the administration of New Zealand, most of the 150,000 or so inhabitants of the country were Maori, and native-speakers of one of the closely-related Eastern Polynesian dialects constituting what at the time was generally referred to as the New Zealand language. Under the Treaty of Waitangi, the leaders of the Maori tribes ceded administrative authority to the British Crown, in return for the protection of their physical patrimony and cultural heritage. Within a decade of the Treaty's signing, massive immigration, mostly from the British Isles, changed the ethnic and linguistic balance, and the combined effects of the land wars of the 1860s, and high infant and adult mortality from introduced diseases, resulted in a rapid decline in the Maori population, which hovered under the 50,000 mark for the last three decades of the 19th century. By 1881, Maori were out-numbered by non-Maori in a ratio of 10.6 to 1; a trend which continued until 1921, when the ratio had risen to 21.3 to 1. By 1976, however, the proportion of persons counted as 'half or more' Maori had risen to the 1881 level, and in 1991, one New Zealander in eight claimed Maori ethnicity. Nineteenth-century immigrants from non-English speaking countries included speakers of German, Serbo-Croatian, Cantonese, and Scottish Gaelic, followed by Danes, Norwegians, Italians, Greeks, Hungarians and Poles. After World War II, Dutch was probably the most numerous immigrant language until the 1970s, followed (and eventually outpaced) by Samoan; large numbers of speakers of other Polynesian languages also entered New Zealand from this period, and together their communities made up almost 4% of the total population in 1991. Since the mid-1980s, immigration from Asia has accelerated, with significant (and growing) numbers of Southeast Asian, Chinese, Japanese and Korean immigrants, as well as a large influx of Indians from Fiji.

Early immigration policies clearly and overtly favoured first British then British and Northern European immigrants over all others, with an influx of Polynesian immigrants from New Zealand's Island Territories, including the Trust Territory of Western Samoa, also supplementing the need of new industries for labour in the early post-war period. Refugees, first from Europe and later from Southeast Asia and other areas of conflict, added to the linguistic and ethnic diversity of the immigrant population. With the deregulated economy following the reforms initiated by the fourth Labour government from 1984, immigration policy also changed radically, with a weighted check-list awarding points for capital, skills, educational qualifica-tions, age and family ties replacing earlier more nebulous criteria.

The language policies developed in response to the presence of speakers of languages other than English generally reflected the theme of the Court of Appeal judgement quoted earlier. Fluency in English was regarded as the goal to which everyone aspired, and it was assumed most people would attain it without the need for much special assistance. The case of the Maori was, however, different. *Ad hoc* measures may have sufficed for immigrant groups, but in education a systematic attempt to engineer a linguistic and cultural shift to English had commenced in 1858, with the requirement that mission schools receiving government funding make English the classroom language. The 1867 Native Schools Act set up a system of secular village day schools in which teaching was to be in English, and 'the ordinary subjects of English primary education' constituted the curriculum. When the Department of Education took over the control of Native Schools from the Department of Native Affairs in 1879, a form of transitional bilingual education was instituted. However, by the turn of the century, the earlier policies aimed at the exclusion of Maori from the classroom, and the playground, were reinstated. (For detailed information on policies and practice in Maori education in the colonial period to the 1970s, see Barrington & Beaglehole, 1974 and Benton, 1981.)

In the 1930s, official policy towards the Maori language became more accommodating, although teachers in many schools continued for some time to discourage the use of Maori by their pupils through sanctions of various kinds, including physical punishment. It was during this period that Maori language was introduced as a subject for the new School Certificate examination. In primary schools, a system of 'junior assistants' was introduced, whereby young Maori-speaking school-leavers could assist the junior class teacher to introduce new entrants to classroom routines, for there were few Maori teachers in the 1930s and early 1940s. However, no attempt was made to promote the use of Maori as the general language of education at any level, except in a few small mission schools in very isolated communities.

From the 1860s until the outbreak of World War II, most Maori people lived in rural communities, concentrated in the northern half of the North Island. These communities were relatively isolated from everyday contact with English speakers, and Maori remained the lingua franca of the community in most of them. The exodus from the countryside began with the need to recruit labour to replace those conscripted for military service overseas, and accelerated at the end of the war. With Maori people now visible outside their former strongholds, the government was compelled to pay increasing attention to Maori education, including the place of Maori language in the schools. In 1958, the Education Department set up a Maori Language Advisory Committee to organise the production of text books and journals for use in the teaching of Maori in secondary schools. In the same year the University of Auckland recognised Maori for the first time as a language subject for purposes of satisfying the requirement that students for the BA degree include a language other than English in their course. By 1962, the Royal Commission on Education had recommended that children in intermediate schools be introduced to a second language, especially Maori or French. The Commission did not, however, consider bilingual or Maori-medium schooling to be a viable option for children even in Maori-speaking communities.

During the 1960s, steady progress was maintained in providing resources for the teaching of Maori as a subject at the secondary school level, with two major textbooks printed by 1964, and 16 issues of *Te Wharekura*, a journal containing traditional and contemporary stories, poems and narratives written entirely in Maori had appeared by 1969. By 1970, a scheme for linking the study of Maori in intermediate and secondary schools had been developed. The 1970s were a decade of intense, at times frantic, activity relating to Maori language issues. In 1972, a petition calling on the government to make Maori language available as of right to all children who wished to study it gained 33,000 signatures. The same year, the organisers of the petition, *Nga Tamatoa* ('The Warrior Youth') set aside a special 'Maori Language Day', which within a few years was transformed into Maori Language Week, observed officially by schools and marked by special programmes in the mass media devoted to Maori language topics or content. In 1973 the New Zealand Council for Educational Research commenced a five-year sociolinguistic survey of Maori language use, which provided background information for the planning of new initiatives in Maori-medium education. The first officially bilingual school since the establishment of state education for Maori in 1867 was approved in 1976. A teacher training scheme to prepare adult native-speakers to teach Maori in secondary schools was also launched. By the end of the decade, 'elements of the Maori language' had become part of the core curriculum in primary education, and 15,000 secondary school pupils in 182 schools were studying Maori (compared with 2500 in 30 schools in 1970).

By 1980, four bilingual primary school programmes had been officially approved, and more were awaiting official confirmation. These programmes required approval directly by the Minister of Education, which was granted only after a lengthy process of community consultation. At the tertiary level, courses in Maori language had been introduced at all universities, and intensive Maori language courses were being offered to government officials and others at the Wellington Polytechnic. Teacher training lagged well behind demand, which was both a cause and an effect of the delay in developing a comprehensive bilingual education policy. Community initiatives included the *Ataarangi* movement, which was involved in extensive home-tutoring of families wishing to learn Maori. The seeds of the *kōhanga reo* movement (which will be discussed later in this chapter) had also been sown.

In the public domain, Maori and English had long occupied very different places. Throughout much of the 19th century, official notices and legislation directly affecting Maori people had generally been translated into Maori. As schooling in English became more widespread, this practice became less common. Maori-language newspapers similarly had ceased regular publication by the 1920s. It was not until 1952, however, that the last of the legal requirements for the mandatory provision of interpreters in cases involving Maori defendants or litigants were revoked (Benton, 1984: 26). By the 1970s, the movements already noted in the educational sphere were being more widely recognised. Politicians had begun to use Maori phrases when greeting foreign visitors and in their opening remarks on other state occasions. In 1978, the Minister of Education opened Maori Language Week with a speech delivered entirely in Maori in which he stated (according to the official translation, quoted in Benton, 1982: 17):

> In past times the Maori language belonged to the Maori people alone . . . Today Maori Language is one of the two official languages of Aotearoa [New Zealand]. Be strong in the teaching and learning of it.

The Minister was in fact a little ahead of his time: Maori did not legally acquire official status until 1987, and English owes its status to custom (reinforced by the Pleadings in English Act of 1362, repealed in England in 1863, but still in force in New Zealand in 1978, and similar precedents), not specific legislation (Benton, 1979: 7).

The mass media were not as forward-looking as some of the politicians and the school system. The National Programme of Radio New Zealand began two daily five-minute news broadcasts in Maori in the 1970s. Television was much slower to respond, first with a brief daily Maori-language newscast on one of the two channels during Maori Language Week of 1982, which subsequently became a regular feature on the same channel, but never moved beyond this token level. Following a successful action before the Waitangi Tribunal in 1985–6, which upheld the claim that the Crown was obliged under the Treaty of Waitangi to foster and protect the Maori language (Waitangi Tribunal, 1986), the Wellington Maori Language Board (*Nga Kaiwhakapumau i te Reo*), in cooperation with the New Zealand Maori Council began a series of court actions aimed at obtaining an equitable allocation of state resources to support Maori language radio and television broadcasting. The Board also established the first Maori-medium radio station. The litigation succeeded in delaying the disposal of state broadcasting assets under the government's deregulation programme until 1993, and was a major factor in securing state funding for Maori radio, resulting in the establishment of Maori-controlled stations broadcasting wholly or partly in Maori in most centres of Maori population.

Until the 1950s, French and Latin were the prestige languages in New Zealand secondary schools in the 19th century; they had been more important than English, as Arnold Campbell (1941: 113) notes in his Centennial Survey of the New Zealand education system:

> In practice foreign languages and mathematics remained the staples for all children in both secondary and district high schools, though, as the century wore on, French tended to replace Greek, and English got a firmer footing.

By the early 1960s, Greek had almost faded from the scene, and, although French was still studied by one-third of secondary school pupils at the beginning of that decade, its star too was waning fast. Other languages on the official secondary curriculum in 1963 were Latin (also in decline, but still second only to French), Russian, German and Indonesian. There was, as Table 4.1 illustrates, a sharp decline in the proportion of students studying languages other than English throughout the 1960s and 1970s. It was only the steadily increasing popularity of Maori, and to a lesser extent German, during this period that prevented a drop in the actual number of students so engaged. A partial turnaround commenced in the 1980s, with a burgeoning interest in Maori and Japanese. By 1993, Italian also was no longer taught in secondary schools, but Chinese, Spanish and five Island Polynesian languages had been added to the curriculum. However, although their numbers had increased substantially, the proportion of secondary school students enrolled in language courses other than English and Maori (i.e. in foreign and classical languages) in 1993 – around 25% – was still about one-third less than what it had been 30 years earlier.

Towards a National Languages Policy

The Maori Language Act of 1987 had established the Maori Language Commission and recognised Maori as 'an official language of New Zealand'. The following year the First National Conference on Community Languages and English for Speakers of Other Languages was held in Wellington. By this time, immigrant communities had sufficient numerical strength and confidence in their future in New Zealand to articulate concerns about the lack of coherent policies in relation to language in education and public life. The Conference was addressed by Joseph Lo Bianco, who had played a key role in the drafting and implementation of a national language policy in Australia, and appointed an organising committee to lobby the government to formulate a languages policy for New Zealand (Waite, 1992a: 10). As a result of these efforts, work began within the Ministry of Education in January 1991 on preparing a report on the development of a national languages policy. After a lengthy process of consultation and revision, the report *Aoteareo: Speaking for Ourselves* was released in mid-1992.

Table 4.1 Numbers and percentage of all secondary school students enrolled in languages other than English, 1963–93

Language	1963		1973		1983		1993	
Maori	1,064	(0.8%)	5,509	(3.2%)	13,456	(5.8%)	21,593	(9.3%)
Modern Indo-European Languages								
French	39,106	(31.2%)	41,309	(23.9%)	33,736	(14.0%)	26,057	(11.6%)
German	1,925	(1.5%)	5,632	(3.3%)	8,348	(3.6%)	9,196	(4.1%)
Russian	58	(<0.1%)	134	(0.1%)	187	(0.1%)	118	(0.1%)
Spanish	—		16	(<0.1%)	51	(<0.1%)	980	(0.4%)
Italian	0		4	(<0.1%)	7	(<0.1%)	—	
Polynesian Languages								
Cook Island Maori	—		—		—		108	(<0.1%)
Niuean	—		—		—		30	(<0.1%)
Samoan	—		—		—		1,015	(0.5%)
Tokelauan	—		—		—		111	(<0.1%)
Tongan	—		—		—		30	(<0.1%)
Other Modern Languages								
Indonesian	—		—		289	(0.1%)	154	(0.1%)
Japanese	—		472	(0.3%)	1,787	(0.8%)	21,991	(9.8%)
Chinese	—		—		—		395	(0.2%)
Classical Languages								
Latin	8,664	(6.9%)	6,155	(3.6%)	4,524	(2.0%)	2,677	(1.2%)
Greek	2	(<0.1%)	6	(<0.1%)	—		—	
Total Students	125,460		172,675		231,998		223,787	
Language Enrolments[a]	50,819		59,237		62,198		85,519	
LOTEM Enrolments	49,755		53,728		48,742		62,862	
LOTEM Percent[b]	39.7		31.1		21.0		28.1	

Source: Education Statistics of New Zealand 1964, 1974, 1984, 1994.
[a] Excluding enrolments in English (98–99% of students were also enrolled in English).
[b] Aggregated enrolments in languages other than English and Maori as percentage of all students. Some students will have been enrolled in two or more languages.

The report was very widely distributed, and individuals and organisations were asked to make submissions on the issues raised in it by 1 October of that year.

The name *Aoteareo* is a pun combining the Maori name for New Zealand, 'Aotearoa', and the Maori word for language, 'reo'. The report surveyed the current situation in relation to the language needs of the New Zealand population and how these were being met. Major attention was given to the areas of education, identity – observing that 'both Maori and English can be proudly affirmed as symbols of our national identity' (Waite, 1992a: 13), human rights, the Treaty of Waitangi (and concomitant guarantees of protection for the Maori language), language maintenance (with particular attention to Maori, NZ Sign Language, and three Island Polynesian languages, Niuean, Cook Islands Maori and Tokelauan, most of whose speakers were New Zealand citizens), broadcasting, inbound tourism, access to information, access to justice, access to the labour market, industrial relations, access to social services, international relations, international trade and immigration. Certain common themes surfaced in many of these areas: the need to facilitate the acquisition of English as a second language on the one hand, and ensure that immigrants and visitors to New Zealand were not unfairly handicapped by a *de facto* 'English only' policy on the other; the economic, educational and social advantages of fostering bilingualism and community language maintenance, as well as the learning of foreign languages, in relation to the development of both the local tourist industry and the expansion of foreign trade; the central importance of the Maori language both to the nation and to the Maori community; and the obvious inadequacy of the *ad hoc* haphazardly reactive nature of responses to language issues on the part of government policy making thus far.

In its discussion of community languages, the report drew attention to the growing need for a corps of skilled interpreters to assist in health care and other social services, as well as in court work. It noted that the then Auckland Area Health Board had set up a system of interpreters, covering 85 languages, but (in late 1991) was able to meet only about 30% of the actual calls for assistance, which were averaging 70 a month. In the first five months that the service had operated, a third of the requests had come from Samoan speakers, with Tongan (17%), Vietnamese (15%), Cantonese (10%) and Cook Islands Maori (6%) the other major users of the system (Waite, 1992b: 60). New Zealand Sign Language was also categorised as a community language; its recognition 'as the preferred language of the Deaf community' and its use in the education of deaf students were advocated.

The report included a considerable amount of information about the linguistic dimensions of both inbound tourism and external trade (Waite,

1992b: 62–68). English-speaking countries accounted for only 44% of New Zealand's trade in 1990; Japan, with 16.1%, was the major non-English-speaking trading partner. Other major linguistic groups in the trading area (accounting in all for just over 25% of trade) were Chinese, German, Arabic, Korean, French, Indonesian/Malay, Italian and Spanish. It was noted, however, that current policies indicated that a number of other languages, such as Thai and Farsi, were likely to become more important in the future. With tourism, English was still predominant, with almost 63% of short-term arrivals in 1989–91 having come from English-speaking countries. Again, Japanese were the second most significant group linguistically, accounting for 11% of such arrivals, followed by Chinese (5%) and German-speakers (4%) respectively. Future expansion was seen as most likely to come from the German, Scandinavian and South-East Asian markets. Stress was laid on the need for a sophisticated and multi-layered approach to language education to respond to the needs of these people, encompassing cultural as well as linguistic awareness.

In discussing foreign language education, the report noted two main features of the situation in secondary schools (Waite, 1992b: 68–75): the split between the 'top four' languages other than English and Maori (in 1991, French, Japanese, German and Latin), and the gender imbalance in favour of female students in these subjects, except Latin. (Enrolments in Latin, as can be seen in Table 4.1, had been in decline for many decades; it would be more appropriate now to talk of the 'top three', with Japanese currently occupying the second place held by Latin until the 1970s, and then by German.) The overall decline in LOTEM ('languages other than English and Maori') over the last few decades was noted with some alarm, as was the high attrition rate: in the 1987–91 period, the percentage of students enrolling in one of the 'big four' language in Form 3 (first year high school) who were still studying the language in Form 7 was 6% for Latin, 10% for French, 17% for German and 23% for Japanese. The report recommended that priority in the expansion of foreign language teaching be given to two 'tiers' of international languages, selected on economic, diplomatic and cultural criteria. The first tier consisted of 'Standard Chinese' (i.e. Mandarin), French, German, Japanese and Spanish. The second tier languages were Arabic, Indonesian, Italian, Korean and Russian. It was also pointed out that employers had an important role to play in fostering the study of economically important international languages.

Overall, the *Aoteareo* report identified six priority areas for the development of a national languages policy:

(1) Revitalisation of the Maori language.

(2) Second-chance adult literacy (in both English, and also in their native language as a prerequisite for adults who lack basic literacy skills in that language to later acquire such skills in English).

(3) Children's ESL and first language maintenance (seen as going hand-in-hand, with sustainable bilingualism for those who already spoke or were exposed to a language other than English as an important educational and social goal).

(4) Adult ESL.

(5) National capabilities in international languages.

(6) Provision of services in languages other than English (and Maori), to assist new settlers adjust, and as a permanent service to Deaf people with the recognition of New Zealand Sign Language as a linguistic system in its own right.

This list was an ordered one, with the report stating explicitly that:

> Setting priorities in any area of public policy that is currently inadequate on a number of fronts is an invidious task, and it must be understood that all of the points . . . are considered to have a high priority. It is essential, however, to determine a ranking upon which decisions can be made about the distribution of limited resources to the language areas [selected]. (Waite, 1992b: 18)

That the ordering might be contested vigorously was clear from the introduction to the report by the Minister of Education, in which the list was rearranged and restated thus:

- the opportunities for all children and adults to learn English;
- the growing need for New Zealanders with skills in major international languages to enhance our competitiveness;
- the place of Maori as an official language of New Zealand;
- the need for increasing levels of adult literacy in the workplace;
- the possibilities for ethnic communities to maintain their own languages;
- the provision of access to social services for all New Zealanders, including those with communication difficulties. (Waite, 1992b: 4)

The Minister and his Ministry were also safely distanced from the report and its findings by the fact that it was published as a 'commissioned report' under its author's name, rather than as the official report of a governmental working party. A follow-up to the report, with an official policy statement taking into account the results of the responses from its readers, was expected early in the new year, but none was forthcoming. Some comments on the report found their way into the press; teachers of classics in particular were incensed by its apparent thesis that modern languages with commercial significance had priority over all others, and that Maori rather than Latin was the language most relevant to New Zealand's cultural heritage. In its Annual Review for 1992–3, the University of Auckland announced the introduction of Dutch language classes (the first at a New Zealand university), and carried an item headed 'Latin Promoted' in which it was stated:

> Latin's place in the New Zealand high school curriculum is threatened by a draft national languages policy entitled *Aoteareo: Speaking for Ourselves*, released in 1992. This document promotes the teaching of the languages of trade, such as Arabic and Korean, at the expense of Latin, despite its position as the fourth most popular language in New Zealand schools.
>
> In several newspaper articles Professor Gray eloquently discussed the importance of Latin which helped shape European culture, tradition and language. In economically powerful countries overseas, she said, Latin is highly valued. More than 50% of high school students in Germany learn it, while Boston University is setting up a private feeder school where Greek and Latin are compulsory for two years. (University of Auckland, 1993: 31)

However, information released in response to a request made under the Official Information Act in June 1993 revealed that 129 submissions had been received in response to the 10,000 copies of the report which had been distributed. The eloquence of the Professor of Classics had obviously been effective: according to the Ministry of Education's analysis, 39% of the responses asked that Latin be given greater priority – the highest level of support for any one issue. There was apparently no clear agreement on the general priorities proposed, although there was a 'high level of overall support for the contents of the report'. There was also a 'high level of support' (28%) for priority to be given to Maori language, for all New Zealanders to have the opportunity to learn Maori, and for the targeting of resources initially to Maori immersion and bilingual classes. Agreement was evident on the benefits of bilingualism, support for the study of another language as part of the curriculum (20%), and on the principle of first language maintenance alongside second language learning in schools. A number of community groups endorsed the promotion of New Zealand Sign Language. Concerns were expressed by teachers of English to Speakers of Other Languages and school principals about the adequacy of ESOL resources and the provision of social services for new settlers. There was, apparently, 'little agreement on the basis for prioritising international languages', and no agreement about 'proposals for wider involvement than the education sector'. About 20% of respondents put forward 'detailed or alternative proposals with implications for further development of a national languages policy' (Ministry of Education, 1993a).

With a response rate of only 1.3%, it is not surprising that the Ministry was in no hurry to formulate a definitive language policy on the basis of this consultation. Most New Zealanders, even within the education sector, obviously had other more pressing matters on their minds. Nonetheless, a policy of sorts, in harmony with if not based on the *Aoteareo* proposals, appears to be emerging, in part as a result of deliberate planning by the Ministry of Education, and in part a natural development of the *ad hoc* response to 'market forces' of one kind or another that has traditionally characterised much of the *de facto* policy towards language in New Zealand. In its 'Ten Point Plan for Maori Education' for 1993/94, the Ministry of Education identified two essential outcomes: (1) 'to ensure the retention of *te reo Māori* [the Maori language]'; and (2) to 'ensure that the achievement rates of Maori students increase through positive achievement initiatives' (Ministry of Education, 1993b: 6). Three of the 10 points directly concerned Maori language: (1) support Maori language initiatives; (5) provide more Maori language resources; and (6) provide more Maori language teachers. Point (10), promoting a 'bicultural perspective in the Ministry of Education', included provisions for ongoing tuition in the Maori language for all Ministry staff. Furthermore, the Minister of Education announced in July 1993 that five more *Kura Kaupapa Māori* were to be funded in 1994, bringing the total number of state funded schools of this type to 28; 14 others were also being considered for funding (Ministry of Education, 1993b: 28).

The *New Zealand Curriculum Framework*, also released in 1993, was published in both Maori and English, and noted that the education reviews of the 1980s, from which it had emerged,

> sought a more equitable curriculum, particularly for those who were found to be disadvantaged by the existing system, such as girls, Maori students, Pacific Islands students, and students with different abilities and disabilities. The reviews acknowledged the significance of the Treaty of Waitangi and its implications for New Zealand society, according particular value to *te reo* and *nga tikanga Māori* [Maori language and culture]. They recommended an increased emphasis on culture and heritage, to reflect a growing awareness of the bicultural identity of New Zealand society and its multicultural composition. (Ministry of Education, 1993c: 27)

The section on language and languages (Ministry of Education, 1993c: 10) showed an openness to linguistic diversity which even a decade earlier would have been quite astonishing. Not only did it affirm the intellectual, social and cultural advantages of language study, and state that 'all students benefit from learning another language from the earliest practicable age', it made provision for languages other than English and Maori, and especially for Island

Languages and Polynesian languages, to be used as media of instruction. Gender and cultural inclusiveness in language and resources, and promotion of 'the use of language that does not discriminate against particular groups of people' were also affirmed. As media of instruction, priority was given to English and Maori, including the teaching of both as second languages, with community languages to be used in programmes whose nature 'will be decided by schools in response to local community needs and interests'. However, for general second language study, provision was to be made for all students to 'choose from a range of Pacific, Asian and European languages, all of which are important to New Zealand's regional and international interests'. It was noted that acquisition of such languages 'furthers international relations and trade'; *Aoteareo* was not mentioned, but neither was Latin.

The publication of the curriculum framework had been preceded by a new draft syllabus for the last two years of secondary schooling. This syllabus took a very broad view of language study, and made explicit reference to the need for students to be able to 'understand the nature and importance of current issues involving language', such as 'language and gender, language and power, language and social class', and 'the ways in which language reflects, conditions, and manipulates attitudes to these issues' (Ministry of Education, 1992: 12). This was followed by a similarly comprehensive draft proposal for English in the New Zealand Curriculum generally. The latter drew a hostile response from the Education Forum, an organisation of educators and business leaders associated with the Business Round Table. The Forum's submission asserted that 'the aim is now not just good citizenship, but individual therapy; and with that emphasis there has been a progressive undermining of academic content' (Education Forum, 1994: 21). The emphasis on New Zealand literature and speech, and concern with certain 'language issues' was certainly not in accord with the Forum's view of an acceptable language policy for education:

> the most specific and absolute requirement [in the study of literature] is that consideration should be given to local and 'gender-inclusive' content (New Zealand/Female/Maori), and that something (anything, the choice is open) of the wider perspectives which 'literature in English' signifies, should be included. By this measure the case for studying the work of a Maori woman writer is made central and specific, without reference to quality, while that for studying work by Dickens and Shakespeare depends entirely on the inclination of the individual teacher. (Education Forum, 1994: 20)

Outside the education sector, an initiative was launched jointly by the Aotearoa Maori Tourism Federation Inc, the New Zealand Tourism Board and the New Zealand Tourist Industry Federation in Nelson in June 1992. There was research evidence to indicate that many visitors to New Zealand were at least as interested in its people, and especially in its indigenous culture, as they were in the physical landscape: a New Zealand Tourism Board survey in 1991 had revealed that 'the key to revealing New Zealand's uniqueness was our indigenous Maori culture' (NZTIF, 1992). A project was therefore undertaken to respond to this need. This was called the 'Kia ora' campaign, and was designed to promote the use of this Maori greeting (meaning literally 'be well', but with many nuances, including thanks, approval, support, casualness and formality) in interactions with tourists and New Zealanders alike. This apparently simple objective – 'to promote the use of KIA ORA as a national greeting and farewell' (AMTF, 1992) – was taken very seriously, with training videos and other materials prepared to ensure that those involved would know as much as any non-native speaker could about how and when to use this expression. The two words were invested with great power: in its material for potential sponsors of the Kia ora campaign, the NZ Tourist Industry Federation claimed that 'Kia ora will enable you to expand your business into an international market worth $1.7 billion annually'. The Maori Language Commission supported the campaign, but hoped it would lead eventually to a deeper knowledge of Maori language within the tourist industry. The *Aoteareo* report had noted that 'it is essential, in this domain, [that] the Maori language is represented in a way that preserves its integrity' (Waite, 1992b: 43). In education and tourism alike, the question of 'who owns the Maori language' is no longer a purely academic one.

Prompted initially by a series of court cases and the finding of the Waitangi Tribunal in relation to the Maori language claim (1986), government support to Maori language radio broadcasting increased significantly in the late 1980s; more will be said about this shortly. Broadcasting authorities were also concerned about establishing standards of acceptability in language use, and commissioned research to ascertain what values held by the community should be reflected in broadcasting policy. One such study looked at swearing and blasphemy, and recommended that the Broadcasting Standards Authority develop 'guidelines regarding swearing and blasphemy on radio and television'. However, the report cautioned against 'expending a great deal of time and energy on this issue', noting that 'although swearing and blasphemy can generate spontaneous and loud complaints, formal complaints to broadcasters on this issue are rare' (Lealand, 1990: 47).

Maori Language: National Resource or Private Property?

Language is studied, experienced and used in many different ways. An especially significant attribute of language as a social and cultural phenomenon is the capacity of particular languages to become resources, exploitable by speakers and non-speakers for a variety of ends. Christina Paulston (1985: 15), for example, stresses that: 'Language can be seen as a resource which is available to ethnic groups in their competition for access to the goods and services of a nation.'

This view draws attention to the economic and political value of language in particular conflict situations, and to the transitory nature of such value: once the economic or political goals have been achieved (or the language loses its effectiveness as a means for obtaining them), a minority is likely to be discarded in favour of another more obviously associated with economic success, power and prestige (cf. Paulston, 1985, 1988).

However, the encoding of collective experience, world view, and cultural priorities and preoccupations is another aspect of language-as-resource which is somewhat more enduring. If it were not, the study of languages like Ancient Greek, Latin, Sanskrit, Classical Arabic, Ancient Chinese and so on would not be so important to the political, philosophical, cultural and religious heirs of the ideas and traditions first expressed in these tongues, their absence from the recommendations in discussion documents on language policy notwithstanding. In a defence of bilingual education, Lily Wong Fillmore summarises what many advocates of language maintenance would regard as the justification for this kind of intervention:

> What is lost in surrendering the native language may be the connectedness with primary group and community that gives an individual the personal stability for coping with adult responsibilities and opportunities. In the long run, however, the greatest loss may be to the society. . . . The learning of English will give [non-native speakers] access to the opportunities offered by the society, but if the unique resources that their cultures have given them are lost in the process they will have less to give back to the society as adults. (Fillmore, 1986: 680)

It is within the framework of language-as-resource that questions of 'ownership', and therefore also of control, inevitably arise. The controllers are not necessarily the owners, although the owners will normally consider that they should also be in control, and they are likely to feel aggrieved if they are not.

The simplest way to resolve ownership may be to say speakers of the language own it. In the case of Maori, such a simple definition is highly problematic. The Maori language is commonly regarded as essential to Maori identity and cultural survival: in a High Court judgement in relation to the disposal of broadcasting assets by the state, for example, this proposition was accepted by the Court as a matter 'of common knowledge and commonsense' (McGechan, 1991: 60). There are over 400,000 people of Maori descent in New Zealand, most of whom identify themselves as ethnically Maori –

in fact, many regard themselves as being New Zealand citizens of Maori nationality. However, only about 10% of the Maori population are fluent speakers of Maori (R. Benton, 1991b), which means that there are a large number of absentee owners who still feel that they have a stake in this resource.

Maori as a language has a number of commonly recognised dialects. The most obvious split phonologically is between the North Island and the local tribes in the central and southern South Island. However, South Island Maori was not extensively recorded before it ceased to function as a community language in the 19th or early 20th century, and it is thus difficult to ascertain whether the phonological differences were symptomatic of other, more fundamental contrasts. There is an East–West split in the North Island, with seven or eight major dialects altogether. However, the distance between these dialects in terms of mutual intelligibility is not great – proficient native-speakers move with ease from one dialect area to another. Nonetheless, in the early stages of government support for the preparation of Maori language materials for schools (in the late 1950s and 1960s) perceptions of favouritism for writers from a particular dialect area provoked intense, if relatively short-lived resentment elsewhere. (The problem was resolved by ensuring that authors from all major dialect areas were included in later publications.) There tends still to be very strong local language loyalty in rural areas, but less concern about dialect in the larger urban areas (where, thanks to massive internal migration since the 1950s, a majority Maori people now live).

As schooling in Maori (rather than just study of the language as a subject) has become an option, questions of ownership and control have become highly significant. There are three major educational movements or developments which have the revitalisation of Maori in a setting outside the home as their focus. These are the *kōhanga reo* ('language nest') movement, the bilingual schools, and the *kura kaupapa Māori* ('Maori-agenda schools') movement. The *kōhanga reo* is a grassroots organisation with wide support in the Maori community. More Maori children are involved in its community-run, Maori-language immersion programmes than in any other kind of pre-school experience. The first *kōhanga* were set up in 1982; in 1993, there were 809 of these centres, with 14,514 students (51% of all Maori pre-school enrol-ments), and supported by almost NZ$50,000,000 in government funding.

The *Kura Kaupapa Māori* are schools which are also community based, but with a much more prominent role for university educated intellectuals than the *kōhanga reo*. They were first organised in the mid-1980s when it became obvious that the public school system neither could nor would provid an adequate education through Maori for children entering primary school from the *Kōhanga Reo*. The leaders of the movement, aware of the success of immersion programmes in Canada, and similar approaches in Ireland and the Basque Country, also rejected bilingual education (i.e. a programme which would give equality to English and Maori as classroom languages) as a dangerous compromise, given the tenuous position of Maori in New Zealand society (cf. Smith, 1990, 1992).

Table 4.2 Enrolments in Maori language learning, July 1993

	Maori students		Non-Maori students	
	Number	%	Number	%
Primary School	92,330		331,180	
Taha Māori	48,342	52.4	221,363	66.8
Te Reo Māori	19,065	20.6	42,347	12.8
Maori medium	15,433	16.7	1,174	0.4
English only	9,490	10.3	66,296	20.0
Secondary School	37,637		186,150	
Taha Māori	3,795	10.1	14,262	7.7
Te Reo Māori	12,255	32.6	6,734	3.6
Maori medium	2,563	6.8	159	0.1
English only	19,024	50.5	164,995	88.6

Source: Education Statistics of New Zealand, 1994.

Although within segments of the *kōhanga reo* movement there has often been uncertainty of the place of 'Pakeha' [Anglo-New Zealander] technologies such as writing in the language revitalisation process, the organisers of *Kura Kaupapa Māori* have no doubts as to the importance of literacy in education, and are working to develop proficiency in the use of Maori in all domains and in all modes by their pupils. They were also able, after intense political lobbying, to obtain statutory recognition of their schools as a type of state school at the end of 1989, and therefore eligible (under carefully prescribed conditions) for full state funding. As noted above, in 1994 there were about 30 of these schools receiving or about to receive government funding. The 23 schools so classified in 1993 had a combined total of 1487 students, 1464 of whom were Maori (1.6% of all Maori primary school pupils; figures supplied by Ministry of Education).

Some among the other 98.4% of Maori primary school pupils were also receiving their schooling through the medium of Maori – more, in fact, as Tables 4.2 and 4.3 show, than were attending *kura kaupapa Māori*.

The options available were divided into three broad classes in the official statistics: *taha Māori* [Maori dimension], *te reo Māori* [Maori language], and Maori medium. *Taha Māori* programmes are those 'where students learn Maori songs, greetings and simple words'. *Te reo Māori* programmes are those where Maori is taught as a separate subject. Maori-medium programmes vary considerably in the extent to which Maori is used in the classroom (see Table 4.3), but in all at least some other subjects in the curriculum, in addition to *te reo Māori*, are taught through Maori. Between 1992 and 1993 the total number of children receiving Maori-medium schooling had increased by 479; the number of *kura kaupapa Māori* receiving state funding was only 13 schools with 510 students in 1992.

Table 4.3 Enrolments in Maori-medium education, July 1993

Type of school		Percentage of instruction in Maori					
		<30	30–50	51–80	81–99	100	Total
Kura kaupapa Māori							
	Students	45	0	40	311	1,091	1,487
	Schools	0	0	0	2	21	23
Primary	Students	2,775	3,965	3,400	2,253	1,992	14,385
	Schools	46	57	65	51	51	270
Composite	Students	190	22	64	229	93	598
	Schools	1	0	1	5	2	9
Secondary	Students	608	1,185	821	245	0	2,859
	Schools	12	19	19	6	0	56
Total	Students	3,618	5,172	4,325	3,038	3,176	19,329
	Schools	59	76	85	64	74	358

Source: Information supplied by Ministry of Education.
Note: School type and class-type are classified independently, so an '80 percent immersion' school may have students in a '25 percent immersion' class.

The official bilingual schools, 20 in number at the time of the structural changes to New Zealand education implemented in 1989 (Benton, 1991a), became administratively the dinosaurs of the revitalisation movement. They predated both *kōhanga reo* and *kura kaupapa Māori*, and were state schools whose communities were able to agree among themselves and then persuade the government to allow them to develop officially a school-wide programme using Maori as a medium of instruction along with English, in ways which each school had to work out for itself. Schools of this type were not recognised explicitly in the new legislation, but those already existing retained their former designation. Some have sought and obtained *kura kaupapa Māori* status. Because it enables pupils to have a bet on both horses, the idea of overtly bilingual education may well have more support among Maori parents than the more radical approach taken by *kura kaupapa Māori*. In a survey commissioned by the Ministry of Education, 57% of Maori respondents (as against 7% of non-Maori), chose a balanced English/Maori bilingual approach as their preferred schooling option; only 7% opted for Maori as the sole language; another 13% favoured Maori immersion initially, followed by introduction of English later (AGB/McNair, 1992: 67–8; cf. also N. Benton, 1991). In theory, under the new educational arrangements, any school could now become bilingual simply by writing such a provision into its charter. However, full community support would still have to be obtained, and even where this exists, the Minister of Education retains the power of veto over such arrangements.

If bilingual classes (where a class rather than a whole school has a dual medium or Maori immersion programme) are added to the bilingual schools, at least 16% of Maori primary-school children have access to some form of bilingual education in Maori and English, and, according to the official statistics, by 1993 another 20% were reached by slightly better than token programmes teaching Maori as a subject. However, about twice as many non-Maori children benefited from this latter type of programme, while many Maori children missed out. The 'owners' of the language obviously have a long way to go before getting access to their resource in formal education, and even further to go to obtaining control of its apportionment.

Another shareholder in the language is the Maori Language Commission, a guardian of linguistic vitality and purity appointed by the government and responsible to the Minister of Maori Affairs. In addition to examining and licensing interpreters and undertaking promotional activities, the Commission has expended much effort on creating new technical vocabulary to meet the needs of both the bureaucracy and the education system, and on purging the written language at least of unnecessary English-derived forms. In what appears to have been a relatively successful move (perhaps because much written material is issued by bureaucratic and educational agencies), it has managed to change the names of the months from the words used since the 1840s to older terms derived from the pre-European Maori calendars. Some Maori-speakers, undoubtedly with good cause, have become concerned about who coins new terms. At a meeting of the Maori advisory body to a government agency, for example, concern was expressed 'that some Pakeha used various Maori words for translation, some of which were inappropriate', and the body resolved that the agency's Maori members 'in conjunction with the Maori Language Commission provide a correct list of translations for key words' (NZQA, 1991: 12). It is noteworthy, perhaps, that although nothing was said about Maori coining inappropriate terms, the Commission is there to guide everyone.

Although Maori certainly wish to control their linguistic resource, it is clear that much of the real control of the language resides with the 'Pakeha' whose linguistic ineptitude worries the Maori Language Commission – that is, with the New Zealand government. The government exercised this control shortly after the turning over of administrative control to the British Crown in the 1840s. As was noted earlier, by the 1850s monetary sanctions had been employed to ensure that schools provided access to English, rather than Maori, as a vehicle for intellectual development. Both moral and physical sanctions were used later to ensure that English became the language for social interaction also, at least within the school grounds. In the aftermath of World War II, urbanisation of rural Maori was actively promoted by the central government, and government housing policy carefully prevented the re-establishment of Maori-speaking neighbourhoods in the larger urban areas. The educational response to the Maori language could be read as one of intermittent support hampered by chronic ineptitude; but such a generous judgement should be tempered by Charles Perrow's (1986: 13) observation that there is a strong possibility 'that what we see as incompetent performance or policy really reflects what some leaders wanted all along'.

A series of judicial hearings (cf. e.g. Waitangi Tribunal, 1986; Fisher, 1990; McGechan, 1991) has established that the Crown has Treaty responsibilities towards the maintenance of the Maori language, and that these extend to ensuring that the language and its speakers are seen and heard on television and radio as well as in courts of law. A High Court judgement in one of the broadcasting rights cases discerned a high measure of wilful ignorance behind government inaction in the past:

> In particular, [the Crown] had left itself inadequately aware of the important assistance which broadcasting could give to the survival of Maori language, protection of which was a Treaty obligation. (McGechan, 1991: 71)

and warned also that this protection must go beyond the archaeological: 'A survival like Church Latin is not a survival' (McGechan, 1991: 59).

However, government and business control of Maori extends well beyond the control of education, housing and the media. It may take the form also of appropriating aspects of Maori material culture (as in the souvenir industry and the design of corporate logos), to the appropriation of the language itself.

At least one other Polynesian language, Hawaiian, has suffered the same fate. At the 1991 Pacific Science Congress I was able to use drinking cups and table napkins emblazoned with 'In Celebration of Aloha – Sheraton's Hawaii'; language, culture and land, neatly packaged for the tourist. Language, culture and ideology are neatly appropriated by the New Zealand education system in the legal declaration of *wānanga* as a defined term in the 1990 Education Amendment Act. A *Wānanga* is defined in section 162b (iv) of the Act as an institution characterised by teaching and research and developing knowledge regarding *āhuatanga Māori* [phenomena pertaining to Maori] according to *tikanga Māori* [Maori ways of doing or regarding things]. The problem here is that Maori themselves, independently of any European-imposed educational system, have had institutions called '*Wānanga*' for centuries. Now, however, it is technically illegal for a Maori to establish a *Wānanga* (or at least to call a *wānanga* a *wānanga* and operate it as a tertiary educational institution) without submitting to an elaborate accreditation procedure determined by the New Zealand Qualifications Authority. On the other hand, the phrase *Kia ora* appears to have been placed firmly in the public domain!

Even when there is the appearance of more Maori control, ownership may be concentrated in an elite, in the interests of a higher agenda. It was suggested by the New Zealand Qualifications Authority, for example, that 'attestation' be an important procedure in the process of determining eligibility for qualifications such as a proposed Diploma of Maori Early Childhood Education, and that 'attestation should be done in Maori and by Maori'. Since most Maori children do not yet speak Maori, and even most Maori adults of diploma-obtaining age cannot speak the language fluently, such a provision would either spur would-be learners on to great efforts to improve their language proficiency, or effectively restrict the eligibility for such a qualification (and to attesting to a candidate's capabilities) to a privileged elite. This in effect has happened with the *Kura Kaupapa Māori*, not because the Maori people organising such schools planned it that way, but because it is the non-Maori bureaucracy, not the local Maori community, that determines whether, where and how many such schools will be established. Indeed, there is a clear and present danger that this most innovative and effective means for revitalising the Maori language may also become an equally outstanding example (on more than one level of metaphor) of what Pierre Bourdieu found to be the case with museums and art galleries in another part of the world:

> The museum gives to all, as a public legacy, the monuments of a splendid past. . . . This is false generosity, because free entrance is also optional entrance, reserved for those who, endowed with the ability to appropriate the works, have the privilege of using this freedom and who find them-

selves consequently legitimized in their privilege, that is to say in the means of appropriating cultural wealth, or, to borrow a phrase from Max Weber, in the monopoly of the handling of cultural wealth and of the institutional signs of cultural salvation (awarded by the school). (Bourdieu, 1990: 214–15)

There are thus many social forces and counter-forces in all aspects of Maori language ownership, control, maintenance and revitalisation. Many paths, however, seem to lead away from Maori concerns to a non-Maori centre. The locus of the centre remains elusive. Will ownership, control, and actual use of the language eventually be evident within the Maori community as a whole? Fishman (1971: 330) thought that by 'judiciously contrasting groups, socio-cultural processes and types of contact situations' we might eventually be able not only to understand these processes better, but also influence them in the direction of diversity rather than homogeneity – to convert the blender into a salad bowl, at least. His subsequent research has resulted in a book (Fishman, 1991) which is realistic about the difficulties and sees grounds for hope that effective counter-measures can be taken, making language shift neither desirable nor inevitable. Others, looking at the same kind of data, have concluded that such efforts to reverse language shift in places like Ireland (and, I suspect New Zealand also) are 'a waste of energy and money' (Paulston, 1990: 14).

Drifting into the Future

A great deal of money has certainly been thrown in the direction of Maori language maintenance and revival, so much in fact that the Maori Language Commissioner, Professor Timoti Karetu, attracted considerable media interest when the Wellington newspaper *The Evening Post* reported comments he had made to the Parliamentary Select Committee on Maori Affairs under the front-page headline 'Up to $300 million "wasted" on Maori lessons' (26 May 1994). The Commission issued a press release the following day, confirming that it had indeed informed the Select Committee that government expenditure 'on Maori education and broadcasting initiatives that have Maori language maintenance as a core focus' in 1993–4 amounted to almost $300 million. (In fact, over a third of the amount quoted was for vocational training for the Maori unemployed, and much of the rest was for similar initiatives in which the language could justifiably be described as tangential rather than as a core focus.) The Commissioner had told the Committee that 'he had serious concerns about the effectiveness and accountability of Maori language initiatives, including *kura kaupapa* and *kōhanga reo*'. There was an 'information gap' about the effectiveness of these measures, because no research had been undertaken to evaluate their linguistic outcomes.

However, the press release pointed out, this did not mean that the initiatives were failing or that the money was being wasted. It did mean, however, that measurements of the benefits derived from them were essential to facilitate forward planning for these Maori language initiatives (Maori Language Commission, 1994a).

The Commission's misgivings in relation to *kōhanga reo* had in fact been prefigured in the Annual Report of the Education Review Office for 1992–3, in which it was stated:

> Even in the *kōhanga reo* where the adults were struggling to use Maori themselves there was a clear commitment to the promotion of Maori language and *kaupapa Māori*. However, Review Officers frequently reported a level of adult–child interaction which at best was described as unimaginative and at worst dysfunctional. (ERO, 1993: 11–12)

The Maori Language Commission has produced its own 'blueprint for a languages policy' (1994b), directed at the public service. The document reviews the current language situation in New Zealand along similar lines to *Aoteareo,* and makes 39 recommendations. While stressing the obligations of the Crown to 'protect the Maori language actively in accordance with the provisions of the Treaty of Waitangi', including the requirement for 'a commitment on the part of all agencies of the Crown to guarantee services in Maori' (p. 4), the Commission also recommends that a languages policy should 'recognise the class of community languages . . . according special status within this class to Samoan, Cook Island Maori (Rarotongan), Tongan, Tokelauan, Niuean and New Zealand Sign Language', and that such a policy should also 'recognise the class of foreign languages, used in the contexts of international contact and cultural enrichment' – although it gives German rather than Latin as an example of a language of the last-mentioned kind. Nonetheless, while supporting the right of speakers of community languages to have their children educated in those languages with state assistance, it notes that 'individuals from that community cannot necessarily expect to be served in their community language if they can speak English'. This is a fundamental distinction between English and Maori, on the one hand, as *de facto* and *de jure* official languages respectively, and community and foreign languages on the other, in the Commission's view; unlike the speaker of a community language, 'a Maori-speaker should not be expected to use English simply because s/he knows English' (p. 5). This view is embedded in the Maori Language Act 1987 (s. 4), and has been tested successfully in the High Court (Fisher, 1990).

The Commission's report discusses in some detail the practicalities of revitalising a minority language, albeit one with official status, in a situation like that obtaining in New Zealand. While supporting the current trend towards dual nomenclature and bilingual signposting, government agencies are urged to go well beyond such symbolic gestures. To get beyond the present 'Catch 22' situation, where the current low demand for services and material in Maori leads to a low level of commitment to developing such materials and providing such services, which are therefore not sought because it is unlikely that they will be found, the Commission states that 'a sense of moral obligation must take over from purely practical considerations, for only by making a firm commitment to English/Maori bilingualism will the perilous situation of the Maori language be improved' (p. 6). A large number of recommendations, from the design of official stationery to the recruitment and training of personnel, are made to help agencies honour this commitment. The question of orthography is also discussed, with the firm recommendation that 'in the case of Maori and other Polynesian languages, the use of the macron . . . must be taken into account when purchasing computer software' (p. 12). The Commission points out that it is Maori, not English, which is threatened as a language, and that Maori therefore needs the support of public institutions to encourage its use. This, the Commission notes, will entail expense. It will also require the reaffirmation of the development of a primarily bilingual language policy in the first instance: 'it is only by developing a policy that addresses adequately the issues of English/Maori bilingualism that the wider issues of multilingualism can be properly considered' (p. 13).

Nonetheless, in terms of immediate practical need, multilingualism has become an issue which many New Zealand schools have to deal with on a daily basis. According to Ministry of Education statistics, there were 46,700 children from 'non-English speaking backgrounds' (excluding Maori-speakers and foreign fee-paying students) in New Zealand schools in 1993, 1915 of whom could speak no English at all, up from 1304 in 1992 (Education Statistics of NZ, 1993, 1994; see also Atkinson, 1992). Only 13,000 of these pupils were considered able to 'read, write and speak English competently' and thus to need no additional special support to enable them to cope with the school programme. There were 3000 to 4000 students at each class level, half to a third of whom in the intermediate and senior classes, and almost all in the first two years of the junior school, who were considered to need comprehensive help to cope with oral and/or written English.

Under policies in force up to and including 1994, schools have been given 'equity funding' by the Ministry of Education to enable them to develop special programmes for such children. Although such programmes were primarily the responsibility of individual schools, the education authorities had provided advisory services and commissioned a series of handbooks for teachers since the influx of non-English-speaking children became noticeable in the

Auckland area in the 1960s, first directed towards the needs of Polynesian children, and later broadened to include guidelines for the assistance of children from various language backgrounds (e.g. the former Department of Education's handbook *New Voices*, 1988). Under new policy proposals, however, special funding will be made available only to schools located in districts identified by the Department of Statistics as having relatively high proportions of *economically* needy families. Several Wellington schools with large numbers of Samoan pupils who had English as a second language were reported as likely to lose funding for their learner support programmes under the new policy as their socio-economic decile rating was too high (Woods, 1994). The reason for the change in policy was not clear; a Ministry spokesperson described it as 'more objective'. On the surface at least, it would appear to have been motivated more by administrative convenience (where 'objective' indicators replace the need for personal decision-making) than by considerations of equity, at least at the individual level. Meanwhile, community language groups and teachers of English as a second language continue to meet with each other annually, following the 1991 conference that led to the development of *Aoteareo*. Their ability to have a substantial impact on the direction of language policy has, however, yet to be demonstrated.

Apart from the administratively imposed need to make provision for the teaching of Maori under the 'Treaty of Waitangi' requirements in school charters (see Benton, 1991b) and other legal obligations, and the practical need to respond to the difficulties encountered by students with limited English proficiency, especially as the latter increase in numbers within the school population, a small number of New Zealand schools have been pro-active in developing language policies of their own, anticipating longer-term needs as well as meeting immediate and obvious ones. Richmond Road School in Auckland was an outstanding example of such a school, and the development and implementation of its programme, which recognised and fostered education through Maori, English and several community languages, along with highly innovative approaches to teaching, administration and school/community relations over a 10-year period have been well documented (Cazden, 1989; Corson, 1993; May, 1991, 1994a, 1994b). However, such cases are rare, and attempts to institute serious and sustained policy formulation along the lines advocated by Corson (1990) and by McPherson & Corson (1989) and practised at Richmond Road seem often to have foundered either through apathy or sheer busyness with other matters on the part of over-worked principals and staff members (see McPherson (1994) for a recent example of this). On the national level, pre-school education shows greatest recognition of the place of heritage languages of one subset of the non-English speaking immigrant population, those from other parts of Polynesia. In 1993,

177 Polynesian language nests, catering for 3877 children, were receiving government funding. Formal curriculum guidelines had been developed for Samoan, and (as Table 4.1 illustrates), the languages of the major Polynesian communities were taught in at least a few secondary schools.

Attention was drawn to both the instability and arbitrariness of language policy making in education when the locus of responsibility was unclear, and individual schools were left largely to fend for themselves, in a longitudinal comparative study by Roger Peddie of the policy-making process in New Zealand and the Australian state of Victoria (Peddie, 1991, 1993). Peddie also noted that 'effective policy implementation needs effective, informed and genuinely committed people at the centre' (1993: 26); the presence of such people was a major factor in the success of policy implementation in Victoria. As a means of bringing some coherence into both planning and implementing language policy in New Zealand, Peddie called for the setting up 'as quickly as possible a New Zealand Languages Institute parallel with that in Australia' (1993: 8). A similar recommendation had been made to the Minister of Education in 1992 by Robert Kaplan, who had been brought to New Zealand from the United States as a consultant on the *Aoteareo* proposals (personal communication from Kaplan, 1992, cf. also Peddie, 1993: 29–30). Peddie stressed the need for the development of a 'comprehensive languages policy', which would cover *all* aspects of language learning and use in New Zealand': this policy would include research into language policies overseas as well as in New Zealand, assistance in the maintenance of minority languages, an examination by government agencies of their own language policies, relating to English and Maori as well as other languages, a campaign to raise public awareness of and sympathetic interest in language issues, and continued recognition of the special place of the Maori language (1993: 7–8; emphasis in original).

Although his research was partly funded by the Ministry of Education, Peddie, like the author of this chapter, had to use the Official Information Act to obtain information about the responses to the *Aoteareo* proposals (1993: 29). In the two years following the publication of *Aoteareo*, official pronouncements on language issues have made no mention of any plans to set up of a special languages institute to help develop policy or monitor its implementation (the current ideology of deregulation and the primacy of market forces does not provide the most hospitable climate for such ideas). Nonetheless, official thinking in regard to second language learning and teaching, at least, is being articulated more explicitly. The Ministry of Education's discussion document *Education for the Twenty-first Century* states:

> One indicator of the school system's ability to provide the skills needed by New Zealand's economy is the number of students who study other

languages. At present 36 percent of students study a language other than English for a period of two years at secondary school. Growth is desirable in this area. (Ministry of Education, 1993c: 26)

In fact, as the Education Review Office points out in its commentary on second language learning, if students of Maori are excluded, this figure is only 26% (ERO, 1994b: 7). Peddie (1993: 34) notes that economic strategy, rather than wider considerations of social harmony, equity, justice or culture seems to be the primary consideration in the language policy implicit in the Ministry of Education's discussion document. The Minister of Education, in his 1994 'state of the nation's education' address in part confirmed that analysis. The cultural and social harmony aspects of language teaching were to the fore in increased emphasis on Maori (a reaffirmation of the policy of approving five new *kura kaupapa* Maori a year, and an announcement that new, comprehensive curriculum guidelines would be issued for Maori language, mathematics and science taught through Maori, and Samoan). The Minister also announced that guidelines would be issued for Spanish and Chinese, and stated his intention

> . . . to look closely at the feasibility of strengthening the teaching of languages other than our two official languages in our intermediate and junior secondary schools. Research shows the links between the foreign language abilities of nations and their foreign trade potential. (Smith, 1994a: 5)

He went on to state that he had asked his Ministry to report on the implications of 'making the study of a foreign language compulsory, highly desirable, or optional in forms one to four'. In May 1994, the Minister launched the promised guidelines for Spanish and Chinese. He reaffirmed his commitment to the teaching of foreign languages in New Zealand, and stated that, while a shortage of teachers made it unlikely that the idea of compulsory second language study would be proceeded with in the immediate future, it was 'more likely' that schools would be required to offer a second language to all students from forms 1 to 4, with compulsion on students a matter for the schools themselves to decide. While stressing that he considered the study of languages important for cultural and intellectual reasons (he himself had won the Pushkin prize for Russian 30 years previously), he noted that 'we need to reflect the changes in New Zealand's international trading situation by including the languages and cultures of our Asian trading partners'. (The Prime Minister was reported as making a similar statement on the importance of second language learning for New Zealanders now and in the future while in Malaysia, also in May 1994; see ERO, 1994b: 4). Economic considerations were clearly to the fore (with political considerations no doubt also attendant) in the decision to develop guidelines for Mandarin, the internationally 'standard' form of the language, rather than Cantonese, the heritage language of most New Zealand-born Chinese (but not necessarily of the latest wave of immigrants). This was underlined in the Minister's comments on the possibility of future guidelines for Cantonese:

> I am aware of the pressure by New Zealand's larger Cantonese-speaking community for a curriculum statement to be developed for that language in the future. I see no reason why that could not occur in the future, when other curriculum statements have been completed. (Smith, 1994b: 3)

The Education Review Office (ERO) subsequently released its own study of second language provision in New Zealand schools. Significantly, the release of this report was announced in a press statement quoting the Secretary of Commerce as saying:

> In the worlds of international linkages and trading partners it is becoming increasingly important for New Zealanders to be able to communicate with each other in their own languages. . . . New Zealand regards itself as a member of the Asia-Pacific rim of nations [sic], while at the same time maintaining strong links with Europe. Encouraging our children to learn foreign languages is one of the best ways of ensuring that we will take our place in the international community. (ERO, 1994a: 1)

The ERO report looked at the reasons why students took foreign language courses. These were largely idiosyncratic, dependent on availability and interest: the possibility of future travel to the country where the language was spoken was a major reason for studying a foreign language, loss of interest the main reason for dropping a language course. The most common reason for not studying a foreign language was that the students concerned considered themselves to be 'not bright enough' (ERO, 1994b: 11–12). The report noted that issues relating to the provision of second language learning in New Zealand schools 'are not necessarily ones that can be addressed satisfactorily by individual Boards and professional staff. There are national ramifications of these findings' (ERO, 1994b: 14). Several key areas of concern were identified: learning opportunities for students (time, availability, starting point); maintaining interest (militated against where the emphasis was on gaining a qualification rather than on enjoyment); staffing (identified as a national issue, but also an area where Boards could 'act strategically' by encouraging language teachers to retrain in languages – like Spanish and Pacific Island languages – 'likely to be sought by future students'. It was noted (p. 15) that 'it is the organisation of the curriculum rather than student ability that perpetuates the perceived elite status of second language in schools'.

Table 4.4 Languages taught at two or more New Zealand Universities, 1994

	Masters programmes	Major for BA only	Specific courses only
Classical Languages			
Ancient Greek	AU,VUW,*CU,OU		MU
Latin	AU,VUW,*CU,OU		
Classical Hebrew	OU		AU
Modern Languages			
Maori	*AU,UW,*MU,*VUW,CU	*OU	LU
Chinese	AU	UW,MU	VUW,CU,OU
Indonesian	AU		VUW
Japanese	AU,UW,MU,CU	VUW	OU
German	AU,UW,MU,VUW,CU,OU		
French	AU,UW,MU,VUW,CU,OU		
Italian	AU		VUW
Spanish	AU	[UW]	VUW
Russian	AU,VUW,CU,OU		
Samoan			AU,VUW
Cook Island Maori			AU,VUW

Key to abbreviations and symbols: AU: Auckland; UW: Waikato; MU: Massey; VUW: Victoria; CU: Canterbury; LU: Lincoln; OU: Otago; * with cultural studies; [ ] Listed but not taught in 1994.

'Retraining', unless through Berlitz or Linguaphone courses, could be somewhat difficult for New Zealand teachers, especially where the 'languages of the future' are concerned. Academic study of languages other than English in New Zealand universities is still restricted, with the expansion of language departments affected by low student demand and the historical entrenchment of a small number of favoured languages. Offerings varied in 1994 from a wide range of classical and modern languages at the University of Auckland, to Maori only at Lincoln University. These are summarised in Table 4.4: in addition, Auckland University offered Classical Chinese and Indonesian to Masters level, Swedish and Korean as majors for a BA, and graduate or under-graduate courses in Ancient Egyptian, Akkadian, Classical Javanese, Classical Malay, Classical Korean, Classical Japanese, Dutch, Norwegian, and Danish. Business people and others needing to learn a foreign language in a hurry could find appropriate courses at some of the larger polytechnics: the Auckland Institute of Technology, for example, listed intensive courses in 11 modern foreign languages in its 1994 Calendar: New Zealand Sign Language and Arabic, which were not taught at any university, and Chinese, Indonesian, Japanese, Korean, German, French, Italian, Spanish and Russian, as well as special courses in Japanese, German and French for business. Waikato University also offered a special course in Chinese for business, and most universities included a range of modern languages in their extension or community education programmes. The Auckland Technical Institute also offered certificate and diploma courses in Maori, vocationally oriented courses in English to speakers of other languages, and advanced training for interpreters.

Despite the top billing given to their needs in the Minister of Education's introduction to *Aoteareo*, there was no coordinated, sustained approach to meeting the needs of students and adult immigrants in learning English as a second language. Schools with large numbers of such pupils were able to provide special assistance through equity funding (although, as noted above, schools located in more affluent districts seemed destined to lose this funding as a result of policy changes announced towards the end of 1994). In 1994, refugees received assistance through resettlement, school-based, and poly-technic courses, and also home tuition through a volunteer network. There were also government-funded multicultural resource centres in Auckland and Wellington, and advisory services based at Colleges of Education and welfare agencies. Private language institutes for teaching English to foreign, fee-paying students had become something of a growth industry. The prepara-tion of teachers in ESOL classes in both schools and private institutes was unregulated, and the Director of the Language Institute at the University of Waikato was sufficiently alarmed about the situation to write that 'this situation endangers New Zealand's reputation as an education provider and is one that is potentially explosive' (Crombie and Poutney, 1994: 1).

Most universities required foreign students to demonstrate their proficiency in English through achieving a certain minimum score on a standardised test such as TOEFL, and provided non-credit courses to assist students to improve their English. Massey University offered a Diploma in Second Language Teaching. The Victoria University of Wellington's English Language Institute offered courses for students whose first language was not English, as well as a diploma in teaching English as a second language and a comprehensive post-graduate programme in applied linguistics. The University of Waikato's Language Institute also offered a wide range of courses in language teaching and applied linguistics, as well as language support for international students and special courses, on a commercial basis, for foreigners wishing to learn English or improve their knowledge of the English language in a New Zealand setting.

Colleges of Education were also developing or extending in-service and pre-service courses for teachers of Maori, community and foreign languages, and of English to speakers of other languages. The infrastructure for New Zealand's language future was thus being developed, but more in response to perceived national and local needs in specific areas of activity, or as a result of local initiatives, than as part of an overall national plan. In the case of Maori, this lack of teachers was recognised as a 'critical issue'; in its report on strategic direction for Maori education in 1994/95, the Ministry stated that:

> Many Maori teacher trainee students are not fluent in *te reo Māori* and do not train to teach in Maori language learning environments. Those who are competent in the language may not have high level subject skills. This is particularly significant at secondary level where there is almost a total absence of Maori teachers in subject areas other than the Maori language. Specific quality programmes need to be established to address these issues. (Ministry of Education, 1994a: 21)

Although the document contained no specific proposals for establishing such programmes, it did link the renaissance of the Maori language with 'greater involvement and success by young Maori in the education system', which in turn, it claimed, was 'bringing new life and energy to the language' (Ministry of Education, 1994a: 36). Support for initiatives such as *kura kaupapa Māori* therefore continued to be high on the Ministry's agenda.

The Crooked Stream

More than two years after the *Aoteareo* discussion documents were released, the comprehensive blueprint for a national languages policy in

New Zealand had not emerged. Nonetheless, certain policy directions, in harmony with, if not based on the options identified in *Aoteareo* were evident. In education, there was a clear thrust to expand the opportunities for students to study languages thought to have strategic importance for commerce and diplomacy, on the one hand, along with increasing recognition of the significance in education, at least, of Island Polynesian languages. Maori language had consolidated its position as an official language, and was taught, albeit often in a token manner, in most New Zealand primary and secondary schools. There was little evidence, however, of any official concern with the possibility that various linguistic minorities might have inherent and inalienable *rights* to the use of their languages either in education or in other aspects of public life (this despite the fact that New Zealand was a signatory to the UNESCO Convention against Discrimination in Education and other international agreements which guarantee such rights).

The *ad hoc* nature of language policy formulation in New Zealand has been a feature of the national political culture since the country's establishment. However, there have always been tacit assumptions underlying the *de facto* policies which have been explicitly stated in times of crisis. One of these, never far below the surface, is the widely held belief that English is the only essentially important language: other languages may have tactical significance, but English is the one that really matters. Added to this, in recent decades, is the acceptance of the special status of Maori, aided no doubt by perceptions of its symbolic value to a nation in search of a unique identity, and indeed of its potential economic value, but grounded in legal obligations reinforced by politically astute and determined activism. Other language policies have also drifted in with the tides and currents of international movements. Although the gender imbalance in foreign language learning (interestingly favouring females in an area of knowledge regarded as reserved for an elite) remains, policies favouring or requiring 'inclusive' language in English discourse have become standard in most public and private institutions, from schools to churches, government departments and newspapers. (This is not such a problem in Maori, which does not have gender-specific pronouns or occupational designations.)

The establishment of a national body to research and plan languages policy development and implementation has been recommended to the New Zealand government by some of those whose advice was sought in relation to *Aoteareo* and its aftermath (see Peddie, 1993: 29, 124). It is unlikely that such a body will be established in the immediate future. Government policy for such institutes in the science area has been to expect them to be 'business units', self-supporting and indeed returning a profit on the investment made in them. The national social science research institute was disbanded in 1994 when it failed to achieve financial viability. Some years earlier, funding had been withdrawn from the National Council for Adult Education, which had been very active in promoting adult literacy. Meanwhile, responsibility for attending to such needs as mother-tongue and second language teaching, as well as the details of foreign language teaching and promotion of adult literacy, are left to local schools and community groups to decide for themselves. In the case of foreign language teaching, this may be a sensible move. There is no guarantee that any individual will actually be able to use the particular foreign language they happen to learn at school when they enter the work-force, so a policy like that articulated in 1994 of encouraging or requiring schools to offer foreign language tuition, without any precise direction about which language is chosen, is probably the most realistic option. The creation of an environment in which learning another language is a normal activity is more important than the languages actually learned at this level. It is oppor-tunities for adults to learn the foreign languages that they need to know when they need to know them that will be critically important in the world of work, and the development of intensive language courses at polytechnics and strengthening of university language departments will be required to meet that need. It is here that policies affecting access to tertiary institutions (for example, the level of government funding as it impacts on fees) will be as important as policies directed at languages *per se*.

From the Maori viewpoint, although access to education through the Maori language is now an option for a growing minority of children, the progress that has been made is still unsatisfactory given the endangered state of the language in its only homeland. This was underlined in a colour photograph and accompanying account on the front page of the *Dominion* newspaper (Wellington) for Tuesday 1 November 1994, describing a march of 3000 people through the streets of the capital to Parliament on 31 October. The marchers were protesting against the 'Government's lack of commitment to Maori language', resulting in inadequate funding and resources and the small number of qualified Maori language teachers. Very similar complaints had been aired at a demonstration of the same kind at the same place in 1972 (see Benton, 1981: 50). Furthermore, the substance of their concerns in relation to teachers was confirmed in the report on the 10-point plan, quoted above, but also in the Education Review Office's 1993/4 Annual Report, which noted that 'some schools would not be willing to or able to provide Maori language tuition' without special funding (which could possibly be removed from such schools under targeting policies), and that:

> An issue of particular concern is the shortage of skilled teachers able to teach the curriculum in both Maori and English. There are too few to meet current demand, let alone an increasing future demand. Colleges

of Education are not producing enough graduates skilled in both languages to satisfy this demand. (ERO, 1994c: 15–16)

Tollefson concludes his book *Planning Language, Planning Inequality* (1991) with the assertion that 'a commitment to democracy means that the use of the mother tongue at work and in school is a fundamental human right', and thus the extent to which a society ensures that individuals may use their mother tongues in education and employment is a measure of social justice. (He defines mother tongue as the native language of a member of a minority group (p. 47)). He sees the major conclusion from his analysis of language policy in a number of widely separated countries as 'that a commitment to democracy requires a commitment to the struggle for language rights' (p. 211). Perhaps the central problem for the development of a just and equitable language policy in New Zealand is that by and large those that really care about such matters are the Latin teachers. Maori activists, and the Maori Language Commission – and the individuals involved, except for the stalwart defenders of the purity of English among the members of the Business Round Table, are more often than not fighting for a mother tongue or heritage language that is not their first or even their stronger language. Elitism, whether in the Latin class or the *kura kaupapa Māori* is also an ever-present danger. With no central agency, not even the government, accepting a primary role in language policy, the energies of those who wish to change the status quo are dissipated among a host of agencies, from government ministries and departments (Education, Commerce, Broadcasting, for example), Crown Agencies (the Education Review Office, the Broadcasting Standards Authority, and the agencies allocating public broadcasting funds) to individual schools, radio and television stations, committees, working parties and private organisations. In this confused and confusing environment, it is covert policy making and the degree to which the assumptions and values of those who are involved in particular activities or institutions converge that has major impact at the national level.

Broadcasting policy is one area that may well be critically important for Maori language survival, and ethnic language maintenance. Although radio broadcasting in Maori has become widely accessible, the much more powerful medium of television is almost monolithically English: only one of the three national networks carries even token transmissions regularly in Maori. Speakers of immigrant languages other than English can listen to 'access radio' programmes in their own languages for a few hours (or minutes) a week (and, in the case of Polynesian languages, a few minutes on national public radio as well), but their languages have no place on television. The commitment of the government and several opposition parties to minimalism in the regulation of the media, makes it unlikely that this situation will change at the national level, although the same policies make it possible for Maori (or other) interests to set up local television channels which could eventually be networked. However, it is difficult to see how these could compete for viewers with the much better resourced and commercially attractive English-medium networks. The logical solution for a home language policy is not watching television at all, until high-quality, full-time broadcasting is available in Maori or another preferred language, thereby depriving the government of revenue it would otherwise have gathered through the public broadcasting fee payable by owners of television sets, and putting pressure on the commercial sector by substantially reducing advertising coverage. Judging by census figures on the ownership of television sets, however, this option does not seem to have been chosen by substantial numbers of Maori or members of other major ethnolinguistic minorities in New Zealand.

The prognosis for the future may perhaps best be expressed in the form of a parable, an adaptation of a story about a venerable sage who had reached the end of his days. In New Zealand he would have been a *kaumatua* (elder) so well versed in traditional knowledge that he headed a famous, but unregistered, *Wānanga*. As the old man lay dying, he was asked by his most trusted and proficient disciple to tell him the real meaning of life. With great effort, he whispered, 'Life is a crooked stream, flowing swiftly to the boundless ocean'. Other members of the *Wānanga* wished to share in this wisdom, so the word was passed along the line and out the door, where the slowest of the old man's pupils was sitting. He considered the proposition carefully, and said to his friend sitting next to him on the doorstep 'What's he mean? I don't get it'. His friend didn't know either, so he passed the word back up the line. Even the senior apprentice had to admit he couldn't explain exactly what the old man meant, so, very reluctantly, he asked his mentor for help. 'You don't understand?', said the old man, sadly. 'No'. 'Oh well then,' he sighed, 'Maybe it isn't', and peacefully breathed his last. Our theories and metaphors about the ownership and control of language, and especially about what these really imply for the maintenance and revival of a unique ethnic language in a setting like New Zealand, let alone the rights of New Zealanders in relation to the other languages they speak now or would like to speak in the future, and the obligations of the state to allocate the resources needed to enable these aspirations to be met, still have both the clarity and the opaqueness of the old man's proverb.

5 Languages and Language Policy in Britain

LINDA THOMPSON, MICHAEL FLEMING and MICHAEL BYRAM

> Language-in-education planning is the process involved in demonstrating how the ideals, goals and content of a language policy can be realised in practice. In case a country does not possess a clearly formulated and stated language policy . . . it is possible to infer a policy from the state's social, demographic, and economic structure, its international relationships, and general developments in policy nationally. (Ingram, 1990: 1)

Paradoxically, the place named in our title does not exist, and an article about languages in Britain is impossible to write. Yet the popular concept of Britain as a country is linked for many 'British' people, and others, with the notion that the British speak English. It is certainly true that many people with British citizenship speak English as their only language, but closer inspection reveals first that they are citizens of 'the United Kingdom of Great Britain and Northern Ireland', and second, that there are many others with the same citizenship who also speak languages other than English. Some are residents of the United Kingdom of Great Britain and Northern Ireland, but some – those who hold Category C UK passports – do not have the right of abode. The situation is complex.

We thus need to define more precisely the territory involved before we can deal adequately with the languages. Politically, the United Kingdom includes the territories of England, Scotland, Wales and Northern Ireland. Ireland (Eire) is not part of the United Kingdom despite a long history of dependence and independence relationships; it is part of the British Isles. In popular parlance, the four territories are separate countries and, though those who live in England often forget it, the Welsh and the Scots are, for the most part, very conscious of their independent identity and languages.

Identity in Northern Ireland, however, is also complicated by sectarian identities and by the history of 'the Troubles', all too familiar from news bulletins around the world. The visibility of the political problems of Northern Ireland should not obscure, however, the politics of nationalism which are a constant issue in Scotland and Wales, even if they are not so well known outside the United Kingdom. Both countries have a degree of political independence from the central British government, located in England; Scotland enjoying greater independence than Wales, with respect to the legal and education systems in particular. On the other hand, though both countries have a language other than English, Wales has greater linguistic independence and a stronger linguistic identity than Scotland.

The issue of language policy is, as a consequence, more explicit and definable in Wales than in the other territories of the United Kingdom. British governments tend to avoid presenting policies on languages unless obliged to do so. The political activity in Wales, including some violent demonstrations of nationalist fervour, has led to clearly expressed language policies, whereas other parts of the United Kingdom have only language practices.

In the absence of language policies, it is not surprising to find a dearth of statistics. The national census, taking place every 10 years, has so far not included any request for information about languages. A debate has begun about the inclusion or otherwise of questions about place of birth or ethnic identity, but this kind of information does not have any reliable relationship to language data, and there are also difficulties in identifying place of birth and country of origin because of the emergence of new nation states and the subsequent change of names of places of origin. Yet in addition to the languages of Scotland (Gaelic) and Wales (Welsh) already mentioned, there are many others – hundreds of others – spoken as first or second languages and in daily use throughout the United Kingdom. Since the mid-19th century, many and varied cultural, linguistic and religious groups have settled in Britain. These include Polish, Ukrainian, Chinese, Yiddish, French, as well as those more recently settled from the former colonies and the New Commonwealth countries. These groups represent a significant number of pupils currently studying in British schools (Bourne, 1990). The Linguistic Minorities Project (LMS, 1985) reported no fewer than 154 languages spoken in London primary schools. However, statistics are in general incomplete, of varying origins and reliability and therefore at best only indicative of the falsity of any concept of Britain as a place where only English is spoken.

It can be argued, of course, that the absence of official policy and statistics on languages spoken in the United Kingdom is itself an implicit policy ensuring the dominance of English. But this does not help us to present an analysis, and in this situation we have to turn to the indirect linguistic policies expressed in other official practices and policies, above all in the regulation of the education system.

It is through official committees of inquiries into the education of speakers of languages other than English, or into the teaching of English in schools, through the recommendations of working parties advising government on curriculum policy and through the introduction of 'national curricula' – varying within the different countries or territories of the United Kingdom – that it is possible to discern and analyse the treatment of the languages of the United Kingdom by government. This is a complex business, because of variation by country, and we have decided to concentrate mainly on the situation in England – and to a lesser degree Wales – where the presence of other languages is most strongly denied in education policy and law, and in relation to Britain's membership of the European Union.

Education policy in the United Kingdom developed slowly throughout the 20th century for as long as schools and universities had considerable independence of central government. Schools were dependent in the first instance on a local education authority and universities were largely autonomous and received government finance through an independent body. As long as this situation lasted – until the late 1980s – government had little interest in policy affecting the curriculum, and with it the language curriculum. National and central influences did, nonetheless, exist in the form of reports and advice from investigating commissions or advisory committees set up for particular purposes, often as a consequence of public opinion and social change. These influential, but in the final analysis only advisory groups, include some devoted specifically to language issues and will be discussed in more detail below.

The powerlessness of national government in matters of curriculum – an exceptional and strange situation seen from a perspective outside the United Kingdom – began to irritate politicians and ministers – including, notoriously, prime ministers – and a slow process of change began in the 1970s. It culminated in 1988 with the first major Education Act since 1944, a law which brought changes throughout the English and Welsh education system, including the curriculum. The powerlessness of national government was replaced by wide-ranging powers being vested in the minister responsible for education. One of the first effects was the creation of advisory committees to review each curriculum area – which was usually interpreted as a 'subject' – and make detailed recommendations for further laws regulating curriculum content and assessment. In the case of the subject 'English', the committee could draw upon the work of an advisory committee of the older type, set up before the abrogation of curriculum power by the Secretary of State for Education and Science (i.e. the Minister for Education). The curriculum committee dealing with other languages in England had less immediate predecessors but was not without a tradition of discussion on policy. Thus, though the 1988 Education Act marked a significant power shift in curricular matters, a degree of continuity can be discerned in the policy development of recent decades.

'National Language' Policy: The Development of English

It is against this background, parts of which will be described in more detail below, that our account of the languages and language policy of Britain is set. We propose to consider, first of all, the position of English by analysing the development of policy about the school subject 'English'. This will lead to a consideration of the other 'national languages', Welsh and Gaelic, before we describe the position of other languages, some of which can be designated as 'foreign', but many of which have an ambiguous and changing status in the linguistic landscape of the United Kingdom.

Examination of the development of English as a subject can help to give some understanding of why, despite significant progress in the 1970s and 1980s towards embracing diversity in language (both foreign languages and dialects of English) the prevailing official drive is towards English ethnocentrism. Attitudes to English as a language derive from wide social, cultural and political contexts, but they also relate to the way English has been conceived as a subject. One of the problems with the term 'English' itself is that it is ambiguous and can lead to a tendency to conflate the subject 'English' with its traditional aims of personal growth and moral development with the language, or, to put it differently, the discipline with the medium. Thus it is possible to speculate that claims about the educative function of English as a school subject can easily become associated in the national consciousness with claims about the superiority of English as a language or the superiority of certain forms of English over others.

Ironically, given the present official reluctance to afford adequate status to other languages, English had to fight hard at the turn of the century to replace the classics as the central literary discipline on the curriculum. English as a school subject had existed in some form as early as the late 16th century but its status was low and even in 1900 largely confined to elementary and girls' schools. It was aimed primarily at providing some basic literacy while the more prestigious boys' public and grammar schools studied classics as a more edifying alternative. The growing pressure that English should occupy a central role in the curriculum culminated in 1921 with the official Board of Education's publication *The Teaching of English in England* (The Newbolt Report) which declared that for English children, 'no form of knowledge can take precedence of a knowledge of English, no form of literature can take precedence of English literature'. One of the members of the committee, George Sampson, published in the same year his *English for the English* and the two documents are seen as constituting a major landmark in the history of English as a subject.

Both Sampson's book and the Newbolt Report were in many ways progressive and pioneering, endorsing the importance of a humane and creative education which would be a preparation for 'life' not for 'livelihood'. Sampson questioned the excessive attention to latinate grammar, to mechanical approaches to learning and emphasised active and relevant approaches to the teaching of reading and writing. In many respects his conclusions about English teaching seem enlightened, the only discordant note coming in relation to diversity of language, and his attitude to language differences. He is uncompromising about the importance of teaching standard English:

> This country is torn with dialects, some of which are, in the main degradations. Enthusiastic 'localists' cling to their dialects – and cling, sometimes, to the merely ignorant mispronunciations, blunders and lapses which they fondly imagine to be part of dialect. (Sampson, 1921: 41)

In Sampson's view it is not the business of teachers either to preserve or to destroy local dialects but to equip pupils with 'normal national speech' if necessary as 'bi-lingual' (his term). He is quite prepared to sacrifice individual differences in language for the sake of conformity: 'Even if the school tends to extinguish a local idiosyncrasy of speech, it is not necessarily doing evil'. Similarly the Newbolt Report refers to the 'evil habits of speech' acquired from the home and the need for pupils' language to be 'cleansed and purified'. Sampson's attitude to standard English has to be seen in its contemporary context and in the light of the prevailing knowledge about language, yet in other respects his views are very forward looking. However, his attitude to standard English demonstrates the very lack of tolerance of diversification in language which has largely characterised the history of English as a subject and owes much to the attitudes of British imperialism and the preservation of national identity.

It was the Newbolt Report which coined the phrase 'every teacher is a teacher of English because every teacher is a teacher in English', an idea which was to be reiterated 55 years later in the Bullock Report (see below) giving impetus to the notion of a policy of language across the curriculum.

Sampson is generally seen as occupying a tradition which owes much to the writing of Matthew Arnold and included much later the considerable influence of Leavis at Cambridge. Under his influence, English continued to be seen as a moralising and humanising force particularly in contravention of the dehumanising effects of the industrial revolution. In literature could be found that vital feel for language which was distinctly absent from mass culture and society. This is not, it should be said, for language as a general human phenomenon, or languages, but for a particular literary style embodied in particular works of literature, the 'great tradition'. In practice the approach to English became associated with 'practical criticism' or 'close reading' of literary texts, an analysis which looked at 'pure' texts in terms of tone, style, structure and so on, as opposed to examining them in their historical, social or cultural context. This conception of English was until the advance of literary theory in the 1960s, dominant in universities and was promoted in schools. It was noble in intent, but because of its narrow conception, implicitly bred a form of insularity and isolation with regard to language:

> To call for close reading, in fact, is to do more than insist on due atten-
> tiveness to the text. It inescapably suggests an attention to this rather
> than to something else: to the 'words on the page' rather than to the
> contexts which produced and surround them. It implies a limiting as well
> as a focusing of concern. (Eagleton, 1983: 44)

Another important influence on the development of English as a subject was the tradition of progressivism originating at the turn of the century. Holmes in 1911 described how teaching in the majority of schools was taking 'the path of mechanical obedience' as opposed to what might be 'the path of self-realisation'. Mechanical drills, rote learning, fierce discipline were to be replaced by more attention to creativity and self-expression. While the tradition recognised the importance of imagination and feeling, at its worst its recommendations were overly romantic and indulgent. The emphasis was on the development of self (The Education of the Poetic Spirit) as opposed to any overt focus on language development in its aims. It was essentially individualistic, and thus in its own way as single-minded and insular as other traditions of English teaching as a subject.

In fact serious attention to language variety had to wait until the work of those writers who influenced the Bullock Report (Britton, 1970; Barnes, 1976, and others), the major government report, *A Language for Life*, published in 1975. Characteristic of their writing was a respect for children's own language, a fresh understanding of the relationship between language and learning, and a belief in the centrality of language in determining personal and cultural identity. The Bullock Report was concerned more with examining language development in the broadest sense than English as a literary discipline, the focus was more overtly on the medium rather than the discipline, and its theoretical origins were derived from linguistics and sociology rather than from particular perspectives on literature. For most English teachers the idea of a language policy is likely to be more associated with a school's policy for language across the curriculum rather than a national policy. It was incumbent on all teachers to develop an awareness of the role of exploratory talk and writing, of the importance of active uses of language and, more significantly, as will be described below, more positive attitudes to language variety. Although originally set up to report on standards in reading, the committee emphasised the interrelatedness of all aspects of language use and outlined a four-part model of language that included reading, writing, speaking and listening.

One of the criticisms levelled at the Bullock Report was that despite its grasp of the complex nature of language, it reduced the status of English as a subject to a form of social studies or linguistics (Abbs, 1982). The National Curriculum for English (1989) and the Cox Report on which it was based deliberately attempted a synthesis of the different traditions of English teaching which had emerged in previous years. To some people English meant a transmission of literary cultural heritage, for others a means of personal growth and fulfilment, for others it was primarily a means of developing language. It is relatively easy to forge a theoretical synthesis; the development of language through exposure to literature (which is language use in a most heightened form) is essentially about personal growth. However, the Cox Committee had the challenge of finding practical solutions, devising a curriculum which would determine the content of what was taught in the classroom and attainment targets which would form the basis of testing. The major challenge with respect to language varieties, including bilingualism, accent and dialect, was to reconcile the need for national standards in education with an appreciation that languages in their many forms have value.

The new emphasis was not just to recognise the importance of explicit attention to the English language (which in many ways had been neglected in the 'language in use' model promoted by Bullock) but to broaden the nature of what this explicit study of language should entail. The idea that knowledge about language should extend beyond mere forms of language to include awareness of language variety marked significant progress. Inasmuch as the National Curriculum could be said to embody something resembling a national policy on language, the initial document (notwithstanding problems with regards to testing which will be described below) was encouraging.

But the story does not end there. LINC (Language in the National Curriculum) was a project funded by the then Department of Education and Science, the aim of which was to produce materials and to conduct activities to support the implementation of English in the National Curriculum in accordance with policies on language outlined both in the National Curriculum and in an earlier report on language, the Kingman Report published in 1988. The materials produced, which were designed primarily for in-service work with teachers, took a dynamic view of language and celebrated its richness and variety.

In the summer of 1991 the government refused to publish the materials. The focus on diversity of language (and such related issues as the relationship between language and power, and language and cultural identity) did not accord with the prevailing preoccupation that knowledge about language should primarily entail training in formal grammar.

The first version of the English National Curriculum was subject to revision. The first set of new proposals published in April 1993 placed considerably more emphasis on teaching spoken Standard English from the beginning of children's education, a prescribed literary canon and lists of set texts to preserve a sense of literary heritage. The conception of knowledge about language was reduced to instruction in formal grammar. The underlying ideology was reminiscent of earlier traditions in the teaching of English. These revised Orders received a very negative reception from teachers and were subsequently modified. The final version, published in November 1994, was less extreme but continued to place more emphasis on the acquisition of standard English than on the celebration of diversity. The Curriculum was adopted by schools in 1995. It is against this broad background of the development of English as subject that the more detailed consideration of attitudes to language will be considered.

Celtic Languages, Bilingual Education and the Welsh Language Act

The history of Welsh and attitudes to the language is too complex to narrate here, but it is important to note that there is a significant difference in the treatment of the indigenous minority languages and those whose speakers have arrived in the United Kingdom in the last hundred years. The struggle has been long and difficult, but in certain parts of Wales bilingual education is well established (Baker, 1985). Schools accept children whose first language is English and thereby allow them to become bilingual. As a result, the Welsh language maintains a presence as an actively used mode of communication. Baker suggested in the mid-1980s that the trend was to increased Welsh language provision (1985: 48), and by 1993 he suggested that there had been a 'gentle revolution' in schools in the last four decades (1993: 9). This means in statistical terms that approximately one primary school in four is Welsh-speaking and almost one secondary school in five (Baker, 1993: 11), where Welsh-speaking means that at least half the subjects are taught wholly or partly through Welsh. This development was accompanied in 1993 by the introduction of the Welsh Language Act which represents the only official, legally founded language policy in the United Kingdom. The main purpose of the Act is to ensure that, in public business and in the administration of justice, Welsh and English should be treated equally. All public bodies must prepare Welsh language schemes to demonstrate how they will realise the principle wherever it is appropriate. Guidelines for such schemes are to be provided by the Welsh Language Board, the establishment of which is the second major effect of the Act. This clearly represents a significant achievement in Wales.

The position in Scotland for Gaelic is by no means as strong, but there has certainly been a revival of interest in recent decades. There are experiments with bilingual primary education in the Western Isles, where Gaelic is strongest. Although these are on a small scale, there has been considerable growth in the last decade, and from the opening of the first Gaelic-medium classes in 1985 there was an increase to 39 units (schools or classes within schools) by 1993 (Johnstone, 1994: 49).

The models of Welsh-speaking and Gaelic-medium education vary according to the environment and local arrangements. Three Gaelic-medium models are cited by Johnstone (1994: 49):

(1) Full immersion for the first two years of primary, with the whole curriculum in Gaelic, followed by a bilingual programme with some subjects in Gaelic and others in English.
(2) A twin-track system within one school where, in the Gaelic track, even English is taught through the medium of Gaelic.
(3) Full immersion in the first two years, with a second phase of a bilingual programme, followed by a gradual shift to English in upper primary, especially for mathematics and science.

The situation in Wales is more complex still. The official typology cites eight kinds of school, from primary schools with Welsh as the sole or main medium, through primary and secondary schools with combinations of Welsh as first and second language, to schools where no Welsh is taught at all. Baker suggests, however, that 'no existing typology of bilingual education in Wales captures the full kaleidoscope of colours that exist' (1993: 19). The practices are determined both by the availability of teachers able to teach through Welsh, and by the particular combinations of first and second language speakers of Welsh in any given locality.

However, neither in policy nor in practice is any explicit link made between bilingual education in indigenous languages and the educational needs of other bilingual children. The crucial difference is of course political representation and action, with the existence of nationalist parties in Wales and Scotland being a significant factor in the response of government to the demands of minority needs. Plaid Cymru (The Welsh Nationalist Party) in particular has made the defence of the language a plank of its policy, and as it has gained votes, the government in London has provided more funding for Welsh-medium broadcasting, for Welsh-medium schools and other facilities to support the status of Welsh. Although Dorian (1981) traced the decline of Gaelic in the North East of Scotland, in the Western Isles after the setting up of a new local government body (Western Isles Islands Council) the first schemes for bilingual primary education were being put in place (Murray & Morrison, 1984), and have been maintained since. It is important therefore to remember, as we turn to policy on the education of other bilingual children, that some bilingual education does already exist in the United Kingdom.

The Education of Bilingual Children in Britain

Although, as we pointed out above, there has been a variety of cultural, linguistic and religious groups settled in Britain since the mid-19th century and earlier, no major educational discussion of their needs began until the 1960s with the arrival of migrants from the countries now known as India, Pakistan and Bangladesh. Only then was it seen as an issue for consideration by society and policy makers. From the outset therefore, the presence of bilinguals from other countries (particularly from the former colonies of the new Commonwealth) provoked a different type of response from society at large and from education authorities in particular. There have been a number of trends and initiatives which have attempted to address the educational needs of these pupils.

The Assimilationist Approach

Throughout the 1960s, the education provided for bilingual children was characterised by its emphasis on assimilation into the dominant British culture through the English language (see Bourne's (1990) review of policies). Its focus on teaching English as a second language (ESL), was frequently at the expense of the wider curriculum and always at the expense of pupils' home language(s). The teaching methodology was 'borrowed' from the British secondary school tradition of foreign language teaching, despite the inappropriateness of this approach for primary-aged pupils, some of whom were as young as five years. Models that were being developed elsewhere, for the teaching of bilingual pupils, were largely unknown in UK educational planning and the classrooms where bilingual pupils were being taught.

By 1966 the need for the intensive ESL teaching was recognised under Section XI of the Local Government Act 1966. This enabled LEAs to claim a grant, at the rate of 75% of the salary paid to each teacher employed for this purpose. One outcome of this separate funding was the establishment of

TESL provision outside of mainstream education. LEAs established peripatetic teams of ESL teachers to serve in primary schools and Language Centres (where older children were placed on arrival in Britain). This form of ESL provision was in keeping with the assimilationist philosophy of separateness. TESL was seen as the key to assimilation and to the newcomers' rapid adaptation to the British way of life. Pupils' existing language skills were disregarded. This led the Swann Report to comment: 'It seems to have been assumed that the children's own languages would simply die out and be replaced by English' (DES, 1985: 388).

In retrospect, current thinking sees this policy as discriminatory in effect, if not in intent. In summary, it can be said that Section XI funding led to separate English language teaching for children whose home language was not English. ESL teaching was made available selectively, and only to children whose community language was accorded language status, but left unserved, for example, those children of Caribbean origin whose first language, Creole, was not accorded this status.

The emphasis on assimilation focused only on language. It did not, however, extend to religious practice in what was becoming a secularised Britain. The central importance of places of worship (for example, the mosque, gudwara, etc.) played an increasingly important role in the everyday lives of these communities. This influence soon spread beyond the initial religious focus, to include cultural transmission and the reinforcement of ethnic group identity. For example, the teaching of home or community languages frequently took place in religious centres. This wider role, encompassing ethnic, cultural, linguistic as well as religious aspects of life, meant that places of worship assumed an increasingly significant role in the maintenance and reinforcement of ethnic identity within some of the settled communities.

Language Teaching

The 1970s witnessed significant developments in the official recognition of the language needs of bilingual children. In 1974 the case of *Lau v. Nichols* established the rights of a non-English speaking child to a meaningful education which acknowledged the child's home language (in this case, Chinese). A year later, in 1975, the move from the assimilationist approach to the education of bilingual children towards integrationist thinking was precipitated from an unexpected source. The Bullock Report, *A Language for Life*, addressed in its recommendations the language needs of children still perceived at that time as 'of immigrant origin', and was critical of language teaching which required a child to 'cast off the language of his [*sic*] home as he [*sic*] passes the school threshold' (DES, 1975: Chapter 5: 20). The report suggested that: 'The school should adopt positive attitudes to its pupils' bilingualism and wherever possible should help maintain and deepen . . . knowledge of the mother tongues' (DES, 1975).

The Report also described bilingualism as, 'an asset . . . something to be nurtured' (DES, 1975: 293), and suggested that schools were in a unique position to fulfil this nurturing role (DES, 1975: 294). This statement, together with a further recommendation for schools to formulate a language policy which included ESL provision, constituted a recommendation to schools to broaden their perception of ethnic minority educational needs, and to offer a wider curriculum that included broader cultural elements. Although the report raised awareness of the existing linguistic skills of ethnic minority pupils, there was little sign of the education system or society at large valuing these abilities as relevant to the pupil's educational achievement and progress. However, another factor combined with the Bullock Report to give impetus to the move away from educational policy dominated by assimilationist philosophy. This was the change in status of black ethnic groups from an immigrant workforce to a settled community of British citizens. The shift in status changed both society's and the groups' perception of their educational and social needs. This change was reflected in the British education system, when assimilationist education gave way to the development of multi-cultural education and the subsequent change in educational provision for bilingual children which ensued.

This national trend was supported by international developments of the late 1970s. In 1977 a draft EC directive on the language education of migrant workers was issued to interested parties throughout the European Community (EC Commission, 1977). It proposed that member states should offer free tuition in the national languages of migrant workers as part of the curriculum for full-time education. However, in 1977, only one year after the draft was first published, a significant modification was made which only required member states to *promote* mother-tongue teaching. An expanded discussion on the specific UK response to the modified directive will be presented in the next section.

Multicultural Education

The development of the concept of multicultural education broadened educational provision beyond English language teaching to include cultural and religious teaching. (Multi-faith celebrations and world religions joined the school curriculum.) More significantly, it expanded language teaching to include mother-tongue teaching (as it was then called) and bilingual support, as part of ESL provision. (The terms 'home language' or 'first language' are now normally used in preference to 'mother-tongue teaching'.) Multicultural education placed increasing emphasis on developing the child's full linguistic repertoire. ESL teaching became sensitive to the existing linguistic competence of pupils for whom English was a second language. Their community languages were seen as a linguistic resource for ESL and other teaching.

However, this wider view of the role of language in the educational experience of ethnic minority pupils impinged only marginally on ESL provision, much of which, in terms of its underlying aims and assumptions, remained unchanged from the earlier days of assimilationist thinking. English remained the medium of instruction in all primary classrooms as well as the medium for testing educational achievement, particularly in the field of language development, reading, writing and oracy, as well as for assessing verbal reasoning or intelligence testing. Thus, bilingual children were compared and assessed in their educational achievements with their monolingual, English speaking peers. By comparison, their seeming lack of achievement (as measured in English) was perceived by educationalists as problematic. Bilingualism remained an unacknowledged resource which still did not feature as significant in educational assessment profiles or pupil records. The development of the home language, in those schools where community languages were taught, was seen only as a means of accelerating children's learning of English, their second or subsequent language, rather than a learning activity of intrinsic worth and value.

Multicultural education has now been seen by both educationalists and ethnic minority groups as failing to meet the needs of ethnic minority pupils in a number of ways. It was perceived as simply another form of compensatory education, essentially no different in form from the assimilationist programmes which preceded it. It also failed to address the institutional practices and procedures identified in the Swann Report (DES, 1985) as the real causes of educational underachievement among some bilingual children. An alternative perspective on the educational underachievement of certain groups of pupils from ethnic minority backgrounds is argued in an article by Troyna (1991), who suggests that bilingual pupils are underrated rather than underachieving. Current institutional practices identified by the Swann Report as disadvantageous to bilingual pupils remain in place even now. These include the testing and assessment procedures which are now carried out annually as part of the 1988 Education Reform Act. Bilingual children are currently assessed through tests in English and their performance compared with mean score that had been standardised on monolingual English speaking pupils. In retrospect it seems that the multicultural education movement with its focus on a curriculum for black, ethnic minority children which taught aspects of their everyday lives (characterised as the tokenism of samosas, saris and steel bands), was no less marginalising than its predecessor, the assimilationist approach. Through this misfocus, the multicultural education movement failed to improve bilingual children's performance in mainstream curriculum activities. This situation, although disappointing is perhaps not altogether surprising, since none of the DES documentation on the education of ethnic minority children addressed educational needs from within mainstream resources. Hence the need for change within educational institutions was not perceived as central or essential. Britain is still not acknowledging the multilingualism of its population and this attitude is clearly reflected in the current education system.

In 1977, only two years after the publication of the Bullock Report, the European Economic Community issued a directive on 'The Education of the Children of Migrant Workers' (July 77/4861). Article 3 stated that it required member states:

> In accordance with their national circumstances and legal systems and in co-operation with the state of origin, to promote the teaching of the mother-tongue and culture in accordance with normal education (Council of European Community, 1977: 2).

EC member states were required to comply with the directive from 25 July 1981, and the Commission issued a report on the implementation of the directive on 10 February 1984. In Britain, Circular No. 5/81, issued on 31 July of the same year, outlined the DES guidelines on compliance with Article 3. It stated:

> For the local education authorities in this country, [the directive] implies that they should explore the ways in which mother-tongue teaching might be provided, whether during or outside school hours, but not that they are required to give such tuition to all individuals as of right (DES, 1981: 2).

Thus it could be inferred that the British education system was not making adequate provision for the self-perceived educational needs of bilingual pupils. A follow-up EC Report in 1984 on the implementation of the 1977 directive showed that Britain was, at that time, lagging behind other member states in complying with the directive, with only 2.2% of the primary school aged children from homes where languages other than English were spoken receiving home language teaching at school, compared for example, with 80% of the children of the same age in the Netherlands.

Furthermore, Article 3 met with a mixed response from within minority communities. It was regarded (from both inside and outside these groups) as separating ethnic minority groups and differentiating their right to educational provision. On the one hand those linguistic minorities from EC states who were not living in the EC state of their birth (and for whom the EC directive was originally intended), were entitled to home language teaching while resident in their host community, while those linguistic minority groups, many of whom were British citizens and living in the EC state of their birth (Britain), enjoyed no such entitlement.

Thus the settled migrant communities in Britain felt disenchantment on two fronts: firstly, with their exclusion from the EC directive and secondly, with the multicultural education initiative which they perceived as conceptually unsound in both its theoretical foundation and its practical implications. This dual disenchantment coincided with a developing political awareness within black ethnic minority groups whose newly found confidence accompanied their change in status from that of immigrant to that of British citizen. The dissatisfaction felt amongst educationalists representing ethnic minority educational rights stemmed from the disregard of education planners for the theoretical and practised models of bilingual education that existed both elsewhere throughout the EC and internationally. It was felt from a number of sources that the multicultural education initiative needed revision. Other criticisms of the Multicultural Education Movement have been based on a broader analysis of the assumptions underlying education policy where it intersects with language planning issues.

Churchill's (1986) overview of the principles used by policy makers in OECD countries in their attempts to meet the educational needs of linguistic and cultural minority groups, for example, identified a number of ways in which the various attempts (including those in Britain) failed to meet the needs of the groups that they were established to serve, namely the ethnic minorities. His view is that the policy making process that emerges from the analysis is one where policy is rooted in societal assumptions about the role of linguistic and cultural minorities, based in turn upon historical factors, of which the strongest is the development of public education, mainly in a context of linguistic uniformity. As a result of these assumptions, the definition of educational problems are focused on the characteristics of the minority populations concerned rather than on an analysis of the majority group and relationships between the two. The solutions provided thus reflect existing educational provision rather than a re-assessment of the needs of both minority and majority groups within society as a whole. Minority aspirations depend in turn, on the level of educational provision made at a given time, and the response to their need is a function of their level of aspiration, a sort of circular relationship (see Churchill, 1986: 155).

Churchill (1986: 3) also suggests that the often abysmal results obtained by educational policies can be traced in large measure to the limits placed by public opinion and by accepted problem definitions on the range of policy options that can be considered and adopted by authorities. His are not the only criticisms, however. Bourne (1990) has identified specific ways in which the recommendations of the Swann Report (DES, 1985) have not been achieved, a decade after its publication. These will be discussed later in this chapter. Thus it was that disenchantment with the multicultural education initiative gave rise to the Anti-racist Education Movement.

Anti-racist Education Movement

Mullard (1984) presents the case for anti-racist education as a development within the Black Consciousness Movement of the mid-1960s. The shift can be traced in the change of name in 1985, from the National Association for Multi-cultural Education (NAME) to the National Anti-racist Movement in Educa-tion, retaining the acronym NAME. For Mullard (1984: 29) the move from multicultural to anti-racist education is not a mere question of alternatives. He perceives the shift in emphasis as linked closely with the change in status of black ethnic minority groups from that of immigrant to black British citizen. He suggests that the anti-racist approach to education reflects the socio-political values of the black ethnic groups in their '. . . struggles and resistances against colonialism, imperialism and metropolitan racism' (Mullard, 1984: 9).

Mullard (1984) and Sivanandan (1982) both view the growth of anti-racist education as a parallel to the life experiences of black people in a white society. Mullard presents the argument for anti-racist education as the re-articulation of black ethnicity through the structural cultural experiences of black people in British society (Mullard, 1984: 24).

The anti-racist movement was not confined to education policy. Although its origins may lie in the development of a philosophy of education, anti-racism as a political ideology and a personal belief system has now spread to other spheres of public life. There are now anti-racist pressure groups in the police force as well as in a number of sports, including football and athletics. The growth within these arenas may be due in part to the increasing numbers of black players who participate in competitive, public sports. This could not of course account for the development of anti-racist groups within public bodies such as the police force and armed forces. In these cases the establish-ment of anti-racist pressure groups can be accounted for by the concern for addressing the negative image these groups inspired among black and ethnic minority communities. Motivated by the need to change their public image and in the hope of recruiting more black and minority members to their numbers, public services and other national bodies established anti-racist or racism awareness slogans (for example, 'Kick racism out of football'). Nor was the anti-racist lobby confined to black and ethnic minority groups. Many white people have expressed ideological solidarity with the humanitarian values and principles of the movement.

The Swann Report – Education for All?

In 1985 a report of major significance for the education of bilingual children was published. The Report, *Education for All* contained the recommendations of the Swann Committee, established in 1979.

Although the primary focus of the committee was on children of Afro-Caribbean origin and their educational under-achievement in relation to their peers, the Report inevitably included a broader discussion of the educational needs of other children of the former migrants. Swann's response to educational provision for bilingual pupils was that: 'Essential to equality of opportunity, to academic success and broadly, to participation on equal terms as a full member of society, is a good command of English and that the first priority in language learning . . . must therefore be given to the learning of English' (DES, 1985: 426).

Although committed to English as the language of education, the Report stated suggested changes in provision. The Report favoured a move away from separate ESL teaching and recommended that the needs of bilingual learners be met within mainstream school as part of a comprehensive programme of language education for all children (DES, 1985: Para 5.2).

The Swann Report acknowledged the importance of fostering positive ethnic identity. They recommended a broader base for doing this through cultural and religious teaching as well as through language use. The committee did attempt to incorporate a broader definition of bilingualism. However, on the subject of bilingual education, the Report did little to advance thinking amongst educationalists. It stated: 'We cannot support the arguments put forward for the introduction of programmes of bilingual education in maintained schools' (DES, 1985: Para 3.15).

The Report was equally unequivocal in its response to the provision for languages other than English. While recommending that community languages and home languages should be valued in the mainstream curriculum, enriching the linguistic awareness of monolingual pupils, the committee remained firmly opposed to any separate provision for language maintenance classes or bilingual forms of education. They stated that mainstream schools should not seek to assume the role of community providers for maintaining ethnic minority community languages (DES, 1985: Para 3.18).

The Committee did, however, make two important exceptions. Firstly, they recommended bilingual support to help pupils make the transition between home languages and English. Secondly, they recommended that community languages should be included in the language curriculum of secondary schools where there was likely to be sufficient demand. The statement recommends that: 'All pupils in those schools where community languages are in demand should be encouraged to consider studying them' (DES, 1985: Paras 3, 19 and 3.20).

While this support was welcome, it was generally felt to have failed to go far enough in its support of community languages within mainstream secondary foreign language provision. It confines the community languages, including Gujerati, Urdu, Arabic, Hindi, Bengali and Panjabi, to those schools where there is a concentration of pupils interested in learning them. This contrasts sharply with the provision and resourcing of the other languages included in the foreign language curriculum and automatically affects the status of these community languages in comparison with those already established within the foreign language curriculum. It also still leaves some community languages outside the official school curriculum.

The omission from the Swann Committee's recommendations pertaining to home language teaching and bilingual support was a disregard of the evidence which exists indicating the central role of languages (first and subsequent) in the learning process. A separate professional report carried out by HMI (the national inspectors for schools) for the DES (the Department of Education and Science, which no longer exists) into *Mother Tongue Teaching in School and Community* (DES, 1984), took a slightly different view on the education issues raised by the topic. Their report stated that progress in community language teaching would depend on: 'Establishing a firmer base of accurate knowledge of pupils' existing language skills in their mother-tongues' (DES, 1984: 24).

The report perceived a gap in existing knowledge (at that time) of the language use of bilingual children and suggested a linguistic description of bilingual children's language repertoire was needed before more concrete recommendations could be made. In their survey report of four LEAs (Ealing, ILEA, Manchester and Walsall) the HMI took a slightly different view from Swann in the question of first language provision within mainstream education. HMI (1984: 7) 'strongly endorsed' the six principles identified by one of the authorities in its documented policy statement. One principle endorsed by HMI is particularly significant. They state: 'It is educationally desirable that bilingual children in primary schools should be given the chance to read and write their mother-tongues and to extend their oral skills in these languages' (DES, 1984: 7).

Current Policy

Since 1988 there has been a National Curriculum in Britain. The Cox Report was the discussion document which preceded the introduction of the National Curriculum for English. The terms of reference of the Cox Committee (DES, June, 1989) stipulated that the Committee concern itself with the English curriculum for all pupils, whatever their first language. The supplementary guidance to the working group stressed that: 'The framework (for English) should ensure, at the minimum, that all school-leavers are competent in the use of English – written and spoken, whether or not it is their first language' (DES, June 1989: Para 10.1).

The Working Group was also informed that it: 'Should also take account of the ethnic diversity of the school population and society at large, bearing in mind the cardinal point that English should be the first language and medium of instruction for all pupils in England' (DES, June 1989: Para 10.1).

In their recommendations (DES, June, 1989) the Cox Committee reaffirmed the Swann Committee's belief that: 'The key to equality of opportunity, to participation on equal terms as a full member of society, is a good command of English' (DES, 1985: Ch. 7 Para 3.16).

The Cox Report included a chapter on Bilingual Children (DES, June 1989: Chapter 10). However, it should be noted that pupils in Welsh medium schools in Wales were to be excluded from the supplementary guidance from the Secretary of State for Education. This exclusion clause once again differentiated between groups of bilingual UK and EC citizens. Dissatisfaction with this differential treatment is now evident from an unexpected source. In 1974, parents in Wales began an appeal to the House of Lords after a five-year campaign against Dyfed (a Welsh local education authority) County Council's bilingual education policy, under which English-speaking children in predominantly Welsh-speaking areas are required to attend Welsh language schools. The appeal (reported in *The Independent* 11 July 1994) is based on the right of the child to be educated in the home language. If successful, the implications will spread beyond Wales. This is but one example of the anomalies of statutory provision within the 1988 Education Reform Act.

The report which was to set the parameters for the teaching of foreign languages in the national curriculum – the Harris Report – also had a chapter on bilingual children (DES, October 1990: Chapter 15). It pointed out that there are several areas where bilingual pupils make up between 10% and 50% of the pupil population and that this should be seen within the framework of national needs for 'more people to use and understand a more diverse range of languages'. As a consequence, it was recommended that bilingual pupils should be given every opportunity to study their 'home language' –

the term used to designate their languages other than English – as foreign languages. The paradox evident in the terminology, and in the practice of treating a language spoken bilingually as a foreign language, did not seem to trouble the authors of the report. Their recommendations led to a list of 19 languages being established as eligible to be taught as foreign languages. These are the eight official languages of the European Union and Arabic, Bengali, Gujerati, Hindi, Japanese, Mandarin or Cantonese Chinese, Modern Hebrew, Panjabi, Russian, Turkish and Urdu. In practice, the languages most widely taught remain French, German and Spanish, and the numbers of pupils taking foreign language examinations in their home language remain relatively insignificant.

English in the National Curriculum and Bilingual Children

The programmes of study for English (and other core subjects of the National Curriculum) are linked closely to age-related attainment targets and pupil assessment. This inevitably means that if all children are to be taught and assessed in the English language, bilingual children are still to be compared with their monolingual English-speaking peers. It will also mean that the full range of their linguistic repertoire will continue to be unrecognised in their learning and formal school assessments. Irrespective of the Cox Committee's disclaimer of inconsistency and unreasonable discrimination, it is likely that the assessment profiles of ethnic minority pupils (a statutory requirement of the 1988 legislation) will record a lower level of performance. Since the assessment will be carried out in English, this will preclude from the assessment other language skills which the pupils may possess. It will not therefore be a comprehensive record of their linguistic repertoire and may result in an inaccurate record of their linguistic competence. This is one way in which the Cox Report and the subsequent legislation can be interpreted as unreasonably discriminatory. In addition, the proviso under Section 19 of the 1988 Education Act allows misapplication of the provisions of the National Curriculum. This enables headteachers to exempt some pupils from the assessment requirements for English if it is considered that those pupils have language difficulties so severe as to render the assessment unworkable.

In practice, this could lead to some bilingual children being separated from their monolingual peers for assessment purposes. Since assessment procedures are to be linked to attainment targets, which in turn are linked to curriculum content, this could also lead to some pupils being separated for teaching purposes. Section 19 (of the 1988 Education Act) is a conundrum. It allows for preclusion from the curriculum by which the Act ensures entitlement. The first assessment takes place at the age of seven. Even if pupils are not excluded from the assessments, it seems reasonable to speculate that some bilingual children will achieve a comparatively low level of performance in their assessment. This achievement will be marked on education records, with the result that the institutional practices and procedures identified by Swann as being discriminatory to ethnic minority pupils have been perpetuated and enshrined in the 1988 legislation. To reiterate Troyna's (1991) point, bilingual pupils will remain underachievers simply because their abilities are under-rated.

The 1988 Reform Act gives each child an entitlement to education. One of its stated aims is to prepare pupils for adult life. This has frequently been represented to mean preparation for the work place. However, there is a broader meaning to preparation for adult life which encompasses active citizenship. The success of the 1988 Education Reform Act is still to be assessed. Its success should not only be judged by the ways in which it creates an appropriately trained workforce but also by the ways in which it develops individuals to take their place in society as citizens who are equipped to exercise their rights and play an active role in their society. In order to achieve this, British schools will need to meet the challenges of both the 1976 Race Discrimination Act and the 1988 legislation. Thus the challenge identified by Swann (DES, 1985: 90) of 'evolving an education system which ensures that all pupils achieve their full potential' should once again be under active consideration by the teaching profession, educational policy makers, politicians but above all by the community groups who speak these languages.

Progress in education provision from assimilation through multicultural education and anti-racist education reflects the change in status of certain ethnic minority groups from immigrants to British citizens. However, despite its heterogeneous, multilingual population, Britain, unlike for example, Canada, Wales and Australia, still does not have an official language policy. In the description and analysis of the education provision for bilingual children in British schools since the 1960s up to and including the introduction of the National Curriculum in 1988, presented here, the inherent value system of education policy makers is clear. English is now firmly established as the only official language of mainstream education in Britain. Foreign languages are taught in secondary schools but these are almost exclusively defined in terms of modern European languages. French and German are widely taught while Urdu and Panjabi are not. This seems a misfocus and a mistake.

And the Future?

The financial support for the education of bilingual children has not been met in full from within the mainstream education budget. Section XI funding, as it is known, is a budget administered by the Home Office. It has been used in the past to fund a number of bilingual support teachers for children in mainstream schooling. However, in 1993 the government announced changes to the existing arrangements. Over a period of three years (1993–96) there will be a gradual reduction in the contribution towards Section XI funding to LEAs. The government contribution will gradually be reduced from 75% to 57%, with a further reduction to 50%. Discussions about policy are needed. However, it is necessary to be mindful of Kroon and Vallon's (1994) reminder that language and education policy are not at all abstract; they form part of people's everyday lives. Recent research in the nursery school (Thompson, 1994, 1995b) suggests that current education policy, with its emphasis on English as the only official language of the school curriculum, exerts a powerful influence on the linguistic repertoire of individual children. Findings to date suggest that there is a quantifiable shift away from the community language (in this case Mirpuri, vernacular Panjabi) towards English after only one term in school (Thompson, 1995).

To return to Ingram's (1990) statement, Britain does not at present possess a clearly formulated and stated language policy. However, it is possible to infer a policy from the education provision. The current situation is that the full linguistic repertoire of some pupils is not being reflected in classroom teaching. It is also ignored as an individual, societal and national resource. By preferring to concentrate resources and teaching in a number of ways that fail to acknowledge bilingualism as a positive intellectual, social and educational advantage for pupils, education provision is undervaluing, undermining and underselling significant groups within British society.

In the Foreword to *Multilingualism in the British Isles* (Alladina & Edwards, 1991) Pattanayak suggests that the multicultural debate in the UK has got bogged down in the spurious controversy between multicultural and anti-racist education. Hence the debate and real issues have been lost. Thompson (1994) suggests that before moving towards a better education provision for all children in the UK, the debate has to be reclaimed and refocused on the real educational needs of bilingual pupils. She suggests that this cannot be achieved without a description of the linguistic repertoires that goes beyond the labelling bilingual or Asian. There is the need to identify more precisely the languages spoken and to draw a linguistic map of the United Kingdom. Education planners need to take account of the distribution of languages in formulating educational policy.

Education provision in Britain is currently in a state of transition. The Education Reform Act introduced in 1988 is still percolating its way through all years of compulsory schooling. This stage of transition has not been without its trauma. However, since change is still in progress it is not too late to reconsider the current provision for bilingual children in two ways. Firstly, their educational needs within mainstream education, and secondly, the type and range of courses that would encourage more active participation in further and higher education. It would be a pity if the 1988 ERA failed to address bilingual pupils. It would indeed be an opportunity lost.

Acknowledgements

An earlier version of the section, 'The Education of Bilingual Children in Britain', appeared in Current Issues in *Language in Society* Vol. 1. No. 2, 'A Response to Kroon & Vallen: A Comparative Overview of the Education Policy for Young Bilingual Children in Britain', Linda Thompson, 1994.

6 Language Policy in the United States[1]

THOMAS RICENTO

Introduction

The lack of an official federal language policy or of any public institution devoted to language issues broadly defined in the United States is rather remarkable for a nation of its size and linguistic heritage. The United States has never had an official language nor a language academy. Recent attempts to enshrine English as the official language by constitutional amendment have proved unsuccessful. In spite of this seeming indifference to the status of English, or perhaps because of it, English has never been seriously challenged as the dominant language of public life in the US. By most measures (e.g. rapid rates of language shift to English, the number (80%) of non-native English speakers above five years of age who report speaking English well or very well on the 1990 census, etc.), there appears to be little threat of social fragmentation along purely linguistic lines. To this point, at least, it would appear that the uncoordinated, *ad hoc* approach that has typified US language policy has been relatively successful. However, such a conclusion overlooks a number of historical events whose effects are still felt today, including the forced anglicisation of American Indians, resulting in the extinction of many languages unique to the Americas, and the destruction of indigenous societies and nations; the historic denial of voting rights and other civil rights to speakers of minority languages and to persons not literate in English; denial of access to educational opportunities for minority language speakers and speakers of non-standard dialects of English, to name a few. Today, matters of great importance to the well-being of individuals, communities, and the nation are often decided on ideological grounds and not on sound research or other principled, and empirically defensible, criteria. I am thinking here not only of the continuing controversy over so-called bilingual education, but also of the sorry state of foreign language education, literacy education and related matters.

In this chapter, I hope to present a broad and balanced picture of language policy in the US. In general, my view is that within the taxonomy provided by Kloss (1971),[2] the US has at best tolerated immigrant minority languages, has frequently moved to suppress them during times of heightened xenophobia, war, and/or economic distress, and has on occasion for purposes of political or economic expediency (as with, for example, the alignment of German-Americans with the Democratic Party in the 1880s) promoted their languages. The languages of indigenous minorities (e.g. American Indians, Puerto Ricans, Mexicans and other Native Americans (Macias, 1990: 1)) have often been repressed. Further, in recounting the immigrant history of the US, there is a tendency to fixate on what John Higham has called '. . . the sunny side of American life . . . the common bonds of an American national character' (cited in Crawford, 1992a: 31). The association of not only a linguistic norm (English), but also a racial (white) and ethnic (Northern European) norm with 'American', going back at least to the Federalist period, is a repeated theme in US history.

This chapter will be divided into four parts: first, I will provide an overview of the linguistic situation in the US, with the goal of exemplifying the rich ethnolinguistic history of the US, from the pre-colonial era to the latest US census figures. Next, I will discuss practices, attitudes, legislative measures, judicial decisions and federal actions which together have constituted *de facto* and *de jure* language policies from the early days of the republic to about World War II. Then, I will comment on current policies at the federal, state, and local level which have had an impact on language use in the public and private sector. The focus here will be primarily on language in education policies. Finally, I will consider the role played by secondary social organisations, such as advocacy groups, in advancing language policies.

Linguistic Background of the US Indigenous Languages

Indigenous languages

At the time the Spanish arrived on the North American continent, 500 different native American languages may have been spoken (Leap, 1981: 129). Altogether, over 1000 languages and dialects were spoken on the American continents in the period just before European contact (Ruhlen, 1987: 6, cited in Molesky, 1988: 36).

Diseases contracted from the white settlers, wars, massacres and the continual encroachment into native lands by European settlers, resulted in a reduction of the native population on the North American continent from 30–40 million at the time of contact (estimates vary; see Ruhlen, 1987: 6, in

McKay, 1988: 36) to a low of 400,000 in 1920 (Molesky, 1988: 37).[3] The eradication of native languages began with the earliest European settlers who viewed the natives as uncivilised heathens, 'destitute of all that constitutes civilization' (Rehyner, 1992: 42).

Although there are some famous examples of missionaries who identified with Indian interests,[4] government policy favoured the replacement of native languages with English. It was believed that the loss of native languages would help natives adapt to reservation life, as exemplified by a federal commissioner of Indian Affairs, J.D.C. Atkins, in his annual report for 1887:

> . . . Through sameness of language is produced sameness of sentiment, and thought. . . . By civilizing one tribe others would have followed . . . Schools should be established, which children should be required to attend; their barbarous dialects should be blotted out and the English language substituted . . . (Crawford, 1992b: 48)

Interestingly, prior to this policy, and after resettling in Oklahoma, the Cherokees had established an educational system of 21 schools and had achieved a 90% literacy rate in Cherokee (Crawford, 1989: 25), as well as '. . . a higher English literacy level than the white populations of either Texas or Arkansas' (according to a 1969 US Senate report on Indian education) (Crawford, 1989: 25). Although the Bureau of Indian Affairs (BIA) rescinded its official policy of repressing Indian vernaculars in 1934 (Crawford, 1989: 26), punishments for native language use continued into the 1940s and 1950s. The dismantling of effective bilingual programmes by the BIA and the imposition of monolingual English instruction at reservation schools led to the inevitable decline in numbers of speakers of native languages. In 1933, John Collier was the first commissioner of Indian Affairs to advocate an emphasis on teaching Indian cultures and languages (Rehyner, 1992: 45).

Today, a majority of American Indians, Eskimos and Aleuts live in six states: Alaska, Oklahoma, California, Arizona, New Mexico and Washington (Roberts, 1993: 83), and 57% of the people who speak Native American languages live in Arizona and New Mexico (Waggoner, 1993). In 1890, 248,253 American Indians were counted in the census; in the 1990 census, 1,878,285 people identified themselves as American Indians; 331,600 people 5+ years of age reported speaking American Indian and Alaska native languages at home. Of that number, about 45% speak Navajo (148,500); 23,200 speak Eskimo languages and there are at least 1000 speakers of Dakota, Apache languages, Cherokee, and Pima and Papago. Altogether, 26 languages/language families were counted in the 1990 census with 1000 or more speakers (Waggoner, 1993).[5]

Colonial languages

Colonial languages refer to languages of settlers who arrived in the US before the birth of the republic. These have been identified as English, Spanish, French, German, Russian, Swedish and Dutch (Fishman *et al.*, 1966: 23, in Molesky, 1988: 38). I will focus here on two of the languages other than English which were most prominent in this era, Spanish and German. For information on other colonial languages, their distribution and functions, see, for example, Heath (1981), Molesky (1988), Crawford (1992a).

Spain was the first colonial power in the New World to establish a permanent presence. Ponce de Leon discovered Florida in 1513, although it was not until 1565 that a permanent colony was established at present-day Jacksonville (Conklin & Lourie, 1983: 10). In 1598, Juan de Onate founded Gabriel de los Espanoles, the oldest continuous Spanish settlement in the Southwest. Santa Fe was established in 1609, followed by other settlements in present-day New Mexico, southern Colorado, Arizona, and western Texas (Conklin & Lourie, 1983: 14). Between 1769 and 1823, Father Junipero Serra founded 21 missions along the California coast, from present-day San Diego to San Francisco (Conklin & Lourie, 1983: 15). The Spanish also held the Louisiana Territory between 1763 and 1800.[6] Between 1800 and 1853, Spain and Mexico lost their holdings in the United States, ending over 300 years of Spanish and Mexican colonialism in the US.

The colonial legacy and the continual influx of Spanish-speakers from Mexico, the Caribbean and Central and South America have made Spanish-speakers by far the largest language minority in the US, with some 17.4 million Spanish-speakers counted in the 1990 census (22.3 million reported Hispanic origin); by way of comparison, the second largest language minority group is French, with 1.9 million speakers. According to projection figures in the 1990 census, by 2050 there will be 80.6 million persons of Hispanic origin, or about 21% of the total US population (compared to about 9% of the total population in the 1990 census).

While persons of Hispanic origin constitute a large ethnic minority group in the US, of those who reported their ancestry in the 1990 census, people of German origin still outnumber all other identified groups of Americans, with nearly one in four Americans (58 million) claiming German ancestry (1990 Census of Population, Social and Economic Characteristics, United States). In 1790, 141,000 Germans lived in the Quaker belt of Southeastern Pennsylvania, constituting 33% of the white population (Kloss, 1977: 140). German was a *de facto* official language in the colonial period; nothing is known about its legal status under British rule, although German had once been the official language of the New Sweden colony (1638 to 1655) (which had its centre in present-day Delaware and New Jersey; cited in Kloss, 1977: 142). Official proclamations, business accounts and bills, and presumably court documents were all published in German (as well as in other languages). At least 38 German language newspapers were published between 1732 and 1800 (Crawford, 1992b: 35–36). However, an attempt in 1828 to elevate German to the second official language of Pennsylvania failed (Kloss, 1977: 143). Although large pockets of Germans on the east coast and in the Midwest remained, the process of anglicisation and assimilation had reduced the influence of German in public life by 1815 (Molesky, 1988: 41). With renewed large-scale immigration from Germany beginning in the 1820s (Schlossman, 1983: 142 in Molesky, 1988: 42), there was a resurgence of German language and culture. By 1850, 75% of the 800,000 foreign born with a non-English mother tongue were German-speaking. The next highest in terms of percentage were the French-speaking, at 13%, and the rest were between 1% and 1.5% of the total (Kloss, 1977: 82). In 1880, 60% of the non-English foreign born were German-speaking out of a total of 3.4 million (Kloss, 1977: 82).

As a result of continued immigration, an active German press, clubs and schools, especially in the Midwest (Wisconsin, Illinois, Minnesota, Ohio, Missouri), German was maintained well into the 20th century. There may have been nine million native German speakers by 1910 (Fishman *et al.*, 1966: 213). By the mid-1800s bilingual German–English schools operated in Baltimore, Cincinnati, Cleveland, Indianapolis, Milwaukee and St Louis (Crawford, 1989: 20). By 1900, more than 600,000 American children (4% of the elementary school population) were receiving at least part of their instruction in German (Kloss, 1977, in Crawford, 1989: 20).

Anti-catholic feelings (although not all Germans were Catholics) and fears of 'the foreign element' led to the passage of laws restricting or outlawing German instruction in the public, and parochial, schools. In the 1870s Cleveland's superintendent of schools claimed that although English was the 'language of our country, it was only natural for German-speaking groups to keep their own language' (Heath, 1981: 14). However, by the late 1880s legislation was passed in several states mandating English as the only language of public and private education (Crawford, 1989: 21). Although many of these laws were struck down by the courts (this discussion will be taken up in a later section), the effects of the 'Americanization' campaign begun in the late 1800s and the anti-German hysteria preceding and continuing through World War I had a permanent chilling effect on the status of German in the schools. By the late 1930s, bilingual instruction of any type had all but disappeared throughout the United States; even the study of German as a foreign language had dwindled from 24% of secondary school students enrolled in 1915 to less than 1% in 1922 (Crawford, 1989: 24).

In 1991, 6500 Germans emigrated to the US (US Immigration and Naturalization Service, Statistical Yearbook, annual), fourth among European countries and less than 5% of the total European immigration.[7] Of the roughly 32 million persons who speak languages other than, or in addition to, English at home, 1.5 million reported speaking German (Bureau of the Census, 1990).

Summary

The United States' multilingual character has continued relatively unabated since the pre-colonial era, thanks to continued immigration.[8] Except in cases of continual or cyclical immigration, the existence and private use of non-English languages has generally, but not always, been tolerated. When large numbers of immigrants were able to claim territorial pockets, especially in relatively unpopulated areas, they were often able to maintain their languages and use them for public purposes, including education. This happened especially with German speakers in rural Pennsylvania, Ohio, Illinois, Wisconsin and Minnesota, and with Spanish-speakers in the Southwest and California. As we will see in the next section, the community pressures against languages mentioned above have led to policies restricting, if not suppressing, non-English languages (see Leibowitz (1971) for a fuller discussion).

In 1965, immigration laws were passed which replaced the national origins quota system that had been in effect since 1924. Preference was given to immigrants based on family reunification and job skills rather than by country of origin. The abandonment of the quota system had a dramatic effect not only on the numbers of new immigrants, but also on the countries from which they came. The biggest change was the great increase of immigrants from Asia and the Americas and the sharp decrease of those from Europe. Between 1961 and 1970, the 'newer' immigrants outnumbered the Europeans 2.1 million to 1.2 million. Between 1981 and 1990, the ratio had grown even steeper: 6.8 million (Asia and the Americas) vs. 705,000 (Europe), a ratio of about 10:1. In the year 1991, 1.75 million Asians and Hispanic Americans and 135,000 Europeans were admitted, a ratio of 13:1.

In the decade ending in 1990, more immigrants arrived than in any previous period except 1901–1910, and from more countries than ever before, at least 65. According to projections of the Bureau of the Census in 1990, the Asian/Pacific Islander and Hispanic groups will experience the greatest percentage growth in population and migration through the year 2050 among five groups identified (these groups are White, Black, American Indian/Eskimo/Aleut, Asian/Pacific Islander, and Hispanic Origin).[9] Thus, the ethnic and racial composition of America is changing rapidly, and this trend will continue under current policy and global conditions, both of which are subject to change. In 1990, nearly 20 million Americans were foreign-born, and the percentage of those who arrived from Asia and the Pacific Islands since 1980 had increased by 108%. In 1990, six Asian-American groups had more than a half million members: Chinese, Filipino, Japanese, Asian Indian, Korean, and Vietnamese (Waggoner, 1992). During the 10-year period 1980–1990, the number of Hmong people increased 1631%, Cambodians 829% and Bangladeshis 801% (although in absolute numbers, these latter three groups are very small). The details of the American mosaic have changed radically.

Language Policies: A Historical Perspective

This section will not address issues of language *corpus* planning, i.e. those issues related to dictionary making, spelling standardisation and/or simplification, document simplification and the like. It will focus on *status* issues, especially as they relate to minority language speakers and their communities,[10] although corpus issues are by no means easily separated from status issues. By status issues, I mean the degree to which a language is recognised and promoted, or restricted or prohibited in specified, and usually public contexts, such as in education, voting, and employment (see Cooper, 1989 for a fuller discussion). The goal of analysis is to gauge the degree to which policy decisions, whether planned or unplanned, further the maintenance of languages by communities, or hasten the shift (replacement) of minority languages by dominant (often official) languages.

Since the United States has never had a coherent and comprehensive language policy,[11] scholars search the historical record seeking patterns by which policy approaches might be characterised. In addition to seeking patterns, scholars often wish to make a case for policy change by demonstrating systemic biases or agendas which inhere in research methods. For example, in recent years, scholars have classified approaches according to possible assumptions underlying research, or the lack thereof. Tollefson (1991) identifies two approaches to language policy/planning: (1) the *neoclassical* approach; and (2) the *historical-structural* approach (another similar scheme is Street's (1984) *autonomous* and *ideological* model). In the *neoclassical* approach, according to Tollefson, the researcher does not judge the equity or fairness of policies nor the historical, structural factors and political and economic interests that benefit from policy decisions (Tollefson, 1991: 28). The *historical-structural* approach '. . . rejects the neoclassical assumption that the rational calculus of individuals is the proper focus of research, and instead seeks the . . . social, political, and economic factors which constrain or impel changes in language structure and language use' (Tollefson, 1991: 31). The work of Leibowitz (1969, 1971, 1974) anticipates the more recent scholarly interest in the *historical-structural* framework, while that of Heinz

Kloss (e.g. 1977) is more neutral in its analytic framework. Among the more recent work in language planning and policy, there has been a discernible shift to a *historical-structural* approach.

In this section, sociopolitical explanations for particular policies are often specified, although not within any particular theoretical framework, such as neo-Marxist or other political-economic models. Nonetheless, the case will be made that language policy decisions reflect sociopolitical agendas in which language is but one, often symbolic, element.

What follows is a historical survey of the status of minority languages, education policy (including literacy), and language rights issues in the US. The discussions in each of these areas will be suggestive rather than exhaustive given the massive amounts of material available.

Status of minority languages

In reviewing the historical record of language policies in the United States, certain themes emerge. One is the often unstated notion that being American is somehow inextricably tied to being an English-speaker; another is antipathy towards the idea that groups should have any special privileges or rights. Although the Constitution is written in English, nothing in it refers to the status of English, nor was such a provision ever considered at the time of its writing.[12]

James Madison acknowledged that 'all civilized societies are divided into different sects, factions, and interests' (Crawford, 1992a: 33). Hence, a constitutional system of checks and balances was created, to safeguard against the tyranny of the majority, but decidedly not with the intention of protecting the rights and interests of groups. Although many tongues and nationalities were in evidence in 1787, these differences were apparently not seen as potential sources of discord. And as Crawford (1992a: 33–34) points out, '. . . in 1787 cultural pluralism was a *concept* [italics mine] yet to be invented'.

It is clear, however, that the seeds for discord did exist at the time of the founding of the republic. John Jay's reference to 'one united people – a people descended from the same ancestors, *speaking the same language* [italics mine], professing the same religion . . . very similar in their manners and customs' (Crawford, 1992a: 32) reflects the myth of homogeneity which has characterised one aspect of the American ethos. Certainly, English speakers constituted the majority of the white population, but German, Dutch, French, Spanish, Italian, Portuguese, Greek, Yiddish and Arabic were spoken not to mention hundreds of Amerindian languages and African languages brought to American shores in the slave trade beginning in the early 1600s. However, concerns about the status of English and of the dangers of 'too many foreigners' overwhelming the American experiment in democracy were voiced early on. Reacting to the growing influence of Germans in Pennsylvania, Benjamin Franklin wrote:

> Why should the *Palantine Boors* be suffered to swarm into our Settlements, and by herding together, establish their Language and Manners to the Exclusion of ours? Why should *Pennsylvania*, founded by the *English*, become a Colony of *Aliens*, who will shortly be so numerous as to Germanise us instead of our Anglifying them, and will never adopt our Language or Customs, any more than they can acquire our Complexion. (Crawford, 1992a: 37)

Franklin complained about the use of German in legal documents and business establishments, worrying that '. . . they will soon so out number us, that all the advantages we have will not in My Opinion be able to preserve our language, and even our Government will become precarious' (Crawford, 1992a: 37). These same arguments and fears have been voiced consistently right up to the present day by groups striving to 'protect' the status of English.[13]

The case of French in the Louisiana Territory is an example of the federal government's lack of any coherent philosophy or approach to linguistic and cultural diversity. But for a few positive political or short-term economic reasons to accommodate differences, both federal and state governments have tended to ignore, or suppress them. When the Louisiana Territory was annexed in 1803, Jefferson appointed a territorial governor who spoke no French and who proposed that English be the official language of local government (Leibowitz, 1969: 325), even though the governor knew that 'not one in fifty of the old inhabitants appear to me to understand the English Language' (Crawford, 1992a: 40). After a failed attempt to take all governmental decisions out of local hands, causing an uproar among the largely French and Creole-speaking inhabitants, Jefferson moderated his policy and rewrote the Organic Act for the Orleans Territory, providing for an elected legislature and promising statehood when Louisiana's free population reached 60,000 (Crawford, 1992a: 41). Jefferson appointed bilingual judges and instructed that records be maintained in both French and English. When Louisiana joined the Union in 1812, it had a large Francophone majority. For most of the 19th century, Louisiana's laws and other public documents were printed in French, and the courts and legislature operated bilingually. However, despite the relatively liberal language policy, the influx of Anglophones hastened the inevitable shift to English. Although rights to bilingual schooling, courtroom interpreters, and translation of legal documents into French survived in Louisiana law until 1921 (Crawford, 1992a: 43), French no longer survives in any meaningful way as a public language. The assumption in 1803 was the same as today: the language of America (if not of all Americans) is English.

While a number of state and federal laws passed during the 19th and early 20th centuries tended to restrict or outlaw the use of minority languages in voting, education and other public venues (see Leibowitz, 1971, 1982 for a thorough discussion of these issues), none of the affected groups, save for enslaved African Americans, was treated with the degree of injustice and brutality as were the native Americans.

Beginning with Congressional appropriation of funds in 1802 (not to exceed $15,000) to promote 'civilization among the aborigines' (Leibowitz, 1971: 30), the aim of federal policy was to remove the natives from the open spaces to reservations in order to open up the Plains for white settlers. As President Monroe put it in 1817: 'The hunter or savage state requires a greater extent of territory to sustain it than is compatible with the progress and must (*sic*) claim of civilized life . . . and must yield to it' (Leibowitz, 1971: 31). In order to speed up the assimilation process, off-reservation boarding schools were established, the first at Carlisle, Pennsylvania, in 1879. The purpose of this school was 'to separate the Indian child from his reservation and family, strip him of his tribal lore and mores, emphasise industrial arts, and prepare him in such a way that he would never return to his people' (Liebowitz, 1971: 32).

What is remarkable is that Indians had been very successful in educating their youth in their own languages; the US government simply refused to acknowledge these achievements or the illogicality of destroying native culture and replacing it with something completely foreign. Although no specific mention is made of the English language in the earliest congressional provisions, the acquisition of it was equated with 'civilization'. By 1886, the US government would not fund any education not conducted in English.

Although questions were asked about the government policy of eradicating Indian languages, and especially in regard to the methods used,[14] the goal of assimilation was never seriously questioned. In 1928, the Meriam Report, prepared by the Brookings Institution at the request of the Secretary of Interior, suggested that the goal of assimilation could be more effectively achieved by strengthening the Indian social structure, not destroying it (Leibowitz, 1971: 34). Among other things, the report recommended that the language of the Indian child be taken into account in instructional programmes. John Collier, Commissioner of Indian Affairs from 1933 to 1945, attempted to implement the recommendations of the Meriam Report. For example, in 1936, the Indian Service Summer School offered classes in Sioux and Navajo, and provided demonstration classes in bilingual education methods (Leibowitz, 1971: 35). This period ended in the early 1940s, and in

1944 the House Indian Affairs Committee recommended a return to the previous English-only policies which had been criticised in previous reports.[15]

By 1950, nearly 150 years after federal funds were first appropriated to 'civilise' the Indians, Congress decided to terminate federal recognition and services and to relocate Indians into cities (Leibowitz, 1971: 35); in effect, the failure of government policies to assimilate the native population was admitted. Whereas in the 1800s, the Cherokees had 'a population 90% literate in its native language and used bilingual materials to such an extent that Oklahoma Cherokees had a higher English literacy level than the white populations of either Texas or Arkansas . . . today 40% of adult Cherokees are functionally illiterate' (Sen. Special Subcommittee on Indian Education of the Committee on Labor and Public Welfare, Indian Education: *A National Tragedy – A National Challenge*, 91st Cong., 1st Sess., 143 (1969), in Leibowitz, 1971: 36).

Throughout American history, the degree of tolerance accorded minority languages often depended on the racial and ethnic background of the speakers. Language, culture and ethnicity have often been lumped together, and the status of immigrant languages often suffered or benefited, depending on the valuation of the other two variables. The fears and doubts expressed by Franklin and Jefferson about the ability of a constitutional democracy to accommodate ethnic, racial and linguistic diversity, have yet to be resolved.

Education policy

In the American political system, education is a concern of individual states and not of the federal government. Some 16,000 local school districts in the US, governed by elected school boards and superintendents, make decisions regarding curriculum, allocation of available resources, staffing and other essential services. (Other jurisdictional boards exist in the District of Columbia, Puerto Rico, Guam, etc. (Macias, 1982: 144).) The federal role has increased in two ways: increased expenditures under titles I, IV, and VII of the Elementary and Secondary Education Act,[16] and an increased role in the enforcement of civil rights laws in education (Macias, 1982: 144). Other areas in which the federal government has appropriated funds for language education programmes are literacy grants and foreign language education.

While most curricular matters are decided by local school boards, from time to time certain issues gain national political attention and engage policy makers at the federal level. This has happened with the Bilingual Education Act, Title VII of the Elementary and Secondary Education Act, approved in 1968 with subsequent reauthorisations mandating modified formulas for allocating funds to different programme types (more on this in a later section). However, local school boards have great flexibility in the interpretation and implementation of federally funded programmes.[17]

In the early days of the republic, schools were financed by private funds. When the notion arose that tax dollars might be used to finance education, several states decided to support existing private schools with public funds (Kloss, 1977: 61–2). Since a number of these private schools had strong religious affiliations, the issue of church–state separation was enjoined. Catholics, many of whom were Germans who wanted separate German schools, or at the least German as a subject, petitioned the state legislature of New York for a partition of the school fund. In 1842, the legislature passed a bill which established non-parochial public schools (Kloss, 1977: 62). Despite subsequent efforts by certain Protestant groups to inject their beliefs in the public schools, and despite also the support of denominational schools in New Mexico until 1891 (Kloss, 1977: 63), separation of church and state finally prevailed.

In many of the earliest school laws, the language question is not touched on. However, individual school laws were passed that established English as the dominant language (e.g. Indiana School Laws, 1824; Kloss, 1977: 86). A number of school districts allowed non-English languages to be used as a tool of instruction or as subject matter. In Ohio and Colorado, German was used as a medium of instruction for immigrants, while all non-English languages were permitted by two Wisconsin laws, in 1846 and 1848 (Kloss, 1977: 86). In Oregon, an 1872 law allowed purely German public schools if demanded by at least one hundred voters (Kloss, 1977: 86). In many states, ethnic languages were offered as subjects within basically English public schools.

As the dominant language minority group for most of the 19th century, Germans were successful in maintaining their language and culture, in part, by developing political alliances with the Democratic Party.[18] However, strong anti-Catholic prejudice aimed at the Irish and Germans found political support in the Know-Nothing party, whose 1855 platform had a plank against parochial schools (Kloss, 1977: 66). Later, the American Protective Association (APA) attacked the parochial schools of non-English groups in the 1880s. These political movements helped end the teaching of German in a number of cities throughout the country in the 1880s (e.g. St Louis in 1881, Louisville, Kentucky in 1889). The main attack against non-English parochial schools began in 1889–90 with the passage of the Edwards Law in Illinois and the Bennett Law in Wisconsin in 1889. Although both Acts were repealed in 1893 after a Democratic coalition elected anti-Edwards and Bennett candidates in the 1890 elections, an important precedent had been set. With the surge of new immigrants between 1880 and 1920, an Americanisation movement gained strength by appealing to nativist fears. Organisations such as the YMCA combined English instruction with citizenship lessons. With the onset of World War I, even the US Bureau of Education became active in efforts to stress the connection between speaking English and being American. After the US entered the war, most public schools in the US curtailed the study of German (Crawford, 1989: 23).

In 1924, the landmark *Meyer v. Nebraska* case was handed down, arguably the most important case in the area of language rights. The Supreme Court affirmed that the due process clause of the Fourteenth Amendment protected certain substantive liberties that the state could not restrict (in this case, the teaching of German to an elementary school pupil).[19] The Court might have ruled differently had German not been singled out as a restricted language. Justices Holmes and Sutherland said, in part:

> We all agree, I take it, that it is desirable that all the citizens of the United States should speak a common tongue, and therefore, that the end aimed at by the statute is a lawful and proper one . . . I cannot bring my mind to believe that in some circumstances . . . the statute might not be regarded as a reasonable or even necessary method of reaching the desired result. (Leibowitz, 1971: 10)

Although the *Meyer v. Nebraska* decision was an important precedent for language minority rights, restrictive measures such as the Edwards and Bennett Laws had a lasting effect on language in education policy. Whereas only three states had laws prescribing English as the language of instruction in private schools prior to 1889, by 1923, 34 states required English (Leibowitz, 1971: 7). The high water mark for voluntary bilingual education in the US was probably around 1900.

The Americanisation campaigns of the late 19th and early 20th centuries had a negative impact on public attitudes toward bilingual education, as well as on the teaching of foreign languages. Attempts were made, ultimately unsuccessfully, to prohibit private Japanese, Chinese and Korean language schools in the territory of Hawaii and in California.[19] Opposition to bilingual and native language instruction was not based on pedagogical concerns, but more typically on fears and anxieties that Germans, Japanese, Koreans, and others might not be trustworthy Americans if they maintained their ancestral language and culture. Such fears were exaggerated during wartime. Edward P. Irwin, editor of the *Pacific Commercial Advertiser*, wrote that 'In many instances it [the German language press] had not actually been preaching disloyalty openly . . . It did not preach anti-Americanism; rather it preached Germanism. So here in Hawaii today, there are Japanese papers that do not actively teach anti-Americanism, but they do teach Japanism, and that amounts to the same thing' (Tamura, 1993: 41).

The case of Puerto Rico provides yet another example of how politics has driven language in education policy, even where the legitimacy of a non-English language, Spanish in this case, is not in question. From 1898 until the adoption of a Commonwealth Constitution in 1952, 10 Commissioners of Education were appointed by succeeding US presidents. Language policies vacillated between English in all grades (1898–1900); to Spanish in the elementary grades, English in high schools (1900–1904); to English in all grades (1904–1916); to Spanish in grades 1–4, Spanish and English in grade 5, English in grades 6–12 (1916–1934); to English in all grades (1934–1946); to Spanish as the language of instruction in all grades with English as a required subject in all grades (1946 to the present) (Resnick, 1993: 274–5). Resnick (1993: 264–5) points out that the fears of identity loss and subjugation to a foreign colonialist power have proven to be powerful deterrents to achieving bilingualism among Puerto Ricans (according to Resnick, not more than 20% of the population functions effectively in English).

Literacy has been a factor in educational and legal aspects of language policy. Laws and custom have determined which language or languages will be used in the classroom, courts, legislative bodies, voting ballots, public offices, private businesses, and more. Although the configurations of these policies and customs have varied, as we have seen in the case of German-, Puerto-Rican-, Japanese-, Chinese- and Korean-Americans, language policy as a means of social control emerges as a consistent theme. A brief review of the historical record will clarify some of these policies and their rationales.

In the colonial era, colonies such as Virginia and South Carolina passed 'compulsory ignorance laws' which made it a crime to teach slaves, and sometimes free-blacks, to read or write (Crawford, 1992a: 35). The concern was that a common tongue and literacy would likely promote rebellion.

Before the latter part of the 19th century, a number of state and local statutes were passed specifying language requirements. As was discussed earlier, beginning in the 1880s, greater restrictions were placed on the use of non-English languages in public and private education, reflecting nativist concerns about the growing number of ethnic communities. Even so, by 1900, about 4% of American elementary school enrollees received at least part of their instruction in German; in California and the Southwest, Spanish was often a language of instruction. In US territories, beginning with the Louisiana Purchase in 1803, both the legislative and executive branches of the federal government have followed policies which have injected English as the language of government, voting, and the courts, regardless of local opposition and whether or not it was expected that the territory would eventually become a state (Leibowitz, 1969: 325). As was the case in the Louisiana Territory, English was mandated in the original territorial decrees of the Territory of New Mexico (1850), Hawaii (1900) and Puerto Rico (in 1902, the Official Languages Act granted official status to both English and Spanish). Although accommodations were later made to the use of non-English languages,[20] the federal government has been insistent that English be the basic language.

Although immigration policies had discriminated against certain groups before the 'great wave' of new immigration began in 1890 (for example, the Chinese Exclusion Act of 1882), the next 30 years saw the passage of much broader restrictions. In 1906, the first law requiring English as a precondition to citizenship was passed; although some of the requirements have been modified, that requirement stands today. In 1907, the Dillingham Commission recommended that passing a literacy test (in any language) be a requirement for immigration. This policy reflected the belief that, according to the Commission 'the new immigration as a class is far less intelligent than the old, approximately *one third of all those over 14 years of age when admitted being illiterate*' (Liebowitz, 1984: 36). Presidents Taft and Wilson vetoed legislation requiring literacy tests. In 1917, a bill was finally passed requiring literacy for immigration. In 1924, the Johnson–Laird bill was passed establishing national origin quotas of 2% of the number of foreign born already in the country as determined by the census of 1890 (Ricento, 1988: 4). The effect of this legislation was to restrict the number and racial distribution of immigrants. In 1965 the quota system was abandoned, ending nearly 50 years of largely northern European immigration, and allowing much greater numbers of non-Europeans to settle in the US.

English literacy requirements beginning in the 1890s had been used to disenfranchise racial and religious minority groups. Some of these statutes were overturned by the US Supreme Court, but it was not until 1965, with passage of the Voting Rights Act, that literacy tests and other educational prerequisites for voting were suspended (Leibowitz, 1969: 343). However, the needs of large numbers of non-English speakers had not been taken into account in the 1965 legislation.[21] The Voting Rights Act was amended in 1975 to require bilingual ballots in those districts in which at least 5% of the population belonged to a single language minority group.[22] In 1992, Congress expanded coverage to districts with at least 10,000 members of a single language minority group (Crawford, 1992a: 197).

While legal barriers to voting were removed, educational policy had not addressed the language needs of tens of thousands of language minority students. The passage of the Bilingual Education Act of 1968 was the first legislative attempt by the federal government to remedy the deleterious effects that English-only education had had on several generations of Mexican-, Puerto-Rican- and Native-Americans who had been denied access to meaningful public education, in part, as a result of English-only policies in the classroom. According to a recent government report, functional illiteracy is a major problem affecting millions of Americans. Language minority persons not literate in English face barriers as a result of restricted access to classes, a severe shortage of classes, and, often, inappropriate instruction and curricula in the classroom (see McKay & Weinstein-Shr, 1993 for a detailed discussion of these issues).

Language rights

Macias (1979) distinguishes two kinds of rights: the right to freedom from discrimination on the basis of language, and the right to use your language(s) in the activities of communal life. There is no specific constitutional right to receive communications in a language other than English (Miner, 1994: 15).[23] The exception to this general principle was established in a decision by the federal Court of Appeals in 1970 (US ex rel. *Negron v. New York*, 434 F.2d 386 (2d Cir.), which held that '. . . the Sixth Amendment's guarantee of a right to confront and cross-examine witnesses gives criminal defendants the right to an interpreter during court proceedings' (Miner, 1994: 15).[24]

Although there is no Constitutional right to receive communications in languages other than English, the US Congress has enacted several laws to remedy the effects of discrimination against individuals on the basis of their race or national origin in specified domains of voting, education, and health care. For example, legislation was passed during the 1960s to bar literacy tests which had been used since the 19th century to deny blacks in the South the constitutional rights they had obtained after the Civil War during the Reconstruction era. In passing the Voting Rights Act of 1965, Congress found that the more fundamental right of suffrage superseded states' rights to stipulate voting requirements. A series of court cases involving literacy in Spanish in New York (*Katzenbach v. Morgan*, 1966; *Cardona v. Power*, 1966) and in California (*Castro v. State of California*, 1970), combined with Congressional hearings on voting and elections discrimination against Hispanics, Asian Americans, American Indians and Aleuts, led to amendments to the Voting Rights Act of 1975 requiring bilingual elections and bilingual services in certain jurisdictions (Macias, 1982: 94).

In the area of education, non-English speakers from specified national origin minority groups who had been effectively denied equal access to educational opportunities received protection under Title VI of the Civil Rights Act of 1964. Although at the time of its passage, the Civil Rights Act of 1964 was aimed at outlawing discrimination against Southern blacks, it did forbid discrimination on the basis of national origin. Groups such as La Raza Unida Party began to file lawsuits in Southwestern states demanding that the schools address the language needs of their children (Crawford, 1989: 34). Such protests eventually required some response by the Office for Civil Rights (OCR). On 25 May 1970, the director of that office, J. Stanley Pottinger, issued the so-called 25 May Memorandum, which instructed school districts with more than 5% national-origin-minority group children to '. . . take affirmative steps to rectify the language deficiency in order to open its instructional program to these students' (Crawford, 1989: 34). School districts reacted with reluctance to the directive; however, a number of important challenges to unsatisfactory school policies were litigated in the federal courts. In New Mexico, *Serna v. Portales* (351 F. Supp. 1279 (10th Cir. 1974)) and in New York, *Aspira of New York, Inc. v. Board of Education of the City of New York* (58 FRD 62 (SDNY 1973)), judges required that bilingual instructional plans for Hispanic children with limited English-speaking ability be provided to remedy past and present discrimination against Hispanic-Americans in public education.

The major court decision on the rights of language minority students was *Lau v. Nichols* (414 US 563 (1974)). In reversing the judgment of the Ninth Circuit Court, the US Supreme Court found that English-only instruction to non-English-speaking public school students in San Francisco was a violation of Title VI of the Civil Rights Act of 1964. In issuing his opinion, Justice Douglas did not mandate bilingual education as the only, or even best, remedy:

> No specific remedy is urged upon us. Teaching English to the students of Chinese ancestry who do not speak the language is one choice. Giving instructions to this group in Chinese is another. There may be others. Petitioners ask only that the Board of Education be directed to apply its expertise to the problem and rectify the situation. (cited in Crawford, 1989: 36)

It is important to note that the basis of the court's ruling was not that the children represented in the case had a right to receive education wholly, or in part, in their native language; rather, it was because of the children's deficiency in English that they had been prevented from meaningful participation in the educational programme offered by a school district.

In the area of employment, Title VII of the Civil Rights Act of 1964, sometimes called the Equal Employment Opportunity Act, provides protection from discriminatory conduct of employers, both public and private. Although discrimination based on language is not covered, employers can not discriminate on the basis of race or national origin (Miner, 1994). The Equal

Employment Opportunity Commission (EEOC), the agency charged with enforcing provisions of the Act, has written guidelines that prohibit discrimination because '. . . an individual has the linguistic characteristics of a national origin group' (cited in Miner, 1994). The EEOC has issued a number of rulings citing discrimination on the basis of accent; if the accent interferes with the employee's ability to perform the duties of the job, then the law does not apply. Courts have not viewed English-only rules in the workplace as violations of the Act, as long as the employer can demonstrate a business necessity for such a rule (Miner, 1994). However, EEOC guidelines stipulate that 'Prohibiting employees at all times, in the workplace, from speaking their primary language or the language they speak most comfortably, disadvantages an individual's employment opportunities on the basis of national origin' (29 CFR, @ 1601.7, cited in Miner, 1994).[25]

In the area of health care, federal legislation mandates bilingual services in federally funded migrant and community health centres and in federally funded drug and alcohol treatment programmes (Miner, 1994).

A number of states have passed laws requiring the provision of state services in non-English languages. For example, in California state agencies are required to hire sufficient numbers of bilingual employees to provide information and services in specified languages. Written materials in non-English languages must be provided if the language is spoken by at least 5% of the people served by the office (Miner, 1994). Other services so covered in California include emergency (911) services, which must be multilingual; applications for and information about government benefits, which must be available in Spanish; property tax forms and instructions must be provided in Spanish; and the summary of motor vehicle laws must be published in Spanish (Miner, 1994).

Concerns have been raised that official English statutes passed in recent years[26] might override current safeguards of access to government and public services in languages other than English. Indeed, such concerns are well founded, given the rise in anti-immigration sentiment since the 1980s. From its inception in 1983, the political lobbying organisation, US English, has raised and spent millions of dollars – $28 million dollars between 1983 and 1990 – (Crawford, 1992a: 4) on a campaign to have English declared the official language of the United States. In 1981, the late Senator S.I. Hayakawa, Republican of California, introduced a constitutional English Language Amendment (SJ Res. 72) in the US Senate, the first such proposal ever introduced into the US Congress. It was not reported out of committee. However, due largely to the intense advertising and lobbying of US English and similar groups, and a growing backlash towards federal and state support of bilingual education and voting, similar legislation has been proposed in subsequent sessions of Congress. In the latest session, the 103rd Congress of the US, four official English bills have been introduced, three in the House of Representatives and one in the Senate. One of the House bills seeks to amend the US Constitution (HJ RES 171); the other three are more narrow in focus. HR 123 would modify Title IV of the US Code, making English the 'official language' of government; the bill offers no specific programmes or funding to achieve its stated goals. A companion bill, HR 124, provides incentives for employers to provide English language training for their non- or limited-English speaking employees. Another bill, HR 739, introduced by Rep. Toby Roth (Republican – Wisconsin), establishes English as the preferred language of communication among all US citizens, 'reforms' current naturalisation requirements, and seeks to repeal all federal bilingual education and voting rights programmes (Inman, 1994: 11). HJ RES 171, introduced by Representative John Doolittle (Republican – California) would amend the US Constitution, requiring that English be used for all public acts, including every order, resolution, vote, or election, and for all records and judicial proceedings of the United States Government. Passage would require a two-thirds majority in both Houses of Congress, and ratification of three-fourths of the states within seven years of its submission.

With control of the 104th US Congress in Republican hands, following the 1994 mid-term election, there is a greater chance that one or all of these bills will be reported out of committee and debated on the floor of the Congress. It is ironic that one of the aims of the 'official English' legislation pending in the US Congress is to overturn state and federal provisions for bilingual services, such as bilingual ballots, which had previously been authorised by Congress to safeguard the civil rights of non-English speaking Americans. The courts, however, might be unwilling to enforce such laws, as has been the case with challenges brought under state statutes[27] declaring English the official language. These rulings, which have found official English laws and initiatives to be more symbol than substance, make it less likely that a Constitutional Amendment officialising English would be ratified. However, there is a real possibility that some form of 'official English' legislation will pass Congress in the near future, with serious repercussions not only for language minority persons, but for the nation as a whole (for a discussion of these issues, see Ricento, 1994).

Current Education Policy Issues

Bilingual education

Much of the US language policy literature deals with approaches for the education of Limited English Proficient (LEP) students and Non-English

Proficient (NEP) students.[28] Although the federal government's role in bilingual education has been relatively small in terms of funding levels, federal guidelines have been influential in policy development and implementation at the state and local levels.[29] Judicial precedents have had at least as much impact on policy development as federal legislation. A number of important Supreme Court decisions led to policy changes at the federal and state levels, which in turn resulted in policy changes in local educational agencies (LEAs). Changes of administration in Washington, DC have resulted in modifications in policy, funding levels, and support for what has been, virtually from its inception, a politically charged issue. The popular press has also played a role in shaping public attitudes towards bilingual education.[30]

The federal government's first attempt to deal with the needs of students with limited skills in English was the Bilingual Education Act of 1968 (Title VII of the Elementary and Secondary Education Act (ESEA)). The original purpose of the legislation, introduced by Senator Ralph Yarborough of Texas, was to address the needs of Mexican-American children in the Southwest who had either been segregated in inferior schools, or had been placed in English-only (submersion) classes (Lyons, 1992: 365). No particular types of programmes were recommended, and funding was modest at 7.5 million dollars. The lack of explicit guidelines in the original legislation, coupled with a shortage of adequately prepared bilingual teachers and non-English teaching materials, made implementation of the 1968 Bilingual Education Act problematic, at best.

After the *Lau v. Nichols* decision in 1974 (discussed earlier), the Office of Civil Rights (OCR) convened a group of experts to recommend approaches to implement the high court's decision.[31] The so-called 'Lau Remedies' outlined the necessary procedures districts should follow to be in compliance with the Supreme Court's decision, including programme selection, identification of student's primary language, personnel requirements, parental notification, and evaluation (Fernandez, 1987: 100). In 1980, as part of a settlement of a case in Alaska, OCR published official regulations which spelled out the obligations of school districts to LEP students (Fernandez, 1987: 101). Students with greater proficiency in their native language than in English had to be in bilingual programmes, while students demonstrating superior proficiency in English could receive instruction in English. Students with equal facility in two languages could choose either an English-only or bilingual programme. However, protests by major educational associations led to the adoption of an amendment in Congress prohibiting the Department of Education from using any money to enforce the proposed regulations. By September of 1980, when the Senate passed a similar amendment, the Lau Remedies were effectively dead. They were withdrawn in 1981; henceforth, the federal government would defer to states and local school districts to assure compliance with judicial and legislative mandates.

Research findings have also played a role in the evolution of policy in language education, although the politicisation of the 'bilingual education' issue has, to say the least, created more uncertainty and hostility than clear advice upon which to develop educational policy.

In the early years of the Bilingual Education Act, no research money was appropriated under Title VII. The first relatively large-scale study was conducted by the American Institutes for Research (AIR) during 1975–6. Their finding that there was no significant difference between bilingual and all-English classrooms has been criticised for significant methodological failures. Another later study (Baker & de Kanter, 1983) which reviewed the research literature was also widely criticised for methodological short-comings.[32] Nonetheless, recommendations based on the AIR and Baker and de Kanter studies found their way into the 1984 reauthorisation legislation of Title VII; these included the use of 'structured immersion' programmes and other innovations. A later study by Ramirez *et al.* (1991) who collected data between 1984 and 1988 found that late-exit programmes, in which students had been taught primarily in Spanish, produced the most sustained achieve-ment. Further, LEP students, regardless of the type of programme they were enrolled in, required five or more years to acquire adequate academic English proficiency. The most significant finding of the Ramirez study is that LEP students who receive all, or most, of their classroom instruction in English are at higher risk of falling behind and dropping out than are children who receive large amounts of instruction in their native language. The idea that earlier and greater exposure to English exclusively will speed up English acquisition, resulting in better learning of subject matter in the early grades, is simply not borne out by the data.

It is not clear that such studies will convince entrenched interests of the benefits of late-exit bilingual programmes. In spite of an impressive amount of qualitative and quantitative research now available on the needs of LEP students, the public debate (to the extent that there is one) tends to focus on perceptions and not on facts. As Fernandez (1987) puts it: 'The real – the only – question is not whether transitional bilingual education should become maintenance bilingual education for some or all children, or whether ESL is better for LEP students than bilingual education . . . The issue is: What is the most effective way to educate the growing number of language minority students in schools so that they can reach the social and economic mainstream of our society? (Fernandez, 1987: 115). Another way of looking at this issue from a purely pragmatic perspective is that, as Padilla (1990: 25) puts it:

'Today's language minority student is tomorrow's wage earner, tax-payer, and participant in the political process.'

Apart from the controversy about which models of so-called bilingual education are most appropriate for LEP students is the issue of federal funding. The number of school-age LEP children in the US in 1993 was between 2.3 and 3.5 million.[33] Of all pupils with limited English language skills served in programmes designed to meet these needs in the 1990–1 school year, only 15% were in BEA-funded programmes.[34] Other federal programmes serve LEP students, including programmes funded under Title I of the Elementary and Secondary Education Act (ESEA) – these include Chapter 1, compensatory education and migrant education – and those funded under Title IV of the ESEA – these include immigrant education and bilingual vocational education. In fact, Chapter 1 programmes serve more LEP students than does the BEA because of its role as the largest federal elementary and secondary education programme providing remedial educational services. The under-funding for LEP students can be seen in the following statistic: in the 1990–1 school year, at least 521,000 LEP children needing English language instruction did not receive any. Fiscal Year (FY) appropriation for the BEA for 1993 was $196,465,000, about a 7% increase, adjusting for inflation, from the 1988 level.

Some notable changes in the 1992 reauthorisation of the BEA are as follows: Special Alternative Instruction: these programmes which do not require the use of the LEP's native language, increased from 6% (FY 1988) to 23% (FY 1992) of part A appropriations (grants to LEAs); Family English Literacy projects: these provide opportunities for the adult family members of LEP children to learn English; funding increased from $4,524,000 (FY 1988) to $6,141,000 (FY 1992), an increase of 26%; Special Populations: supports bilingual preschool, special education, and gifted and talented projects; funding increased from $5,868,000 in FY 1988 to $8,009,000 in FY 1992, an increase of nearly 27%.

Other changes in funding levels between the 1988 and 1992 reauthorisation occurred in Part B and Part C grants. Part B Grants support data collection, evaluation assistance centres, studies and a national clearinghouse, awarded on a competitive basis to states. Since 1988, funding has decreased 12% after adjusting for inflation. Under Part C Grants, which consist of Personnel Training, the support of 16 Multifunctional Resource Centres, and a Fellowship Programme, there has been a 20% decrease in overall funding since FY 1988.

An important issue in reauthorisation debates has been whether or not to allow LEP children to be served in Chapter 1 solely on the basis of their language needs. Many advocates of bilingual education argue for greater coordination between Chapter 1 and Title VII programmes.

Another issue is whether or not to increase the cap of 25% on instruction projects which do not make use of LEP's native language, such as ESL; the demand for special alternative projects has increased in recent years, suggesting the trend that began with the withdrawing of the Lau Remedies is still in force, despite the evidence that late-exit bilingual programmes may be superior to basic ESL programmes.

Indigenous languages

Prior to 1978, children of native American backgrounds were not eligible for Title VII bilingual programmes because English is usually the dominant language in their homes (Crawford, 1989: 143). However, linguists and educators have discovered that the variety of English these children speak at home has been influenced by the ancestral language to such a degree that the resultant variety ('Indian English' code) causes difficulties in the English-only classroom (cf. Leap, in Crawford, 1989: 144–5). As with Spanish–English bilingual programmes, not enough qualified teachers and insufficient native language materials, as well as modest federal funding, have made implementation of bilingual programmes problematic. In 1986–7, only about 11% of Title VII bilingual education grants to school districts were earmarked for Indian children (about $10 million) (Crawford, 1989: 151).

In 1992, the Indian Nations at Risk Task Force reported to the Secretary of Education on its goals for the year 2000 for American Indian and Alaska Native students. Included in their recommendations are that: (1) all schools serving Native students will provide opportunities for students to maintain and develop their tribal languages; (2) all Native children will have early childhood education providing the needed 'language, social, physical, spiritual, and cultural foundations' for school and later success; (3) state governments will develop curricula that are 'culturally and linguistically appropriate', and will implement the provisions of the Native American Language Act of 1990[35] in the public schools, and provide model schools 'designed to meet the unique language and culturally related needs of Native students' (Waggoner, 1992: 3). A number of factors, in addition to those mentioned above, prevent implementation of the policies recommended by the Task Force. For one thing, there is a lack of unanimity among tribal leaders that bilingual education is appropriate; many elders remember a time when speaking their native language resulted in punishment and shame. In other cases, traditional elders have resisted writing the ancestral language, feeling that '. . . this will open its last cultural bastion to whites' (Crawford, 1989: 247). In other cases, local public (and private) schools refuse to provide bilingual classes, or find ways to sabotage programmes. As Crawford so aptly puts it: 'Coercive anglicization has taken more from Native Americans than a set of linguistic skills. It has isolated them from cultural resources they need to define themselves, leaving many unprepared to enter a wider society, still far from color-blind, that is likely to reject them regardless of their English-speaking ability' (Crawford, 1989: 248). Inappropriate language-in-education policies, coupled with feelings of cultural dislocation and limited economic opportunities, only hastens the erosion of native languages and cultures while slowing the acquisition of appropriate English academic skills.

Despite the good intentions of linguists wishing to preserve indigenous languages, and despite recommendations of task forces and the passage of federal legislation, it is difficult to be optimistic with regard to the future of these languages. A number of tribes have taken matters into their own hands and adopted official language policies in the 1980s, including the Navajo, Red Lake Band of Chippewa, Northern Ute, Arapahoe, Pasqua Yaqui and Tohono O'odham (Papago) (Crawford, 1989: 246). Without the support of local public and private schools, and as long as Anglo-conformist policies remain in effect, North American indigenous languages and cultures will continue to remain vulnerable.

The education of deaf students

In recent years, a movement has emerged within the Deaf[36] community with important language policy implications. One aspect of this movement is the assertion by a number of leaders and scholars that deafness is not a malady or handicap, but rather a condition to be accepted and affirmed, and that deaf persons are deserving of the same respect granted other ethnic or linguistic minorities.[37] Related to this is the assertion that deaf children born of hearing parents in the US should be allowed to develop the language which comes naturally to them, American Sign Language (ASL). Deaf children born to English-speaking parents should learn English in school as a second language, preferably in a bilingual–bicultural programme (Kuntze, 1993: 15). This recommendation is based on research showing that the English reading skills of deaf students instructed in a sign system known as Manually Coded English (MCE) plateau at the third-grade level (Kuntze, 1993: 15). In contrast, those students who have had access to ASL during their formative language acquiring years do much better in reading and writing. At this point, there are only a few such bilingual–bicultural programmes in the US and Canada. However, this approach is not without its critics. Many argue that the families of deaf children should decide what is best for their children; further, there is the concern that removing deaf children from their hearing parents to learn ASL and acculturate into the

Deaf community will result in a permanent separation and rejection of English.

A great deal of work has been done by linguists validating ASL as a fully legitimate natural language, with the implication that it deserves the same respect and support as any other minority language.[38] There is a movement to address the rights and interests of Deaf persons in the Bilingual Education Act. Whether this will happen and in what precise configuration and funding levels remains to be seen. The issues here are complex and challenge some of the assumptions which have guided bilingual policy with other non-English languages.

English as a second language

The demand for English as a second language classes continues to be robust for both K-12 and adult populations. According to a recent survey, the total reported K-12 enrolment of limited English-proficient students for the 1991–2 school year was 2,254,592, an increase of nearly 70% from school year 1985–6. California reported that more than one in every five students was identified as LEP in 1990–1[39] (Winn-Bell Olsen, 1993). The same survey found that there were approximately 1,200,000 adult ESL students for the 1990–1 school year, an increase of about 40% from the 1985–6 school year. While these increases may reflect, in part, changes in reporting LEP student information, continued migration of non-English speakers is the principal factor.

The National Literacy Act of 1991 and the Immigration Reform and Control Act (IRCA) of 1986 have also had an impact on the number and types of ESL programmes available. IRCA mandates English literacy and knowledge of US history and government to qualify for legal residence; the NLA addresses broad goals for all legal residents to improve literacy standards. In addition, reauthorisations of Title VII (BEA), beginning in the 1980s, have tended to fund a higher percentage of special alternative instruction programmes which do not require the use of the LEP students' native language. ESL and English immersion programmes are typically used in these projects. Although bilingual programmes using the native language of children have been upheld by the courts as appropriate under existing guidelines[40] (see *Keyes v. School District No. 1, Denver Colorado* (1983)), a lack of qualified personnel and funding, and multilingual classrooms (among other reasons) have restricted the number of fully bilingual programmes. In 1988, only 12 states and Guam mandated bilingual education, and another 12 states had legislation permitting it (Malakoff & Hakuta, 1990: 40). A 1984 study by Developmental Associates of K-5 in 335 schools in 19 states found only half of the teachers responsible for teaching language minority students were able to speak a second language (in addition to English), and only 28% had received bilingual education certification. Fully 93% reported that English was the central ingredient in the programme, while only 7% said the native language was emphasised (Malakoff & Hakuta, 1990: 40). The rapid mainstreaming of children (20% were reported to be mainstreamed each year) suggests that students are increasingly expected to develop appropriate academic English skills and move into mainstream classes as quickly as possible. Given the research findings that suggest children need two to seven years to acquire a second language (Malakoff & Hakuta, 1990: 42), early exit bilingual programmes are more likely to produce students who will be candidates for pullout ESL programmes or, eventually, adult ESL programmes.

In addition to ESL programmes in public and private K-12 schools, classes are offered in proprietary schools, community colleges, churches, and in a variety of vocational and adult basic education programmes funded by federal, state, and local programmes. Federal funding earmarked exclusively for ESL programmes is rather limited; funding through family literacy and other job-training programmes is also available.[41] As is the case in Canada (see Burnaby, 1994), programmes are not coordinated among government or state agencies, although high priority has been assigned to the development of English literacy skills by non- or limited-English speaking students by the US Department of Education (Hornberger, 1989).

Apart from lack of coordination and insufficient funding for these literacy programmes, considerable controversy exists about what sorts of programmes should be provided. Different views of literacy result in different types of programmes. On the one hand is the view that ESL literacy programmes should provide learners with the tools to enter the workforce (the economic/ autonomous view); on the other hand is the idea that literacy should empower individuals within their communities to achieve personal growth, to develop critical thinking and decision-making skills through a participatory process (social/ideological view) (see Crandall, 1992: 89–91 for a discussion of these views). Following these general orientations to literacy education, two basic curricular approaches have been identified: competency-based and participatory, respectively. According to Crandall (1992: 91), however, both of these curricular approaches '. . . seem to be using much more of a top-down, whole language approach . . . drawing on techniques such as dialogue journals, language experience stories, process-based writing', etc.

In both competency and participatory programmes, issues of programme design and implementation have been raised in the literature. Critics of current programmes argue that, for example, only English literacy, rather than mother tongue (L1) literacy, is valued; Wiley (1991) points out that most national surveys fail to collect statistics on L1 literacy. In most programmes, students literate in their L1 are placed with preliterate students, with negative results for the latter group. Further, students' L1 is typically not valued or exploited pedagogically in classrooms in which English is the only allowable language. Other issues in ESL literacy include lack of opportunities for literacy education, inappropriate classroom methods (including a failure to build on L1 literacy where it exists), inappropriate outcome-based assessment protocols, pressures to place students in any job, and access problems to training (especially for undocumented immigrants) (see McKay & Weinstein-Shr, 1993, for a fuller discussion of these issues).

The preparation and certification of ESL teachers is another area which has generated much discussion in the professional literature. In general, '. . . adult ESL and adult literacy instructors work part-time without contracts or benefits . . . and are often volunteers' (Crandall, 1993: 499). There is a lack of training programmes for adult ESL instructors, since most graduate programmes in TESOL focus on the needs of primary, secondary, or university students (Crandall, 1993: 500). Within the field, there is also a debate as to whether certification is appropriate, given that the skills required for successful adult ESL instructors are not necessarily taught in traditional MA programmes. What is clear is that low and non-continuous levels of funding for adult ESL literacy programmes and the relative lack of teacher preparatory programmes, coupled with an indifferent national language policy, will create continuing challenges for the field.

The status of ESL teachers in elementary and secondary schools is somewhat more recognised. In a survey conducted by TESOL (Teachers of English to Speakers of Other Languages), 38 states (out of 47 that responded to the survey) reported having a certificate or endorsement in the field of TESOL for either the primary or secondary grades, or both (Kornblum & Garshik, 1992: 216). Professional education associations have lobbied state and federal agencies and legislatures for greater support and recognition of the specialised training required in teaching non- and limited-English speaking students. TESOL has published a *Statement of Core Standards for Language and Professional Preparation Programs*, as well as *Guidelines for the Certification and Preparation of Teachers of English to Speakers of Other Languages in the United States*. Other organisations, such as the National Council of Teachers of English (NCTE), the Modern Language Association (MLA), among others, have developed alliances with TESOL, NABE (National Association for Bilingual Education) and other groups that deal especially with language minority populations in order to share information, sponsor programmes and develop position papers on various aspects of the education of language minority speakers.

Foreign language education

Despite the presence of many foreign languages in the United States, 'US residents remain remarkably uninterested in developing second language proficiency or even in acquiring basic information about other peoples and their values, attitudes, and traditions' (Tucker, 1994: 1).

Although in absolute terms, more college students are studying foreign languages today than 30 years ago, in relative terms, enrolments have actually decreased from 16.1 per 100 college students in 1960 to 8.5 per 100 in 1990 (Brod & Huber, 1992; cited in Tucker, 1994: 4). Fewer than 5% of elementary school children and 40% of high school students study any foreign language (Draper, 1991). As distressing is the fact that the language resources of non-English speaking students are wasted in early exit bilingual programmes, or English-only programmes. Rather than producing fully competent bilinguals, schools tend to undervalue the non-English languages of students, helping to perpetuate pervasive monolingualism.

In the late 1970s, a presidential commission studied the issue of foreign language and international education in the US. Its report, released in 1979 (the President's Commission on Foreign Language and International Studies), called for more programmes and greater funding to help fortify US competitiveness in the 'global economy'. The statistics cited above reveal the relatively little progress that has been made since the commission issued its report. In some areas of the country, and for certain socioeconomic groups, studying foreign languages and travel abroad are seen as economic assets and career-enhancing skills. However, on average, in the area of foreign language study, Americans seem not to be '. . . achieving the level of success . . . necessary for them to compete effectively in the commercial world of the 21st century' (Tucker, 1994: 4).

There are some bright spots, however. Some states have added requirements for foreign language study in recent years. The State Department of Education in Arizona has mandated that school districts provide foreign language education at every grade level by the year 2000 (Ruiz, 1994: 117). Pennsylvania has added a foreign language 'fluency' requirement for graduation from secondary school, and North Carolina requires foreign language study for all students from kindergarten through fifth grade (Tucker, 1994: 5). The federal government has been less involved in promoting foreign language study, although a number of scholars argue that with the passage of trade agreements such as NAFTA (North American Free Trade Agreement), greater emphasis will be placed on language education programmes at all levels. It is also argued that the availability of enhanced technology, including interactive, computer-based programs, will increase access while allowing for more individualised study of foreign languages. However, given the cost of technology, without significant subsidies from the federal government, more affluent school districts will have greater access to such technology.

The Present and the Future

The same xenophobia that led to the adoption of restrictive, and sometimes repressive, policies towards non-English speaking indigenous and immigrant groups and their languages in the first two decades of this century are in abundant evidence today in the United States. President Calvin Coolidge's warning in 1924 that 'America must be kept American' (Crawford, 1992a: 60) has currency in today's public discourse. Even among political liberals, immigration reform, curtailment of public services to undocumented aliens, and increased sanctions against employers who hire undocumented workers are viable campaign issues. Tensions between established residents and newcomers have escalated, especially in high immigration states such as California, New York and Florida. Just as with the Americanisation campaigns of the late 19th and early 20th centuries, grass roots organisations have sprouted up to exploit these fears and support candidates for office who will implement their agendas. National organisations, such as US English and the Federation for American Immigration Reform (FAIR) have raised millions of dollars to support restrictionist language and immigration policies. US English has been effective in spreading its message: by 1988, 48 of the 50 states had considered legislation to declare English their official language (Crawford, 1992a: 150). Although US English and FAIR have been tainted by scandals in recent years,[42] they have regrouped and continue to pursue their anti-immigration and, in the case of US English, language restrictionist agendas.

Meanwhile, grass-root movements continue to spring up in states which have been affected by large-scale immigration. One example is seen in California, where Proposition 187, called the Save Our State (or SOS) proposal by its sponsors, was approved by California voters in the 8 November 1994 election by a 3:2 margin. The proposition seeks to discourage illegal immigration by denying publicly funded benefits to undocumented aliens; the most legally problematic provision would bar illegal immigrants from public elementary and secondary schools (*Los Angeles Times*, 10 August 1994).[43] One of the most troubling, and potentially divisive, aspects of Proposition 187 is the requirement that public schools and offices providing health and welfare services verify the status of 'suspected' undocumented persons. In effect, teachers and public officials will become agents for the immigration service, an Orwellian concept even for those who are sympathetic with the stated goals of the proposition. Clearly, non-English speakers, even persons with 'foreign' accents, will be suspect. Many undocumented persons will not seek medical services even in emergency situations (although the proposition does not bar undocumented persons from receiving emergency care), risking not only their own health and well-being, but also that of the general population. For this reason, many clinic workers and public school teachers have indicated their unwillingness to comply with the reporting provisions of Proposition 187 (*New York Times*, 11 November 1994). Several restraining orders have been issued by federal and state judges, blocking implementation of the measure's education provisions until hearings are held. The issues surrounding Proposition 187 will likely be litigated for years to come. Even so, initiatives such as Proposition 187 will likely stimulate public debate and galvanise support for significant changes in immigration and language policy.

Countering the efforts of such anti-immigration groups are coalitions and professional associations concerned in promoting the interests and rights of language minority persons. These include the National Association for Bilingual Education (NABE), Teachers of English to Speakers of Other Languages (TESOL), the Modern Language Association (MLA), among many others. Other, more ethnically oriented, groups include the League of United Latin American Citizens (LULAC), the Puerto Rican Defense and Education Fund, the Mexican American Legal Defense and Education Fund (MALDEF), and the National Council of La Raza. These groups have been effective in presenting testimony at congressional hearings, at lobbying members of Congress, and in preparing reports and policy statements and guidelines for school districts and other educational associations.

The courts continue to be the policy battleground for the interpretation of English-only rules in the workplace. In California, where Proposition 63 passed with 73% of the vote in 1986, amending the state constitution making English the official language of the state, a number of cases have been adjudicated with very mixed results. Courts have been reluctant to review the constitutionality of 'English-only' rules in the workplace. In one case in 1994, the US Supreme Court refused to hear arguments in which Latino employees sued their employer (Spun Steak Co.) for requiring them to speak only English while on company property. This ruling left intact a ruling by the US Court of Appeals in San Francisco which gives free rein to employers to impose English-only rules, at least in several western states. Elsewhere, the US Equal Employment Opportunity Commission rule which bars English-only rules unless an employer can show a business necessity would prevail (*San Francisco Chronicle*, 21 June 1994).

In another case relevant to language policy, the California Supreme Court in *Ramirez v. Plough, Inc.*, 6 Cal. 4th 539 (1993) was asked to decide whether drug manufacturers were required to place warning labels on their products in languages other than English (Miner, 1994). The case involved a Spanish-speaking woman whose child developed Reye's syndrome after taking St Joseph's Aspirin for Children. Because she could not read the label, Jorge's mother brought suit against the manufacturer, Plough, Inc. The court found that the issue of what information should be provided in which languages should be addressed by the legislature, not the courts. Since current law required labelling only in English, the court reasoned that the legislature must have intended not to require warnings in other languages (Miner, 1994). What is most interesting is that attorneys for Plough, Inc. argued that the Official English amendment in California eliminates any obligation to print warnings in languages other than English. The court, however, did not address the argument nor did it even mention the Official English provision in its decision. As with earlier cases in which plaintiffs have invoked the Official English argument (e.g. *Gutierrez v. Municipal Court*), these provisions have been viewed as largely symbolic and irrelevant in adjudicating these issues.

With significant demographic changes anticipated for the foreseeable future, local, state and federal governments will be required to deal with the stresses and strains such changes bring. What is needed as much as a coherent and humane policy towards language minority groups is leadership at the highest levels of government. The possibility for inter-ethnic tension and conflict exists in many parts of the United States, and is exacerbated by campaigns which often blame undocumented aliens for problems not of their making. Immigration policies which take into account the interests of all residents are more likely to benefit the commonweal than are policies which select scapegoats for endemic social and economic problems.

Conclusion

Language policy in the United States is a composite of legislative, govern-mental, and judicial instruments which have evolved within and as a reflection of a particular history of nation-building. Many of the particular characteristics of the American ethos have remained relatively constant over the past 250 years, and have helped shape public attitudes and policy: the belief in indivi-dual rights and responsibilities, as opposed to group-oriented or territorial rights, as exist by custom or law in many other countries; the notion that being American entails speaking the English language; tolerance (if often grudging) towards immigrants, especially for purposes of economic expansion; a relatively low tolerance for the use of non-English languages in schooling and in the public domain; less favourable attitudes towards certain indigenous and immigrant groups (usually non-white or non-European) compared to others (white, European); a tendency towards cultural isolationism and monolingualism; a belief that immigrants should give up their native cultures and languages in becoming 'American'. There are other lessons to be drawn, and the material presented in this chapter will no doubt lead readers to other conclusions.

The lack of any coherent policy, and the absence of a language planning commission or other permanent governmental body is not, in and of itself, a bad thing. There is no guarantee that such a body could operate effectively without broad public support, and such support is hard to come by in a country run by majority rule with a surfeit of dissatisfied and polarised minorities. Many other countries with such policy/planning bodies have not been able to achieve the degree of stability that the United States has without such bodies. Still, the continued politicisation of important issues in education, immigration, and public policy, generally, often wastes the resources which are deployed to benefit specified groups, such as limited-English proficient students. The American infatuation with contentiousness threatens to consume the good intentions and great possibilities for enlightened progress, which are always in abundance. Only time will tell whether American society will evolve to a point in which multiculturalism and multilingualism are recognised as resources to be valued and respected, and not merely tolerated as temporary aberrations requiring 'remediation'. At the time of this writing, it is difficult to be optimistic. Multiculturalism has been portrayed by its opponents as antithetical to 'American' interests; politicians have jumped on the 'anti-multicultural' bandwagon; perhaps the latest in a series of Americanisation campaigns has already begun.

If the United States cannot come to terms with its multicultural/multilingual roots, with its own history as a country once populated by peoples who were not willingly subjugated, with its legacy of forced servitude of Africans who were unwilling 'immigrants', then it will be difficult to move beyond multiculturalism as a stigmatised slogan. Clearly, the historical record shows that some groups (and languages) have fared better than others at various times in the past. We seem to have entered a period in which the profile of 'American' is once again being transformed in a way that discomfits many of the older immigrant groups. Such a transformation (whatever form it takes) is, of course, inevitable, as are the tensions which accompany such changes. Appropriate language policy and planning can play an important, and constructive, proactive role in the development of equitable and humane social policies. Unfortunately, or perhaps inevitably, language policy is rarely planned and is nearly always formulated in the behest of dominant political interests. It is rare in most polities that the academic approach to language policy and planning is heard, let alone given credence, by the political culture.

However, in multilingual/multicultural societies throughout the world, governments have been forced to come to grips with the difficult task of balancing the interests of the state with the rights of individuals to learn and appreciate their native tongues and cultures, while at the same time being educated in their native, regional and/or national language, and even in a language of wider communication.[44] In the United States, the unreasonable and unfounded fear that linguistic pluralism will weaken national unity may lead to the adoption of policies – language restrictionism, enforced English monolingualism in education and voting, etc. – that are most likely to promote the disunity that Americans fear.

Notes

1. The author is grateful to the following persons for their readings of earlier versions of this chapter: Barbara Burnaby, Nancy Hornberger, Robert B. Kaplan and Terrence Wiley. A number of their suggestions, both substantive and editorial, have been incorporated into the final version. However, responsibility for the ideas expressed, as well as any errors, factual or otherwise, is assumed by the author.
2. Kloss argues that nationality laws for ethnic groups can be either *promotion-oriented* or *toleration-oriented* (Kloss, 1977: 2). At times, minority rights have been suppressed, especially during times of war, and more frequently in the case of new versus established, immigrant groups.
3. However, if one takes into account the considerable amount of intermarriage, or so-called race-mixing, that occurred in many parts of North and South America, the picture is more complex (Terrence Wiley, personal communication 10/24/94). It is clear that native cultures as they existed prior to European contact were transformed, if not completely eradicated.
4. For example, Samuel Worcester went to jail fighting the removal of the Cherokees to Oklahoma during the 1830s; dictionaries prepared by missionaries, such as Stephen R. Riggs's *Grammar and Dictionary of the Dakota Language*, helped preserve Indian languages (Rehyner, 1992: 42).
5. American Indian and Alaska native languages (including language families) with at least 1000 speakers (estimated) counted in the 1990 census are (in descending order by numbers of speakers): Navajo, Eskimo languages, Dakota, Apache languages, Cherokee, Pima and Papago, Choctaw and Chickasaw, Keresan, Tewa and Tiwa and Towa, Zuni, Muskogee, Hopi, Ojibwa, Crow, Shoshoni, Ute, Tlingit and Haida, Mohawk, Cheyenne, Paiute, Athabascan, Aleut, Kiowa, Cree, Blackfoot, and Arapaho.
6. In 1800, Spain secretly retroceded the Louisiana Territory to France. In 1802, President Jefferson sent a delegation to France with the intention of purchasing New Orleans and West Florida for $2 million. However, to the surprise of the delegates, the French offered to sell the entire territory for $15 million. The Louisiana Purchase covered the area west of the Mississippi River, north to the Dakotas, and as far west as Montana. The area of the US was doubled with this acquisition.
7. The European countries with more immigrants than Germany in 1991 were: the Soviet Union (57,000), Poland (19,200), United Kingdom (13,900) and Romania (8100).

8. According to US census records, since 1860, there have been no fewer than 2.3 million immigrants legally admitted during each 10-year period except for the depression years and years of World War II. The decades of 1901 to 1910 and 1981 to 1990 saw the greatest absolute numbers of immigrants admitted to the US: 8,795,000 and 7,338,000, respectively.
9. Persons of Hispanic origin may be of any race.
10. Excluded from consideration here is the status of non-standard varieties of English, such as Black English Vernacular (for an excellent discussion, however, see S.S. Williams, 1987), Acadian dialect, etc., the status of creoles such as Gullah and Louisiana Creole, as well as broader issues such as language and gender, each of which warrants a chapter of its own.
11. Plans, to the extent they have existed, tend to be politically driven, as in the case of language education policy in Puerto Rico throughout most of this century. Often, policy comes in the form of judicial decisions which at best provide suggestions for possible courses of action, as was the case in the landmark *Lau v. Nichols* decision of 1974.
12. In 1780, John Adam proposed to the Continental Congress that a society be established for '. . . refining, improving, and ascertaining the English Language' (cited in Crawford, 1992b: 32). Adam's proposal was rejected, as were other subsequent schemes, as being elitist. A national language academy, it was argued, would involve government in matters best decided by individuals.
13. As the German–American community assimilated and the 'Anglo-conformity' model was affirmed, Franklin softened his position, eventually spearheading a drive to establish the country's first German-language institution of higher learning, Franklin & Marshall College.
14. W.N. Hailman, Superintendent of Indian Schools in 1896, questioned this policy, noting that the imposition of 'severe penalties upon the unfortunate children who were caught in the use of Indian speech . . . is so manifestly unreasonable and so pernicious in its perverting and destructive influence upon the child's heart-life . . .' (Leibowitz, 1971: 34).
15. The Meriam Report, published in 1928, recommended strengthening the Indian social structure, not destroying it, and that the child's native language should be taken into consideration in schooling (Leibowitz, 1971: 34).
16. Titles I, IV, and VII with their various chapters serve children who are limited in their English language skills. However, the overall financial contribution is relatively small; for example, of all pupils with limited English language skills served in programmes to meet these needs in the 1990–91 school year, only 15% were in Bilingual Education Act-funded programmes. The rest were served primarily in state and locally financed programmes (CRS report for Congress 25 January 1993: CRS-2).
17. See Fillmore, 1992, for a discussion of the various ways so-called bilingual programmes are run in the US.
18. For example, the Pennsylvania legislature granted a charter in 1840 to the 'German convention for promoting education' which would sponsor a seminary to '. . . promote the cause of education particularly among the German population' (Kloss, 1940: 287–8).
19. In the *Meyer v. Nebraska* decision, it was noted that in 1923, 21 states besides Nebraska had laws prohibiting the teaching of foreign languages in primary schools. In California (1921) and Hawaii (1920), a series of laws were passed aimed at abolishing Japanese language schools. The Ninth Circuit Court of

Appeals in 1926 declared the territorial language school laws and regulations unconstitutional, relying on earlier Supreme Court decisions, including *Meyer v. Nebraska*. The ruling was appealed, and in 1927, the Supreme Court upheld the lower court ruling, voiding not only the Hawaii and California anti-Japanese language school laws, but also laws prohibiting the teaching of other non-English languages in at least 22 two other states (Tamura, 1993: 44–5).

20. For example, New Mexicans resisted the conditions imposed by legislation requiring 'a system of public schools, which . . . shall always be conducted in English', and further stipulating that English literacy be a requirement for 'all State officers and members of the State legislature'. Delegates to the 1910 convention passed antidiscrimination protections for Spanish speakers in voting and education (Crawford, 1992a: 52–3).

21. An amendment introduced by Senator Robert Kennedy of New York stated that no person who had completed the sixth grade accredited by any state, territory or Commonwealth in which the predominant classroom language was other than English shall be denied the right to vote in any federal, state, or local election because of his inability to read, write, understand, or interpret any matter in the English language (cited in Liebowitz, 1969: 346).

22. However, in 1982, the criterion was narrowed to 5% of potential voters who 'do not speak or understand English adequately enough to participate in the electoral process'. The effect of this amendment was to cut the number of districts required to provide bilingual ballots from 369 to 160 (Crawford, 1992a: 272n).

23. For example, in *Castro v. State of California*, 2 Cal.3d 223 (1970), the California Supreme Court ruled that a bilingual voting system is not required by the constitution. In *Guadalupe Org v. Tempe Elem. School Dist.*, 587 F.2d 1022 (9th Cir. 1978), the federal Court of Appeals found no constitutional right to bilingual education. In *Guerrero v. Carlson*, 9 Cal.3d 808, cert. denied 414 US 1137, the California Supreme Court found that welfare notices need not be given in Spanish. In *Frontera v. Sindell*, 522 F.2d 1215 (6th Cir. 1975), the federal Court of Appeals ruled that civil service examinations need not be given in Spanish (all of the above cited in Miner, 1994: 15).

24. A later case held that this right did not extend to participants in civil litigation.

25. The courts have not entirely accepted the view of the EEOC that English-only rules are a form of national origin discrimination. The only case to find an English-only rule invalid is *Gutierrez v. Municipal Court*, 838 F.2d 1031 (9th Cir. 1988).

26. By 1990, 17 states had passed laws proclaiming English as the offical language, with differing provisions and degrees of specificity as to application and enforcement. Interestingly, 12 of these laws were passed during the 1980s, a decade which saw nearly unprecedented numbers of immigrants from Asia and Latin America.

27. In 1990, US District Judge Paul Rosenblatt declared Arizona's official English amendment unconstitutional, in violation of the First Amendment's guarantee of free speech (Draper & Jimenez, 1992).

28. Fernandez (1987) shows how public policy in bilingual education was shaped by legislation, regulation and judicial precedent.

29. In 1974 in the wake of the *Lau v. Nichols* Supreme Court decision, Congress reauthorised Title VII (Bilingual Education Programs); enforcement of policies by the executive branch through the Office for Civil Rights resulted in the adoption of educational plans by several hundred school districts; these plans had to comply with suggested federal guidelines weighted in favour of transitional bilingual education (Fernandez, 1987: 94–5).

30. On the one hand were polemical attacks of bilingual education, such as Noel Epstein's 1977 book *Language, Ethnicity, and the Schools: Policy Alternatives for Bilingual-Bicultural Education*, which argued the federal government should not have a role in financing and promoting ethnic languages and cultures; on the other hand were works such as Alex Haley's *Roots* (1976) and Rodolfo Gonzales' epic poem *I am Joaquin* (1972) which formed part of the ethnic revitalisation movement of the 1970s.

31. In reversing the decision of the Ninth Circuit, the court said, in part: 'There is no equality of treatment merely by providing students with the same facilities, textbooks, teachers and curriculum; for students who do not understand English are effectively foreclosed from any meaningful education . . . Imposition of a requirement that, before a child can effectively participate in the educational program, he must already have acquired those basic skills, is to make a mockery of public education. We know that those who do not understand English are certain to find their classroom experiences wholly incomprehensible and in no way meaningful.' (*Lau v. Nichols*, 414 US 563 (1974)).

32. For example, the researchers did not take into account that two-thirds of the students in the comparison group had previously been enrolled in bilingual classrooms, where, presumably they benefited from native language instruction, enabling them to 'graduate' to the mainstream English-only classroom (Crawford, 1992a: 220).

33. According to a survey by R.E. Winn-Bell Olsen, there were 2,524,592 LEP students in K-12 for the 1991–2 school year; this represents an increase of nearly 69% from the 1985–6 school year (Winn-Bell Olsen, 1993).

34. In 1990–1, states reported that about 1,698,000 LEP students were served in federal, state and local programmes designed for them; only 251,000 LEP students were served in BEA programmes (US Department of Education. *Conditions of Bilingual Education in the Nation – 1992*. Washington, 1992. Tables C and E.)

35. In an attempt to reverse the loss of indigenous languages, the Native American Language Act of 1990 was passed. In fairly sweeping language, the bill endorses the preservation of indigenous languages, and requires government agencies to ensure that their activities promote this goal. However, no new funds are committed to achieve the goals of the legislation.

36. The use of the upper-case D here is significant; it serves as a marker of cultural identity, as opposed to a clinical description of a medical condition.

37. See, for example, Harlan Lane *The Mask of Benevolence* (1992) and *Looking Back: A Reader on the History of Deaf Communities and their Sign Languages* (1993) for an exposition of these views.

38. Random House has published the *American Sign Language Dictionary*, first edition, 1994.

39. Winn-Bell Olsen (1993) notes that these statistics may understate the actual number of LEP students due to non-identification or non-reporting of LEP students by state agencies. This is because identification criteria vary from state to state, and a state may change identification criteria or reporting procedures from one year to the next. The same caveats apply for reporting of statistics of adult ESL student populations.

40. In *Castenada v. Pickard* (1981), the Fifth Circuit Court of Appeals developed a three-prong test to judge whether a school district's programme met the needs of LEP students. The programme had to be based on a sound educational theory; the programme had effectively to implement the educational theory; the outcome

had to be analysed and, if necessary, revised in order to achieve the desired results (Fernandez, 1987: 105–6). This decision allowed districts more flexibility in choosing a method to instruct LEP children.

41. For a discussion of these issues see, for example, Chisman *et al.* (1993) *ESL and the American Dream*, Washington, DC: Southport Institute for Policy Analysis; Wiley (1993) Issues of access, participation and transition in adult ESL. Working paper, Southport Institute for Policy Analysis, Washington, DC; and Wrigley *et al.* (1993) *Sparks of Excellence: Program Realities and Promising Practices in Adult ESL*. Washington, DC: Southport Institute for Policy Analysis.

42. An internal memo written by Dr John Tanton, co-founder of US English, revealed the author's fear of an Hispanic takeover of the US. Among questions posed in the memo were: 'Will the present majority peaceably hand over its political power to a group that is simply more fertile?' 'As whites see their power and control over their lives declining, will they simply go quietly into the night? Or will there be an explosion?' (Ricento, 1991: 6). Disclosure of the memo led to the resignations of both Tanton and Linda Chavez, then President of US English, who was outraged at the anti-Hispanic, anti-Catholic views expressed.

43. The proposal also stipulates that US citizen children born of undocumented parents will be expelled from school, even though they have grown up in the US, speak English, and know little about their parents' native country. The proposal does not address the rights of children born in mixed status household, i.e. in which one parent was legalised under a 1986 law which extended amnesty to undocumented persons who had arrived in the US before a particular date, while the other parent might be undocumented. Such uncertainty will ultimately be resolved through the courts, a process likely to take many years (*New York Times*, 11 November 1994: A17).

44. Kaplan (1994) describes some of the complexities involved in developing a National Languages Policy in New Zealand. The study is noteworthy for its comprehensiveness and relevance for similarly configured multilingual/multicultural nations in which an important world language (English, in this case) dominates a number of threatened indigenous languages, whose speakers are increasingly marginalised within the broader society.

7 Language Policies in Canada[1]

BARBARA BURNABY

Introduction

The aim of this chapter is to provide an overview of significant areas of language policies in Canada. The ways in which Canadians have chosen to deal with language issues can serve either as good examples or object lessons for those promoting language policy change. The definition of policy here is extremely broad; it includes everything from constitutional provisions to the role of small community organisations. Attention is paid to how and why policies have developed, or not developed, and what their outcomes, in general, have been. This overview is of necessity superficial, and only the most salient and broadest policy issues are touched on.

Following this introduction, the chapter is divided into five sections. First, some background is provided on Canada as a country and the languages used by its citizens and residents. The next section details relationships between Canada's two official languages, English and French, in legislation and policy, and the application of those measures. The third section deals with issues for speakers of all non-official languages, except the Aboriginal languages, and how policies affect relationships between those languages and the official languages. Then follows a section on Canada's Aboriginal languages and their formal treatment by governments. Finally, there is a concluding section. In each section an attempt is made to cover the impact of policies on both adults and children.

Background on Canada

Though in area Canada is the second largest country in the world, and smaller only than Russia, its total population was just over 27 million in the 1991 Census (Statistics Canada, 1992a). At the time of initial European contact with northern North America, Aboriginal people lived in areas spread across what is now called Canada, speaking an estimated 450 languages and dialects belonging to 11 different language families (Office of the Commissioner of Official Languages, 1992: xiii). Immigration, starting with the basic colonisation by Great Britain and France, has greatly increased the population and changed its ethnic/racial mixture since the 16th century. Although immigration from northern and western Europe predominated for most of this period, especially since the 1890s, immigrants from other continents have considerably increased in proportion, particularly since the 1960s. According to the most recent census:[2]

> In 1991, 28% of the population reported British only origins compared with 34% in 1986. . . . The population in Canada reporting French only origins decreased slightly from 24% in 1986 to 23% in 1991. . . . In 1991, 31% of the population reported ethnic origins which were neither British nor French, up from 25% in 1986. . . . 470,615 persons reported Aboriginal single origins [less than 2% of the total population], up from 373,265 in 1986. (Statistics Canada, 1993a: 1)

With respect to languages, the latest census figures indicate that:

> English was reported as mother tongue for 63% of the population. . . . French was reported as mother tongue of 25% of the population. . . . A non-official mother tongue was reported as the only mother tongue for 13% of the population. . . . Aboriginal languages were reported as mother tongue by less than 1% of the population . . . (Statistics Canada, 1992a: 1)

> In 1991, 73% of the population . . . had English as first official language spoken, 25% . . . had French as first official language spoken, 1% had English and French, and the remaining 1% spoke neither English nor French. (Statistics Canada, 1993c: 1)
> In provinces where French was [in the] minority, the percentage [of Francophones] was highest in New Brunswick (33.9% . . .) and Ontario (5.1% . . .) and lowest in British Columbia (1.5% . . .) and Newfoundland (0.5% . . .). . . . In Quebec, the English . . . minority made up 13.3% of the population. . . . (Statistics Canada, 1993c: 1)

Canada is a federal parliamentary democracy and a member of the British Commonwealth of Nations. It was created as a country in 1867 by an Act of the British Parliament called The British North America Act. By the early 20th century it had consolidated most of its present territory into nine provinces and two territories. In 1949 Newfoundland joined this confederation as the tenth province. In the early 1930s, Canada gained full national powers (i.e. over foreign as well as domestic affairs) from Britain, and in 1982 the Canadian federal government 'patriated' the constitution by passing The Constitution Act which superseded The British North American Act, with provisions for making amendments and the addition of a Canadian Charter of Rights and Freedoms. For the purposes of the current discussion, it is important to note that The British North America Act and The Constitution Act have divided legislative responsibilities so that, among many other things, the federal government deals with Aboriginal affairs while the provinces deal with education. Both levels have powers concerning immigration. The federal government is responsible for the territories directly, but over the years the territories have been permitted to create legislative assemblies of their own with responsibilities including education.

The provinces, roughly from east to west, are Newfoundland and Labrador, Prince Edward Island, Nova Scotia, New Brunswick, Quebec, Ontario, Manitoba, Saskatchewan, Alberta and British Columbia. The territories are the Yukon Territory and the Northwest Territories. The Northwest Territories have recently voted to split into a largely Inuit territory (Nunavut), and a Dene territory (Denendeh). In general, the population tends to reside in an area in the south of the country along the Canada/US border. The smallest province in area and population is Prince Edward Island with about 130,000 inhabitants, while the largest is Ontario with a population of over 10 million (Statistics Canada, 1992a: 8). According to the 1991 census:

> Newfoundland and Quebec were the provinces having the highest proportions of their populations reporting a common ethnic background. In Newfoundland, 88% of respondents reported British origins only, while in Quebec, 75% reported French origins only. . . . The proportion of British origins was highest in Atlantic Canada [Newfoundland and Labrador, Prince Edward Island, Nova Scotia, and New Brunswick]. . . . In the Northwest Territories, the majority of the population (51%) reported single Aboriginal origins. (Statistics Canada, 1993a: 2)

Perhaps the most central factor in this chapter is the continued and pervasive power of English to dominate all other languages in the country. This tendency is greatly strengthened not only by the country's history but also by the fact that Canada's only close neighbour is the United States. Figures given below will document this tendency.

According to federal terminology, English and French are called the official languages and all other languages except Aboriginal languages are called non-official languages. Aboriginal languages are sometimes called Native, First Nations, or Indigenous languages. However, the tricky term is 'linguistic minorities'; this refers *not* to populations of non-official language speakers, but to Francophones living outside of Quebec, and Anglophones living in Quebec.

The Official Languages of Canada
Basic information

The recorded history of colonial and post-confederation Canada is dominated by discussion of the struggles and politics of relations between first France and Britain and then Francophones and Anglophones in Canada. According to Neatby (in Office of the Commissioner of Official Languages, 1992: v–ix), in the 19th century the focus of the legal expression of rights for the 'English' and 'French' populations was on religion rather than language. Legislation specifically on language therefore was rare in Canada and the provinces. However, in the early 20th century, increased secularism, industrialisation, national attention on Canada's role in the British Empire, and massive immigration encouraged a movement to 'Anglo-conformity', especially through legislated use of English as the medium of instruction in schools in most provinces. Francophones in Quebec were isolated in a French medium, church-run school system and the social and political use of French in areas of Quebec where Francophones dominated the population. Only on the surface did the federal government recognise the supposedly equal status that French had (through The British North America Act) with English in Parliament, in federal courts, and in the legislature and courts of Quebec. Thus, for example, by the middle of this century the federal bureaucracy was 90% English and the Quebec bureaucracy was almost 100% French (Wardhaugh, 1983: 50).

After World War II, increasing industrialisation, immigration, and low birth-rate among Francophones threatened the critical mass of French even in Quebec (Neatby in Office of the Commissioner of Official Languages, 1992: vii). Non-French immigrants to Quebec, the majority of whom settled in Montreal, mostly chose English as their second language. This was undoubtedly due in large part to the fact that English was the dominant language of business in Quebec, and Montreal was the centre of large business in the province. Being ethnically Quebecois and unilingual Francophone put one at the bottom of the economic heap in terms of salary in the early 1960s (Wardhaugh, 1983: 74–80). In the 1960s, Francophones in Quebec, through a movement called the Quiet Revolution, moved to gain control in the province. In 1960, a separatist movement, the Rassemblement pour l'indépendance nationale, was formed, and by 1963 the Front de libération du Québec (FLQ) had begun to use violence to press its cause. On the other hand, other Quebecois were pressing, not for separation, but for increased Francophone power within the federal state (Labrie, 1992: 25). In 1963, the Quebec government created a Ministry of Education to take provincial control over what had been an entirely parochial education system (comprising French Catholic and English Protestant systems, the latter involving English Catholics and most other ethnic minorities).

Such pressures moved the federal government to take the matter of the constitutionally 'equal' status of the French language in national-level governance seriously, as Francophones made up a quarter of the voters in federal elections. The following is an outline of the major federal government initiatives and provincial responses relating specifically to French and English taken since 1960.

Federal legislation and provincial actions

The Royal Commission on Bilingualism and Biculturalism (1963–71)

In 1963, the Committee of the Privy Council of the federal Parliament established the Royal Commission on Bilingualism and Biculturalism:

> To inquire into and report upon the existing state of bilingualism and biculturalism in Canada and to recommend what steps should be taken to develop the Canadian Confederation on the basis of an equal partnership between the two founding races, taking into account the contribution made by the other ethnic groups to the cultural enrichment of Canada and the measures that should be taken to safeguard that contribution. (Royal Commission on Bilingualism and Biculturalism, 1967: 173)

Federal government institutions, including Crown corporations, public and private organisations (particularly the media), and education (even though it was not a federal responsibility) were to be studied (1967: 174). Indigenous peoples, then called 'Indians and Eskimos', were to be excluded from consideration in the study since they were perceived not to form part of the 'founding races' as understood in the terms of reference for the Commission, nor were they included as 'other ethnic groups', which were those others who had immigrated to Canada. 'Other bodies', federal and provincial, were supposed to be considering the issues of Aboriginal peoples (1967: xxvi–xxvii). Given that most Aboriginal people in Canada did not get suffrage at the federal level until 1960, it is perhaps not surprising but ironic that the federal government was not used to thinking of them as citizens much less as among the 'founding races'.

The Office of the Commissioner of Official Languages summarises the six books produced by this massive and detailed study as follows:

> In Book I of its Report (1967), the Commission concludes that Francophones in Quebec constitute a 'distinct society' . . . [and] recommends that Parliament adopt an Official Languages Act to establish the equal status of English and French in Canada and appoint a commissioner of official languages to oversee its application. It urges the provincial governments to follow suit.

Book II (1968) recommends that parents be able to select the official language of their choice for the education of their children. It urges that minority language schooling . . . be provided by the provinces, especially in the bilingual districts it proposes.

Book III (1969) says that the federal Public Service, as an institution, should be bilingual, and that each public servant, subject to certain conditions, should be free to work and make a career in English or French.

Book IV (1969) recommends that governments extend support to cultural groups other than those of British or French origin.

Book V (1970) recommends that all levels of government work together to make the National Capital Region truly bilingual.

Book VI, which concludes the Report in 1970, explores the role of voluntary associations in furthering language reform. (Office of the Commissioner of Official Languages, 1992: 13)

The impact of the Report was first seen in changes in the federal public service. In 1964, language training was created for public servants, and in 1966 secretaries were paid 7% extra if they used both English and French 10% of the time. In 1966, the Public Service Employment Act included language as one of the positive points for appointment of public servants. In 1971, the Treasury Board released objectives for making French as well as English a language of work in the civil service, for providing all correspondence with the public in both languages, and for increasing the numbers of bilingual personnel (Office of the Commissioner of Official Languages, 1992: 14–17). Finally, Parliament passed a resolution in 1973 which provided measures to make both English and French equitably the languages of work in the federal civil service and to ensure full participation of members of both language groups in that work (Beaty, 1989: 186).

Some of the provinces clearly anticipated the impact of the Report and federal action on it. Between 1967 and 1969, Saskatchewan and Manitoba had amended their Education Acts to permit French to be the language of instruction for about half of the day. Ontario authorised public elementary and secondary schools in which French might be the language of instruction. Alberta permitted French to be used as a language of instruction to the end of secondary school in 'bilingual schools' (Office of the Commissioner of Official Languages, 1992: 14–15).

In St Lambert, a suburb of Montreal, a group of Anglophone parents in 1965 persuaded a school board to teach their children through the medium of French so that the children would learn the language as a second language faster and more effectively (Lambert & Tucker, 1972). This event was the beginning of the now popular 'French immersion' programmes across the country for Anglophone children to learn French as a second language.

The Official Languages Act (1969)

The main anticipated outcome of the Report of the Royal Commission on Bilingualism and Biculturalism was the declaration in law of French and English as the official languages of Canada. This came about in 1969, even before the Commission had completed all of its report. According to Beaty:

> In addition to declaring that English and French are to have 'equality of status and equal rights and privileges' for all the purposes of the Parliament and Government of Canada, the Act specifically imposes duties on all federal institutions to provide their services in either English or French: in the National Capital Region and in such 'bilingual districts' as might be subsequently designated, at their head offices, and in any other locations where there was 'significant demand' for such services. The Act also created the position of Commissioner of Official Languages to oversee its implementation and generally act as official languages ombudsman. (Beaty, 1989: 185–6)

As noted above, the Report of the Royal Commission started a move towards the bilingualisation of the federal civil service and its relations with the public, and the Official Languages Act followed through. Keith Spicer was appointed the first Commissioner of Official Languages in 1970. Beaty summarises the main programmes to support the Official Languages Act by encouraging 'a more general climate of respect and support for Canada's official languages in other jurisdictions and in Canadian society as a whole' (1989: 190). The plan was to create this climate:

- by supporting minority groups in their attempts to achieve provincial recognition of their legal rights and their special linguistic needs;
- by fostering and helping to finance minority language education;
- by giving similar financial encouragement to the effective learning of English and French as a second language country-wide; and
- by supporting the efforts of national, private and voluntary organisations to develop their own capacity to do business in both official languages. (Beaty, 1989: 190–1)

In 1970–1, the federal government began its Official Languages in Education (OLE) Programme. Since education is a provincial responsibility, the Official Languages Act could not legislate on education directly, but the federal government was able to encourage compliance with the spirit of the Act by offering funding. The Report of the Royal Commission had recommended that the federal government support the provinces for their extra costs in providing minority official language education for Anglophones in Quebec and Francophones in the other provinces and for improved second official language instruction. The OLE has continued to address these aims through transfer payments to provinces (Peat *et al.*, 1987). This programme is monitored by the Commissioner of Official Languages. While the number of minority official language children in schools using their mother tongue as medium of instruction has not changed substantially since 1971, numbers of children in second language programmes of various sorts have (Peat *et al.*, 1987: Section III). Anglophone parents, anticipating among other things that French would become a career asset for their children, were encouraged by the Commissioner of Official Languages to form the national organisation, Canadian Parents for French, in 1977, to promote French-as-a-second-language programmes in schools. The popularity of French immersion programmes increased rapidly starting in the early 1970s (Canadian Education Association, 1992: 3).

Similarly to the education field, the federal government is not in a position to force provincial governments to legislate official languages for themselves; however, some provinces responded to the Official Languages Act at least in some measure. The Bilingual and Biculturalism Commission recommended that New Brunswick, Quebec and Ontario officially become bilingual. In 1969 the Ontario government went part of the way by beginning to provide provincial government services in French on the basis of feasibility, and in 1970 permitted speeches in the legislature in either English or French. New Brunswick, which has the largest proportion of Francophones outside Quebec, went further in 1969 legislating the province as officially bilingual, giving equal status, rights and privileges to English and French in all matters under the jurisdiction of the provincial government, and providing for the use of both languages in schools and courts (Office of the Commissioner of Official Languages, 1992: 15–16).

In Quebec in 1969, feelings were running high. Some Francophones, experiencing strongly the assimilative pressure towards English even within their own province, wanted French medium education not only for themselves, but for the immigrants of language backgrounds other than English or French (called Allophones). Others, including the English and most Allophones, wanted free choice of language of instruction. The upshot was resistance to extended French medium education including a violent confrontation over language of instruction between groups of Allophones and Francophones in a suburb of Montreal. The provincial government created a Commission of Inquiry on the Situation of the French Language and on Language Rights in Quebec (the Gendron Commission), but before that Commission could report, the Quebec government adopted Bill 63, An Act to Promote the

French Language in Quebec. It recognised the right of parents to choose English or French as the language of instruction for their children, indicated that children being educated in English must acquire a practical knowledge of French, and instituted the 'Office de la langue française' to intervene in respect to the use of French, especially in the promotion of French as the language of work. Anger among Francophones towards Bill 63 helped bring down the provincial government in 1970. Separatist action culminated in a British diplomat being kidnapped and a Quebec cabinet minister being murdered by a cell of the FLQ. This event caused the federal government to invoke the War Measures Act. Public tension between the English and French in Canada was at an all-time high (Labrie, 1992: 26–8).

At the federal level, issues relating to language moved along. In 1973, following discussion about permitting the use of French in air traffic control that had begun in 1962 and got more sensitive as tensions in Quebec developed, the federal government began an inquiry that resulted in 1975 in French being allowed in air traffic control at five airports in Quebec; the matter went on until 1979. Ordinary Canadians began to feel the effects of the changes through the use of both languages on all federal forms and in federally controlled buildings, such as airports and post offices. Although not directly related to the Official Languages Act, the Consumer Packaging and Labelling Act of 1974 began the process through which all products were to be labelled in both languages. Between 1970 and 1977, the federal government tried to set up bilingual districts, including the entire provinces of Quebec and New Brunswick, but abandoned the initiative (Office of the Commissioner of Official languages, 1992: 9, 16, 18, 21). In 1971, the prime minister announced a multiculturalism policy focusing largely on the non-official language and cultural groups. This policy and later legislation will be discussed in more detail in the next section of this chapter.

In Quebec, the Gendron Commission recommended in 1973 that French be declared the official language of Quebec and that English and French be its 'national' languages. In 1974, Quebec passed Bill 22, the Official Language Act, making French the official language of the province with provision on language in public administration, public utilities, the professions, labour, and business. It gave French a predominant position, yet most clauses also provided for bilingualism. The Régie de la langue française (Canada) was to monitor and implement the provisions. With respect to education, it withdrew parental choice of language of instruction, introducing English language tests primarily for Allophone children wishing to enter English medium schools. Opposition to the new measures was great in various quarters, and some schools moved to subvert the language tests. Then in 1978, the Charter of the French Language (Bill 101) was passed. It covered much the same territory as Bill 22, but the role of French was strengthened, especially with respect to business and commerce, and a number of new agencies were created to enforce the measures. Only those children whose parents or older siblings had attended school in English in Quebec were permitted to attend public schooling in English; all new immigrant children were enrolled in French schools. Some individuals and businesses left the province over Bill 101. The Supreme Court of Canada (in the Blaikie case, 1979) ruled that Bill 101 clauses concerning the language of the legislature and the courts were unconstitutional in light of the British North America Act. The Blaikie case was the first of several modifications to Bill 101; others are alluded to later. In addition, since separatism was still a driving force in the province, the provincial government in 1980 lost a referendum to gain a mandate to negotiate 'sovereignty association' (Quebec nationalism within the Canadian state) with the federal government (Office of the Commissioner of Official Languages, 1992: 18, 20, 22; Labrie, 1992: 30–2).

In this climate, the country as a whole was worried about national unity. Provinces and the federal government continued to take measures with respect to their legislation, administrations, courts, and education that were generally favourable to French language rights (Office of the Commissioner of Official Languages, 1992: 18–22). At the national level, efforts were made to do something to prevent a total rift with Quebec. A constitutional conference in 1971 had proposed a charter of language rights but failed to get Quebec's agreement because its provision were not protective enough of Quebec's interests. A Task Force on Canadian Unity, created in 1977 and reporting in 1979, recommended constitutional changes to protect minority language rights with a greater role for the provinces. Nine provincial education ministers agreed in 1977 to work towards minority language education where numbers warranted. In 1978, the federal government attempted a constitutional amendment which would have included a guarantee of linguistic equality for English- and French-speaking communities. In 1979, a federal-provincial constitutional conference failed to agree on a charter of language rights.

In 1980, the federal government took the major step of beginning the process to 'patriate' the constitution, providing a major opportunity to make constitutional changes. The initiative was a calculated risk between the separatist feelings in Quebec and the fact that the Quebec government's bid for a mandate to negotiate sovereignty association had been voted down.

The Constitution Act, 1982

Since Canada's constitution, as the British North America Act of 1867, was established by an Act of the British Parliament, patriation meant negotiating with the British Parliament to enact some form of it through the

Canadian Parliament. This was to be done leaving its major structure, the responsibilities of the federal and provincial governments, the same. An amending formula was added together with the Canadian Charter of Rights and Freedoms. In this Charter were put many things, including central matters on language that had arisen since the early 1960s, such as the official language status of English and French for the governments of Canada and New Brunswick. Once in place, items in the Charter could not be changed by the federal government alone, but required agreement through a formula needing provincial support. They were to be a yardstick against which all federal and provincial legislation and policies could also be measured and challenged in court.

The Department of the Secretary of State describes, for public information, the aspects of the Charter that concern language as follows:

The *Constitution Act* of 1867 (formerly known as the *British North America Act*) included provisions concerning the use of the English and French languages. These were strengthened by the *Canadian Charter of Rights and Freedoms* in 1982, with the result that, in terms of the federal government:

- the English and French languages have equal status and rights regarding their use in all federal institutions;
- everyone has the right to use English or French in the Parliament of Canada;
- everyone has the right to appear before federal courts in either English or French;
- the public has the right, in the circumstances set out in the *Charter*[3] to be served in English or in French when dealing with federal government departments and agencies.

The Constitution also sets out certain rights regarding the use of English and French at the provincial government level:

- everyone has the right to use English or French in the legislatures and courts of Quebec, New Brunswick and Manitoba;
- laws must be enacted in both English and French in those provinces;
- both languages have equal status in the institutions of the legislatures and government of New Brunswick and the public has the right to service in English or in French from the provincial government;
- Canadian parents who are members of the English or French linguistic minority in the province in which they reside have the right to have their children educated in that language at the primary and secondary school levels, in the circumstances set out in the *Charter*. (Department of the Secretary of State, n.d.)

In the words of the Charter itself, the circumstances concerning access for children to minority official language education are:

> 23. (1) Citizens of Canada a) whose first language learned and still understood is that of the English or French linguistic minority population of the province in which they reside, or b) who have received their primary school instruction in Canada in English or French and reside in a province where the language in which they received that instruction is the language of the English or French linguistic minority population of the province, have the right to have their children receive primary and secondary school instruction in that language in that province.
>
> (2) Citizens of Canada of whom any child has received or is receiving primary or secondary school instruction in English or French in Canada, have the right to have all their children receive primary and secondary school instruction in the same language.
>
> (3) The right of citizens of Canada under subsections (1) and (2) to have their children receive primary and secondary school instruction in the language of the English or French linguistic minority population of a province a) applies wherever in the province the number of children of citizens who have such a right is sufficient to warrant the provision to them out of public funds of minority language instruction; and b) includes, where the number of those children so warrants, the right to have them receive that instruction in minority language educational facilities provided out of public funds. (Section 23)

The Office of the Commissioner of Official Languages (1992: 27) indicated that:

> The Charter also states that Sections 16 to 20 (on official languages) do not affect the rights and privileges of any other language, or the rights and freedoms of the aboriginal peoples of Canada. Also, the Charter 'Shall be interpreted in a manner consistent with the preservation and enhancement of the multicultural heritage of Canadians.'

An essential factor in this important event was that Quebec did not agree to its terms on the basis of concerns about the amending formula of the Constitution Act. At this time, more than 10 years later, it has not yet agreed despite several attempts at resolution (to be discussed below). This fact leaves federal relationships in an uneasy position with the inclusion of Quebec in the constitution unresolved. However, Quebec is still bound by the Charter, and, in 1983, it relaxed its Charter of the French Language to include recognition of the contribution of English-language institutions, the bilingual designation of a number of institutions, and the easing of conditions for admission to schooling in English for children from other provinces.

The signing of the Constitution Act and the Charter was followed by activity in the Manitoba and New Brunswick governments to adjust to their new status in the federal level legislation. In 1984, the federal government tried to get the Official Languages Act applied to the Northwest Territories and the Yukon Territory. These eventually agreed, but with conditions concerning Aboriginal languages (to be discussed below). As noted already, the nature of the Charter is such that it encourages court challenges rather than the legislative ones that were more common in the past. Therefore, actions on official language issues since 1982 have gone to courts. They have largely involved the testing of provincial legislation and practices concerning education, the language of the courts, and government services in light of the Charter. The cumulative effects of these cases on language in education will be discussed below. Most notably, in 1984, Quebec's Charter of the French Language, which stipulated that only parents who had been educated in English in Quebec could send their children to English schools, was deemed unconstitutional. The courts ruled that parents who were educated in English anywhere in Canada should have the same rights (Office of the Commissioner of Official Languages, 1992: 27–34).

In an attempt to bring Quebec into the Constitution, the prime minister and the 10 provincial premiers came up with a draft amendment to the Constitution in 1987. The proposed addition, called the Meech Lake Accord, embodied Quebec's basic conditions for its inclusion in the constitution, and read:

(1) The Constitution of Canada shall be interpreted in a manner consistent with

(a) the recognition that the existence of French-speaking Canadians, centred in Quebec but also present elsewhere in Canada, and English-speaking Canadians, concentrated outside Quebec but also present in Quebec, constitutes a fundamental characteristic of Canada; and

(b) the recognition that Quebec constitutes within Canada a distinct society.

(2) The role of the Parliament of Canada and the provincial legislatures to preserve and promote the fundamental characteristic of Canada referred to in paragraph (1)(a) is affixed.

(3) The role of the Legislature and Government of Quebec to preserve and promote the distinct identity of Quebec referred to in paragraph (1)(b) is affirmed.

(4) Nothing in this section derogates from the powers, rights or privileges of Parliament or the Government of Canada, or of the legislatures or government of the provinces, including any powers, rights or privileges relating to language. (Office of the Commissioner of Official Languages, 1992: 34)

The Accord put Quebec in the position of having to defend both the distinct, primarily French character of Quebec society, and the linguistic duality of the country (Labrie, 1992: 36). Nevertheless, the Quebec premier signed. It was established that the Accord would have to be ratified by Parliament and all the provincial legislatures within three years. As it turned out, Quebec was the first province to ratify, but since by 1990 two provincial legislatures had not ratified it, it was not added to the Constitution.

The Official Languages Act, 1988

In the meantime, Parliament passed a new version of the Official Languages Act in 1988. A great deal had happened since the first Act (in 1969), much of it to do with federal policy concerning the public service, and the Charter had added substantially as well. According to Beaty, the new Act

is a lot more than a patching up of the more obvious holes in the [old] Act. It has, of course, tried to embody and articulate certain principles which, while logically derivable from the overall declaration of English–French equality, were neither explicit in, nor easily enforceable under, the [old] Act. The 'participation' and 'language of work' provisions are obvious examples. It has also, one might say, taken advantage of the constitutional broadening of official languages rights (to include minority education in the Charter) to make it plain that the new Act's scope embraces a much wider commitment to upholding the language duality which the recent Meech Lake constitutional proposal affirms to be fundamentally characteristic of this country. (Beaty, 1989: 191)

The most recent constitutional initiative began in 1991 when the federal government convened a number of multilateral meetings to try to get a statement on the Canadian Constitution that all provinces could accept. The Meech Lake Accord was highly criticised because it was formulated by the prime minister and the 10 premiers without public consultation. Therefore, the federal government undertook a consultation process involving many groups. In 1992, it came up with a lengthy statement (The Charlottetown Accord) which included enough of the essence of the Meech Lake Accord to satisfy the Quebec premier, the prime minister and the other provincial premiers. A non-binding public referendum was called on its acceptance but the public voted it down because various aspects of it were controversial. The initiative was then shelved, indicating that the public was tired of trying to solve the French–English struggle through constitutional means. The debate has now moved to the House of Commons where, ironically, the Official Opposition is a party from Quebec in favour of sovereignty association.

Outcomes concerning official languages

In the span of 30 years, then, we see a shift from a country where Anglo-conformity was not significantly questioned to one in which issues of language and culture between the Francophones and the rest of the country are central even to the Constitution. Official language rights are enshrined in the Charter of Rights and Freedoms so that not even the federal government may change them unilaterally. The federal government, two provinces, and one territory have formulated their official language policy even though no language had had official status in Canada before 1969. The legislatures and public administrations of most of the provincial governments have at least in some way moved to accommodate the interests of official language minorities. Quebec has created a Ministry of Education, and education in all provinces has been altered to take both official languages into account. The shape of official-language education, both as first and second languages, has radically changed. Every product is labelled in both languages. Issues such as air traffic control and signs outside of and inside stores become matters of national attention when language is involved. Crucially, the political struggle between Quebec and the rest of the country is not only unresolved, but is perceived by many to threaten the fabric of the country.

What are the impacts of these changes? The attraction of English to speakers of other languages is still present. Language retention from census data is usually calculated by looking at the language used in the home of speakers of various mother tongues. A study comparing 1971 and 1981 census data of English and French mother tongue speakers found the following:

> Overall, the level of [French or English] language retention [in minority situations] declined slightly over the ten year period, with significant interprovincial differences. The percentage [of French] in 1981 ranged from 90 percent in New Brunswick to under 40 percent in Saskatchewan and British Columbia. In general the rate of transfer has been much higher in western Canada.

> Four provinces showed a decrease both in minority population and in the number speaking that language at home. In New Brunswick, Alberta and British Columbia, however, there was an increase in both of these groups. In Alberta and British Columbia, one reason for this increase is inter-provincial migration patterns.

> In Quebec . . . the level of language retention for the minority language group was very high in both years (about 90 percent), but there was a slight decrease over the ten-year period. (Peat *et al.*, 1987: III.7)

The 1991 census indicated patterns of language shift as follows:

> In 1991, less than 1% of the population with English as mother tongue spoke another language most often at home. For those with French as their mother tongue, 6% had another language as their home language, while 44% of those whose mother tongue was other than English or French spoke one or both official languages at home.

> The transfer rate from French mother tongue to English home language, very low in Quebec (1%), reached 35% in the rest of the country. This percentage was 10% in New Brunswick, 37% in Ontario and more in Newfoundland, the Western provinces, and the territories.

> The transfer rate from English mother tongue to French home language was negligible in all provinces except Quebec (9%). In Quebec, the number of people with French mother tongue who reported that they spoke English most often at home . . . slightly exceeded the number of those with English as mother tongue who indicated they spoke French most often at home.

> Amongst those living in Quebec whose mother tongue was other than English or French, 63% of the transfers were toward English as home language . . . and 37% French. (Statistics Canada, 1993b: 1)

> In Quebec, the transfer rate from English mother tongue to French home language increased with age to reach 12% for the 35–39 age group and 13% for the 45–49 age group. The rate then declined to 8% for the population 65 and older.

> In the rest of the country, the transfer rate from French mother tongue to English home language also increased with age, reaching 45% for the 50–54 age group. (Statistics Canada, 1993b: 2)

Clearly, English has more drawing power than French, even within Quebec. Although trends in census statistics only show changes over long periods of time, the fact that the transfer rates are greater with older age groups may indicate some impact from the language measures in the past 30 years. The Commissioner of Official Languages (1994: 112) sees the causes of weakness in the official language minority populations as follows:

> Uncertainty over the demographic aspects of linguistic vitality continues to top the list of concerns among both English- and French-speaking minorities. The causes, many of them common to both groups, are well

known. They include low birth rates, immigration (which generally favours the majority [*sic*]) and increased mobility among young people. This last factor is a source of great concern in the English-speaking community of Quebec. Although the exodus of English-speakers from Quebec has slowed in recent years the departure of the young and better educated weakens the vitality of the community. As well, assimilation continues to threaten French-speaking minority communities across Canada, particularly the smaller ones.

On a more sanguine note, however, the Commissioner points to the growing number of French–English bilinguals (Commissioner of Official Languages, 1994: 141).

According to Statistics Canada the ability of Canadians to speak both official languages has increased steadily over the past 20 years to 16.3% in 1991 from 13.4% in 1971. Among Canadian youth (15- to 24-year-olds) the rate of bilingualism is even higher – 22.7%, an increase of 6.5% since 1981. In actual numbers bilingual Canadians increased by more than 50% between 1971 and 1991. . . . While Francophones, both inside and outside Quebec, have traditionally been the most bilingual group in Canada, the increased learning of French among Anglophones means that, when measured in numbers, the gap between the two groups is narrowing.

From all the legislative and policy activity, what has actually happened in terms of programmes? The Commissioner of Official Languages (1994: 57) reported that 'in general, the participation of the two linguistic groups in the federal administration reflects their presence in the Canadian population'. Improvement is being made to address the current imbalance of Anglophones over Francophones in upper levels of management (1994: 59). Each year the Commissioner deals with a large number and range of issues in his capacity as ombudsman (e.g. 1994: 39–106). On an economic note, concern that Francophones were discriminated against has been substantially redressed. Bloom and Grenier (1992) show that the gap between the earnings of Francophone and Anglophone men in Canada is greatly narrowing.

In addition to changes in legislatures, bureaucracies, and government services, the other main focus for change has been in education. The federal Official Languages in Education (OLE) programme, which has provided funding to the provinces for official language minority schools and for second official language training, has been in place since 1970. A major study of it impact (Peat *et al.*, 1987) found, remarkably, that minority official language enrolments (that is, English-medium schooling for Anglophones in Quebec and French-medium schooling for Francophones elsewhere in Canada) has declined. For demographic reasons, all school enrolments in Canada have declined in that period, but the minority official-language enrolment drop has been greater proportionally.

> Outside Quebec, the number of majority language students has declined by some 11 percent over the 15-year period [1970–1985], while the number of minority language students has dropped by 23 percent. . . . Within Quebec, the number of majority language students dropped by some 30 percent over the fifteen year period, while the decline in minority language enrolments was even greater (51 percent). (III. 4–5)

The Commissioner of Official Languages (1994: 137) indicated that in 1970–1 there were approximately 444,942 students enrolled in minority language education programmes, whereas in 1992–3 there were only 256,145.

On the positive side, Peat *et al.*, (1987: viii–ix) note improvements in minority language education programmes.

> Several provinces which, at the end of the 1960s, offered virtually no programs in French for the Francophone minority, now provide such programs.
>
> Programs offered in French in the late 1960s were often so-called bilingual programs attended by both Francophone and non-Francophone students. In practice this meant that a major portion of the teaching was usually offered in English. . . . Most provinces have made progress in eliminating such environments by setting up schools or classes in which French is the dominant mode of instruction.
>
> Even well into the mid-1970s, lack of curriculum materials in French was a major impediment for teaching some subjects. Increasing numbers of curriculum materials have been made available, usually with direct assistance from the OLE program.
>
> Provincial ministries and departments of education have improved the quality of their central services for supporting minority Francophone education.
>
> At the beginning of the period, considerable confusion existed both in policy and practice about the intent of schools and classes established in French for the minority. As a result, the practice in many areas of the country was to enroll non-Francophones in the classes and schools nominally intended for the minority. Most jurisdictions have by now adopted formal policies which distinguish between the two types of institution.

Continuing problems identified included:

The network of classes and schools for minority Francophones is still incomplete, so that some children are still totally denied opportunity for access to such classes.

The programs offered in nominally French-language schools for the minority are often taught only partially in French, often under conditions where lack of well-adapted curricular materials renders the task of teachers doubly difficult.

In some jurisdictions, there have been serious delays in establishing the distinction between programs for the French minority and French immersion programs. (1987: ix)

It seems remarkable that these official language minority programmes should actually decline in a period in which so much attention is being paid to them. Not only were they a central recommendation of the Royal Commission on Bilingualism and Biculturalism Report but they were singled out, along with official languages for some governments, for specific mention in the Canadian Charter of Rights and Freedoms. On the other hand, perhaps it is because they are difficult to deal with that they have been so carefully chosen and put into the Constitution. In the intentions of the federal official language policy, the crucial matter is the rights of all, and especially minority Anglophones and Francophones to choose with equal freedom, not necessarily to make a large number of individuals bilingual. At any rate, while the official language minority programmes themselves have been improving, changing, but shrinking, they have also been the target of dozens of court cases seeking interpretation of Section 23 of the Charter, the part on rights to minority language instruction quoted above. It certainly does not help in the implementation of Section 23 that the Charter concerns national constitutional policy on education, a provincial responsibility.

A great deal of ink has been spilled in trying to make overall sense of the court decisions concerning Section 23. The most comprehensive studies are Foucher (1985) and Martel (1991). Problems with the interpretation of Section 23 are grouped around six issues by Martel. One issue is that parents may ask to have their child put into a minority language programme. Questions raised include: Does the child have to be Francophone? (no); and Can guardians as well as parents be eligible? (yes). A second issue is about rights to instruction. Cases on this matter have determined that children in such programmes should have a complete education, paid for by public funds, in the minority language, and that immersion programmes primarily or partially for Anglophone children do not count as such instruction. A third issue is the right to facilities. Facilities have been interpreted to mean schools where numbers warrant, but classrooms in premises shared with the majority may also be acceptable. A fourth issue concerns the right to management. This matter is especially complicated because it relates to the measure of control the minority has in each of the 12 unique education systems in the country. The implementation of the minority's right to management control is seen as an area of provincial jurisdiction. A fifth issue is equality of services to those in the majority. Again, it is up to the provinces to ensure equal quality. Equality with respect to management is the most difficult aspect of equality in general. A final issue has to do with the 'where numbers warrant' limitation in Section 23. Provinces are left to establish criteria for the two critical levels – enough children with the right to instruction and enough for the right to minority facilities (Martel, 1991: 38–43). These issues, especially the one relating to management, are still being wrestled with. Indeed, the Commissioner of Official Languages (1994: 110) has recommended that several national bodies cooperate on 'the creation of a centre of expertise on problems and solutions relating to the implementation of minority language education rights at the local and provincial levels'.

Compared with official first language minority programmes, official language as second language programmes for Anglophones and Francophones have had a relatively successful and uncontroversial history since 1960. Although the intent of official language policies is not to make everyone bilingual, these programmes, which aim at least in that direction, have been funded, along with the official language minority programmes, under the OLE. Peat *et al.*, (1987), therefore, included the provision of second official language instruction, that is English to Francophones and French to Anglophones, in their OLE evaluation. They report that:

> Since 1970–71, there has been a large increase in the percentage of students learning French as a second language outside Quebec: from 38 per cent in 1970–71 to 49 per cent in 1984–85, representing almost 1.7 million students. Participation in French language instruction has increased every year at the elementary level; participation at the secondary level declined between 1970–71 and 1980–81 but increased every year thereafter. In Quebec, study of the second official language has been required for many years so changes in enrolments in these programs have been fairly stable. (1987: x)
>
> . . . The figures on participation rates by grade reveal that five provinces have moved to make FSL compulsory for at least a portion of elementary schooling . . .
>
> Since the inception of the OLE program, the most fundamental change in teaching techniques has resulted from the rapid development of what are called 'immersion' programs . . . (1987: xi)
>
> . . . it should be remembered that the bulk of increases in enrolments have occurred in programs of FSL which are so-called 'core French'

programs of 20 to 40 minutes of instruction per day, which is widely recognized not to produce functional bilingualism in all except a few exceptional persons following the programs. The impact of immersion programs is likely to be much greater since, by all accounts, almost all children in them attain some level of bilingualism during the course of a few years of attendance . . . (1987: xii)

Concerns identified in the study concerning second official language programmes included:

Elementary level FSL participation rates remain low in a number of provinces. Levels of participation by high school students in FSL have still not returned to the levels of the early 1970s.

The expansion of French immersion programs is notoriously below public demand from parents wishing to enroll their children in them.

'Bridging' programs in high school to help pupils from elementary immersion programs retain their knowledge of French are few in number and insufficient by comparison with demand.

The duration of many elementary school FSL programs in terms of the number of minutes out of the school day devoted to them is often at the minimum level of twenty minutes per day. The effectiveness of this amount of instruction in promoting effective, functional language use remains subject to serious doubt. (1987: xii–xiii)

Figures provided by the Commissioner of Official Languages (1994: 152–5) comparing second official language enrolments between 1977–8 and 1992–3 indicate that French immersion enrolments have increased substantially, elementary core programme enrolments (proportionately) slightly, and high school core numbers and proportions have dropped.

With all the publicity about French immersion classes, what about English in Quebec French schools? Quebec legislation has made it difficult or impossible for boards to offer intensive English medium instruction for the purpose of second language learning. The Commissioner of Official Languages (1994: 147) reports:

In the French school system . . . insufficient learning time devoted to English is the principal deficiency. At the elementary level some school boards offer less than the suggested two hours per week from grade 4 onwards (a total of 216 hours over three years). Those students who arrive in high school with less than this face problems in catching up. Also, some school boards have difficulty in recruiting teachers with sufficient mastery of English to teach it well.

Therefore, 216 hours over three years is proposed as the mandatory minimum for elementary students. The successful intensive-English approach will be made more widely available (currently 31 school boards offer this program).

Training for adults in second languages has come about as part of the official language movement, but has been less extensive and less visible. The chief programme has been for employees in the federal civil service, including members of the armed forces. A number of provinces have paid for language training for their bureaucrats and legislators as well. Otherwise, large numbers of adults have taken French or English classes through expanded adult education classes in school boards, colleges, universities, and so on.

What do official language programmes cost? The Commissioner of Official Languages (1994: 17–18) reported the 1993 costs associated with the Official Languages Act to be 'approximately 30 cents per $100 of service provided or 0.2% of the federal budget. Per capita, it is about the cost of a cup of coffee per month ($12 a year)' (1994: 17). The OLE programme was $269 million, of which $243 million went for official language minority and second official language programmes ($83 million for English and $160 million for French). The rest of the money went towards administration of these programmes and to the Council of Ministers of Education which runs a summer language bursary programme for young people and an official language monitor programme which provides native speakers of the target language to school programmes. The Commissioner noted that the OLE programme pays $586 per child in an official language minority school (about 10% of the total cost) and $32 per year for a child learning a second official language. In total, the OLE is about 1% of the total Canadian education budget. Added to this is the amount it costs the provinces to administer government services and education according to their and federal policies. The costs of court challenges or the translation of texts for cornflakes boxes can only be wondered at.

The evolution of English and French as official languages and languages of education, work, commerce, and other facets of life over the past 30 years provides a contemporary model for others concerning the creation of relationships between language groups. This model certainly is not perfect, especially since it has not found resolution in satisfying either party. However, as will be discussed below, it has set a certain standard for some other language minorities in the country. The intense negotiations between Quebec and the rest of Canada still dominate discussion at the national and many provincial levels. Has this whole process been one of language planning? It has certainly had more of a reactive than a proactive character. It has also concerned status planning with relatively little attention to corpus changes. (See Office de la langue française and Université du Québec à Chicoutimi, 1994 for examples of corpus changes.) Wardhaugh's 1983 perspective on the impact of the Official Languages Act is still worth considering:

Designed to increase the visibility of the French in Canada, it at the same time denied them any special status. Because of that denial the policy has had little effect in Quebec, where it was largely regarded with indifference, being perceived as largely irrelevant to the province's needs. However, that increase in visibility was seen in many parts of Canada as the conferring of a special status on the French at a time when citizens in various regions outside of Quebec were also seeking special status because of local needs and interests. The special status that bilingualism appeared to give to the French seemed to many to be at the expense of the status of the people of almost every other province but Quebec . . . [and] may have increased feelings of regionalism, even separatism, throughout Canada outside of Quebec. *Status is often perceived to exist in fixed amounts. It can be gained only at someone else's expense* . . . It seems not to matter that another value system might show benefits accruing to all: the only thing that counts in a status-oriented system is who benefits more, who less, and who not at all. Such is the characteristic tenor of debates about language in Canada. (Wardhaugh, 1983: 60–1) [emphasis added]

Language Issues for Speakers of Non-official Languages in Canada

In reading most of the documentation on the official languages of Canada mentioned in the section above, one might scarcely believe that languages other than English and French are spoken in the country. Policy statements about official languages carefully refer to groups who speak other languages as other *cultural* groups. However, given the important role and history of diverse immigration in Canada's demographics, to say nothing of the special position of the Aboriginal peoples, non-official languages are very much in evidence in various parts of the country. In this section of the chapter, language issues for speakers of non-official languages (other than Aboriginal languages) are discussed. Aboriginal peoples and their languages are the sole topic of the following section. For simplicity's sake, the term 'immigrants' will be used in this section to refer to the group under consideration, although language issues can impact upon the generations subsequent to immigration. After considering some background information, the two main issues of learning an official language and recognition of non-official languages will be considered. Finally, there is discussion of the implications.

Basic information

Canada's large area, rich resources, affluence and, even today, relatively small population have made it attractive to immigrants for several centuries. Immigration levels have fluctuated in the present century.

Since World War II, 1957 was the year of highest immigration with over 282,000 arrivals. In recent years, numbers have been as low as 84,300 in 1985. Until the 1960s, immigration was almost entirely from Europe, especially northern Europe, but changes in policy since have meant that a much higher proportion of people first from southern and eastern Europe and then from other continents have been admitted (Reimers & Troper, 1992). The demography of the post-war baby boom and the resultant drop in the numbers of young Canadians entering the labour force in the past decade, international pressures on Canada to accept economic migrants and refugees, and other factors, have prompted Canada to raise its immigration intake since the early 1990s to about a quarter of a million a year. This policy has generated a public sentiment that the levels are too high. According to the World Refugee Survey of 1992, Canada has the highest proportion of resettled refugees in its population (1 refugee to every 82 in the general population compared, for instance, with 1 to 171 in the United States) (Immigration Canada, 1992a: 5).

The demographic impact of this has been substantial. As noted above, the 1991 census indicates that 31% of the population reported ethnic origins which were neither British nor French, and 13% had as their only mother tongue a non-official, non-Aboriginal language. Other information deduced from the 1991 census included:

> The immigrant population [that is, first generation immigrants] represented 16% . . . of Canada's population in 1991, almost unchanged since 1951 when 15% of the population were immigrants.
>
> Of Canada's total immigrant population, 48% arrived in Canada before 1971, 24% between 1971 and 1980, and 28% between 1981 and 1991.
>
> While the majority of the immigrant population was born in Europe, this proportion declined from 62% in the 1986 Census to 54% in the 1991 Census. The percentage of immigrants born in Asia increased from 18% in 1986 to 25% in 1991.
>
> Almost half (48%) of recent immigrants who came to Canada between 1981 and 1991 were born in Asian countries. A further 25% were born in Europe, 10% in Central and South America, 6% in the Caribbean, 6% in Africa, 4% in the United States and 1% in Oceania.
>
> Most immigrants (94%) lived in the provinces of Ontario, British Columbia, Quebec and Alberta in 1991.
>
> Immigrants are more likely to live in urban than rural areas.
>
> Toronto had the largest immigrant population of any metropolitan area: 38% . . . of Toronto's population were immigrants. (Statistics Canada, 1992b: 1)

Among non-official languages, the most frequently reported mother tongues were Italian (512,000 people), Chinese (492,000 people) and German (193,000 people).

Of Canada's 25 census metropolitan areas, Toronto had the largest percentage (32%) of its population reporting a mother tongue other than English or French. Vancouver was second with 27%, followed by Winnipeg with 21%.

Slightly over half (54%) of the population reporting a non-official language as their mother tongue were living in Montreal, Toronto or Vancouver.

Some language groups were characterized by an 'older' population: 59% of the Yiddish and 42% of the Ukrainian language group were aged 65 or over. In comparison, 11% of the English language group and 11% of the French language group were aged 65 and over. (Statistics Canada, 1992a: 1–2)

In Quebec, for those whose mother tongue was other than English or French, the transfer rate to English rose to 28% for the 25–29 age group, while the transfer rate to French reached a peak of 17% for the 40–44 age group.

In the rest of the country, amongst those whose mother tongue was other than English or French, the transfer rate to English increased with age from 27% for the 5–9 age group to 53% for the 55–59 age group. (Statistics Canada, 1993b: 2)

Nationally, among Canadians with a non-official language as a mother tongue, 7% were classified as part of the French official language minority. (Statistics Canada, 1993c: 1)

Asian, Arab and African single origins increased from 4% . . . in 1986 to 6% in 1991. (Statistics Canada, 1993a: 1)

These data show that Canada has a large number of immigrants, most of whom are living in a handful of specific urban areas. The rate of linguistic, ethnic, and racial diversity has also increased substantially recently. While only 1% of the population reported that they did not speak an official language well enough to carry on a conversation, this measure is very rough. There is no very satisfactory way, given measures currently available, of estimating the real need and/or demand for official language training either at the survival level of basic conversation or at more sophisticated levels that might enable an immigrant to work at a job more commensurate with his/her training in the home country. Also not clear is the extent of the potential demand for official language training among those who have been in the country for some time as opposed to those who are recently arrived. From the data immediately above and others quoted in the earlier section, English seems to draw non-official language speaking immigrants more than French, even in Quebec.

Non-official Language Speaking Immigrants Learning Their First Official Language

Federal legislation

The Commissioner of Official Languages (1992: 27) explains that the sections in the Charter of Rights and Freedoms 'do not affect the rights and privileges of any other language, or the rights and freedoms of the aboriginal peoples of Canada'. Whatever such rights, privileges, or freedoms there might be will be raised where relevant below. By contrast with the provision in federal legislation on official languages for those who speak an official language already, there is nothing in federal legislation that even suggests that people who speak neither English nor French have the *right* to support in learning one of those languages as their first official language. However, there is considerable legislation that impinges on, and some programmes that relate directly to issues of language for residents of Canada who do not speak either of the official languages. Also, unlike federal legislation and policy on official languages in education for official language minority groups (which refer almost entirely to education for children), for federal legislation and for policy on official language training for non-official language groups, adults are the main target. This is in large part because the federal government links immigration strongly to economic matters.

The following is a brief description of the most significant federal acts and programmes affecting official language for immigrants and their impact. First federal actions will be described and then provincial and other responses and initiatives. For reasons detailed below, the teaching of English as a second language (ESL) to immigrants in Anglophone Canada will be considered *en bloc*, and French as a second language (FSL) in Quebec will be discussed at the end of the section. Also, a new federal official language training programme was announced in 1990. In the commentary below, programmes up to that point are described first and then the new programme is outlined separately.

As context for the discussion below, the following quotation from McManus (1992), (commenting on Vaillancourt's 1992 paper comparing Canadian and US policies on language training for immigrants) indicates the critical emphases:

> In Canada, he [Vaillancourt] claims, the federal government's role in language policy derives from its role as the arbitrator between the two

language groups, while in the United States it derives from the federal government's role as the defender of individual civil rights. In recent decades, however, U.S. affirmative action and civil rights policies have tended to define and defend protected groups rather than individual persons. Thus, the only remaining distinction is that *in Canada only two groups are protected*, while in the United States the number of protected groups is limited only by the ethnic, racial, and sexual composition of the population. Practical policy implications follow: in Canada allophone [non-official language speaking] immigrants are encouraged to acquire English or French, but in the United States, because of a tendency to protect minority group rights, there is less official encouragement to acquire English. (McManus, 1992: 301) [emphasis added][4]

Since it is clear that the Official Languages Act makes no provision for the learning of official languages by residents of Canada who speak neither language, that Act will not be discussed here.

The Multiculturalism Act

In 1971, two years after The Official Languages Act was made law, the federal government declared itself to be, by policy, multicultural. Clearly aimed at calming the backlash among non-official language and cultural groups over the declaration of official languages, the multiculturalism policy pledged to promote respect and support for all languages and cultures in the country. The original policy included, as its fourth tenet, that 'the government will continue to assist immigrants to acquire at least one of Canada's official languages in order to become full participants in Canadian society' (Saouab, 1993: 4). The policy passed through various stages in the years that followed, none of which included direct support for official language training for immigrants, and evolved into the present Multiculturalism Act of 1988 which has concerned itself mainly with fostering the non-English and French cultures, with anti-racism, and affirmative action in support of visible minorities. Developments from this policy concerning non-official language classes in schools are discussed at the end of this section.

The Immigration Act

Changes in the 1960s and 1970s to the Immigration Act opened the door to immigrants previously restricted in access to entry. Hawkins (1989) lists the 10 basic principles of the 1976 Immigration Act, the framework for immigration legislation which is still largely in place. Emphasis has been added to those items which will come up in the discussion below.

. . . enriching the cultural and social fabric of Canada, *taking into account its federal and bilingual character*; family reunion; *federal–provincial– municipal and voluntary sector collaboration in immigrant settlement*; the fostering of trade, commerce, tourism, cultural and scientific activities, and international understanding; non-discrimination in immigration policy; *economic prosperity in all Canadian regions*; the health, safety, and good order in Canadian society; and the exclusion of persons likely to engage in criminal activity. (Hawkins, 1989: 71)

For various reasons, numbers of immigrants had fluctuated over the years. In 1990, the federal government announced a new immigration plan with the goal of 220,000 immigrants in 1991 growing to about 250,000 per year until 1995. Objectives for the implementation of the plan included improvements in support for the integration of immigrants into Canadian society (Employment and Immigration Canada, 1992: 17).

The defined classes of immigrants identified family, refugees, independent immigrants, assisted relatives, business immigrants and retirees. In 1967, a point system was set up to evaluate applicants for some immigrant classes, and though revised several times its principle structure remains. Hawkins (1989) describes it as follows:

Numerical weights are attached to a set of 10 factors . . . to assess the qualifications of an applicant . . . in the broad areas of *education, training* and experience, occupation and intended destination, age, *knowledge of English and/or French*, personal suitability, and the presence or otherwise of relatives in Canada. . . . Members of the family class and retired persons are not selected according to these criteria. Three of the 10 factors do not apply to assisted relatives . . . refugees are assessed by means of the point system, to enable immigration officers to learn about their background, qualifications, and experience, but are not given a point rating. (1989: 77) [emphasis added]

Targets are set each year for numbers in each class and quotas for some (Employment and Immigration Canada, 1993: 3–5). Family class, which has no selection criteria, normally represents the largest group of immigrants (84,000 out of 206,000 in 1991) (Immigration Canada, 1992: 3). Over several decades, immigrants have overwhelmingly chosen to settle in the greater Toronto area, Vancouver and Montreal. To counteract this, immigrant applicants with certain occupational skills can strengthen their case by voluntarily agreeing to settle for a specified period of time in a particular area of the country (Immigration Canada, 1993: 4–5).

The above criteria indicate that Canada emphasises the economic impact of immigration. One form this emphasis has within the point system is recognition of skills in one of the official languages. The use of the Canadian point system may mean that Canadian immigrants are more fluent in English or French than, for example, US immigrants (who are not assessed by such language criteria) are in English. Chiswick and Miller's (1992: 257) study of the role of language in the US and Canadian immigrant labour market shows that employed immigrant men in Canada have a slightly higher rate of fluency, but that comparison is risky because of the use of rather different measures of language skills in the census forms in Canada and the US.

Canadian government structures have influenced the direction and emphasis of immigration policy. Given the importance of balance and negotiation between the federal and provincial levels in Canada, it is not surprising that the immigration principles stress collaboration among various sectors. Such a balance is reflected in federal interests in shouldering only part of the costs of immigrant settlement.

> The government's increased funding represents a significant commitment. However, EIC [the Employment and Immigration Commission] never has and never will act as the sole provider of language training. EIC is counting on sponsors and on training providers to continue to make other opportunities available. The federal government wants overall training opportunities increased. It does not want its increased expenditures to replace existing sources. (Immigration Canada, 1992c: 1)

This balance also means that provinces can negotiate for power in administering immigration intake and services. Since the Cullen–Couture Agreement in 1978 and the Canada–Quebec Accord in 1991, Quebec has taken control of some aspects of immigration and virtually all aspects of settlement in its jurisdiction, probably because immigrants historically have turned to English rather than French even in Quebec. Since the birth rate in Quebec is very low, the province is concerned to support its Francophone culture by immigration that will preserve it as a French rather than English society (d'Anglejan & De Koninck, 1992).

> The federal government retains responsibility for establishing immigration levels and general classes of immigrants, admitting immigrants and granting permanent resident status, while Quebec gains sole responsibility for selecting independent immigrants destined for Quebec and for integration services for permanent residents of Quebec. Additionally, the Accord compensates Quebec for the federal withdrawal from settlement and integration services. (Immigration Canada, 1991: 15)

Ontario has recently shown interest in negotiating such an agreement as well. As noted above, one of the objectives of the 1991 immigration plan was to improve immigrant settlement services, including language training.

Up until that time, language training was more directly linked to economic skills planning. Those important new programmes will be discussed below following more background information on the federal legislative context.

The Citizenship Act

The Citizenship Act (officially An Act Regarding Citizenship) defines the procedures and criteria for achieving Canadian citizenship. For present purposes, relevant clauses are that applicants must demonstrate three years of residency in Canada and a 'reasonable' knowledge of one of the official languages and of Canada's political and social systems. Until recently, citizenship court judges were political patronage appointments and although some have been accused of asking unnecessarily difficult questions at citizenship hearings, generally they are extremely lenient on the language and national knowledge criteria. Thus, lack of knowledge of an official language is not really a barrier to citizenship and many people who are not functionally fluent in an official language have been granted citizenship.

In the 1970s and early 1980s, the Act was administered by the federal Department of the Secretary of State. Since official languages and knowledge about the country are criteria under the Act, that department was considered to be somewhat obliged to support applicants for citizenship in meeting those criteria. In the 1970s, it initiated Citizenship Instruction and Language Textbook (CILT) agreements with individual provinces. Under these agreements, provinces could bill the federal government for half the cost of teachers' salaries and the cost of learning materials for certain citizenship and language classes. There was no ceiling on the amount that could be billed and the provinces had considerable latitude on how the money was spent. In the late 1980s, one province decided to opt out of the other federal language training programme (to be discussed below) and, instead, to apply to CILT for all its immigrant language training programmes because the federal government, under CILT, exercised no restrictions on how the money was to be spent. Whether to stop such practices or for other reasons, the CILT agreements were terminated in 1990.

An important facet of the CILT agreements was that they respected provincial jurisdiction over education by letting the provinces administer the money. On the other hand, this meant that the federal government did not get credit for the programme because it was cost-sharing with provincial programmes. Most provinces that had active immigrant language training programmes made good use of the money, but the federal government could not use CILT to press other provinces to provide services.

In 1988, a Department of Multiculturalism and Citizenship, which later became the Department of Canadian Heritage, was formed to administer the two Acts and other programmes.

Federal Acts and programmes concerning adult training to 1991

In the economic, population, and immigration boom of the 1960s, the federal government wanted to exercise some control over the labour force. While it was not permitted constitutionally to get involved with education, it did become involved with training of adults in skills related to work.[5] It began by passing Acts whereby it would purchase training seats from provincial institutions. Thus, the provinces still controlled the training itself but officials in federal employment offices chose the students. Students' tuition fees were covered and they were given a training allowance to support them while they studied. The provinces had not, up to that time, had much of a system of public, non-university post-secondary institutions, but in considerable part to take advantage of this federal programme, community colleges expanded across the country. The programme involved various levels of academic upgrading and pre-vocational training in a wide variety of occupations for all Canadians.

A large part of this programme was language training for adult immigrants. Although circumstances varied from province to province, immigrants who were selected by federal officials could get about 24 weeks of full-time language training with an allowance. On the whole, only independent class immigrants (those selected on the basis of the point system) got seats with training allowances. The purpose of the programme was explicitly to 'unlock' their occupational skills for the labour market. Most of the training was general purpose, classroom-based language training, but one province, at least, used some of the training programme to offer English in the workplace.

Over the years, there has been considerable controversy over this sought-after programme. The community colleges in urban, immigrant receiving areas developed large ESL sections to handle the trainees, but some were criticised for keeping their teachers on temporary contracts, for using unqualified teachers, for providing general, regimented programmes that did not respond to varieties of student need, for excluding potential students who were ineligible for the federal funding but who wanted the same kind of training on a fee paying basis, and for exploiting this lucrative programme to support less profitable facets of their activities. In the 1970s, selection of students by federal officials targeted the 'head of the household', meaning many women were excluded. Candidates also had to be deemed by officials to be destined for the labour market with the consequence that many women and older people (mostly immigrants from the family or assisted relative classes) were excluded (Boyd, 1992). The programme was legally challenged under the Charter of Rights and Freedoms for discriminating against women (Doherty, 1992). Before a decision was reached the programme was discontinued. The language assessment and intercultural communication skills of the federal officials who were the gatekeepers to the programme in such matters as language assessment and intercultural communication were considered to be inadequate (e.g. Belfiore & Heller, 1992). (See Canada Employment and Immigration Advisory Council (1991: 3–21) for a more detailed discussion.)

Because of its labour related objectives, this programme was administered from the Employment side of the Department of Employment and Immigration. In 1986, in response to some of these criticisms, the Settlement Branch of the Immigration side of Employment and Immigration launched a pilot language training programme aimed specifically at immigrant women not destined for the labour force. It called for proposals from educational institutions, and especially from non-governmental organisations (NGOs) already involved in immigrant settlement activities, to mount one-year projects to provide language training with support, if needed, for child minding (not daycare, which is highly regulated) and transportation. The training would be part-time and with no training allowances. In doing this, it took a significant step over the line of provincial responsibility for education since it would be federal not provincial officials who would make decisions about which proposals to fund and who would monitor the projects. In order to counteract possible provincial objections, an advisory council was to be set up in each participating province or region with representation from the federal and provincial governments and appropriate NGO groups. It suited federal interests to take this step since it would break the hold the provinces had on the federal government to buy seats exclusively from the community colleges with their unionised teaching force which was perceived to be expensive.

This pilot, which became the Settlement Language Program (SLP), has been remarkable in its demonstration of at least some of the kinds of potential learners who have not been reached by other kinds of programmes.[6] Each project was unique: some attracted immigrants who had been in the country for as many as 20 years; others attracted isolated and older people; still others in areas where there is not much immigration reached the kinds of learners that would be served by other federal and provincial programmes in high immigration areas; many appealed to people who were not literate in their mother tongue. In an assessment of the first year of the pilot (Burnaby et al., 1987), it was found that none of the participants wanted to be considered as not destined for the labour force.

A year or so later, another small pilot programme, Language at Work (LAW) was initiated on a similar basis for combined workplace and language skills training for immigrant women. While the SLP and LAW are considered to have the advantage of providing well-targeted training by organisations in good touch with the community, there are concerns about the stress on small organisations to maintain and juggle various sources of funding for short-term projects, the lack of consistency or standards, the qualifications of staff (in some situations), and the ability of federal officials to make informed judgements about choosing applicants for programme delivery, funding, and evaluating the projects. (See Canada Employment and Immigration Advisory Council, 1991: 17–20.)

For a perspective on the relative sizes of these programmes, the following is a quote from Immigration Canada (1992b):

> In 1990/91, 92 per cent ($99M of $107.3M) of federal language training funds provided full-time institutional training related to labour market needs. The two other language training programs, the Settlement Language Program (SLP) and Language at Work (LAW), primarily targeted immigrant women. They offered only part-time training and accounted for a relatively small portion of federal funding.
>
> At present, EIC-funded language training programs only reach some 28 per cent of newly arrived adult immigrants in need of language training. (1992b: 2)[7]

Some notes on other factors concerning federal responsibilities

The federal government does not support official language education services for children who speak neither English nor French in primary or secondary education, except in the case of some Aboriginal children as discussed below. This is a matter of considerable contention in some areas (Flaherty & Woods, 1992; Ashworth, 1992). English and/or French are almost universally the medium of instruction in public education in Canada (see below for further discussion of ESL and FSL for immigrant children).

There is a greater gap between the less and more educated in the immigrant group than native born Canadians. The numbers of immigrants with low levels of education in their mother tongue have been growing for more than a decade (Klassen & Burnaby, 1993). Analyses of a federal literacy study data showed that immigrants as a group did not contribute greatly to the overall illiteracy levels in the country but that some groups of immigrants, particularly women, were especially at risk (Jones, 1992; Boyd, 1991). Academic studies (e.g. Klassen, 1987; Cumming & Gil, 1992; Boyd, 1992) have shown that immigrants with low levels of literacy in their first language experience considerable and specific internal and external barriers to access to ESL and other kinds of training.

It has been a major criticism of general ESL policy and provision that ESL literacy learners are not accommodated. Issues of training for immigrants who do not speak an official language and who are not literate in their first language are normally considered to be an ESL rather than an adult literacy concern in Canada nonetheless (Burnaby, 1992b). Bilingual ESL and mother tongue literacy programmes, developed at local levels in high immigrant density areas, are dealing with some of the demand. One federal strategy for dealing globally with specific problems among immigrants with low levels of education has been, in 1993, to try to discourage such immigration by raising the point value of education for those immigrants whose applications for entry to Canada depend on points. This approach, however, will not affect the main groups of immigrants in need of ESL literacy (that is those who are not evaluated on the basis of points). Boyd (1992) shows that the ESL literacy group in both Canada and the US consists predominantly of women, and that women more than men face external barriers to access to ESL training. One further point here is that, under some conditions, immigrants (though not those with low levels of education) have taken major advantage of expanded provisions of literacy classes since the mid-1980s to meet their ESL needs (Burnaby, 1992b).

The provinces and other parties

The impact of the federal policies cannot be addressed without first considering the roles and contributions of other players, because the federal programmes are offered in cooperation with other parties and other agencies contribute financially to ESL programmes, either in conjunction with the federal government or independently. It will come as no surprise that a precise and comprehensive picture is impossible to paint. Significant factors contributing to the complexity of the situation include the fact that: (1) all the federal programmes are, to some degree, negotiated with individual provinces so that the programmes in each province have their own characteristics; (2) some provinces, particularly the four Atlantic provinces, receive very little immigration so that the federal government works fairly directly in these situations with the delivery agencies for what services there are; (3) each of the other provinces (sometimes through as many as five provincial ministries) funds its own configuration of services, largely through school boards and colleges but through NGOs as well; (4) school boards, which are basically financed through property taxes, sometimes take their own initiatives; (5) other organisations provide direct services, funding, volunteer labour, and resources such as meeting space; (6) immigrants are concentrated in urban areas and scattered elsewhere, with unique needs and resources in each locality; and (7) there are no clean lines between ESL, other settlement services, multiculturalism and anti-racism initiatives, adult basic education, community and women's development work, training for labour market skills, and so on.

The only published attempt at providing an overview from a national perspective of adult immigrant ESL policy and delivery (Burnaby, 1992a) is based, through necessity, on examples rather than comprehensive data on types of programmes, levels of funding, numbers of students, explicit policies, etc. However, we are fortunate to have the results of recent large studies of ESL in two provinces, British Columbia and Ontario, the two provinces with the highest concentration of immigrants (Cumming, 1991; Cumming *et al.*, 1993).

The negotiated character of the federal–provincial relationship (and that of colleges, NGOs and school boards within the provinces) has permitted a considerable degree of flexibility in ESL programme development. Inevitably, what one gains in flexibility one tends to lose in comprehensiveness. National standards for student outcomes are just being developed, yet there are none for teacher qualifications; programmes are not evaluated comparatively much less competitively.

Churchill (1986: 97) assesses Canadian language programmes as having a high degree of freedom from central control on four critical administrative factors (at the initiation of service; choice of population and numbers served; choice of mode of service; and accountability and inspection after grant). Not all the Canadian federal ESL programmes for immigrants described above allow as much freedom as the Official Language Act grants for official language programmes for Anglophones and Francophones (e.g. the employment-related ESL training was low on the choice and numbers of population), but in general Canadian programmes are not held strictly accountable. As well, it is impossible to track immigrant language education funds as they are transferred from the federal level to the provinces, and from the provinces to, for example, a college, and within the college to a specific programme. Only programmes like the SLP, where federal monies go directly to the delivery agency, are fiscally accountable in the public view.

ESL for immigrant children

ESL for schoolchildren is simpler to describe than other programmes because it is delivered almost exclusively by school boards. In areas in which there is little immigration (especially in the Atlantic provinces which have no ESL policies for the schools), immigrant children may be poorly served, if at all, but in high immigration regions they are likely to get at least minimal attention in special classes, withdrawal from regular classes for part of the day, or sensitisation of regular teachers to their needs. (See Ashworth (1992:

36–40) for an overall description.) Bilingual programmes are not used. In some provinces, part-time classes for immigrant women have been funded by provinces and/or school boards as 'parents and preschoolers' programmes so that children are given some language training as well. In some of the SLP classes, the child minding provision has been used to provide English language and orientation for small children (Burnaby *et al.*, 1987). How many children in the target populations are reached? Churchill (1986: 103), comparing the 'coverage and effects' of national school programmes for linguistic minorities in all the OECD countries, reports that:

> The most optimistic results are found in the Canadian case study [which reported on the programs under the *Official Languages Act* and not on ESL or FSL for immigrant children]. The fact that the latter refers to an established minority and the others to 'new' minorities makes it unlikely that the role of regulatory measures is the main causal factor. *The status of the minority appears, rather, to determine in large measure the regulatory approach adopted.* The overall impression derived from the studies is that the indigenous and new minorities are poorly covered in most instances, and that the nature of the provision is not clear. [emphasis in the original]

As far as one can tell from (inadequate) data available, non-official-language speaking children in schools are considerably less well served than are children learning a *second* official language. Cumming *et al.*, in their 1993 study (of supply and demand for ESL, ESD, or French language instruction for recent immigrants from Francophone countries or for students from Francophone backgrounds lacking some proficiency or literacy in French in Ontario) report:

> In this context [of reservations about the quality of the information], our impression is that school boards in the province with well established, well supported ESL/ESD programs consider they are managing relatively well at this time, although they would welcome greater resources and other supports, whereas school boards that are just now having to expand or refine their ESL/ESD programs because of new population growths are experiencing rather more difficulties providing such services and accommodating changes in their students' characteristics. (1993: 51)

Of ESL for immigrant children in Canada, Ashworth (1992: 37) says: 'Data collection regarding ESL funding and figures across Canada is inadequate and lacks uniformity, which means that Canada has little idea as to whether it is investing sufficiently and properly in children.'

Adult immigrant ESL

Before the 1960s, adult ESL learners were almost exclusively served by charitable organisations and school board adult education classes intended for academic upgrading. Now school boards offer free part-time (and, rarely, full-time) monolingual or bilingual ESL programmes on their premises, in a few instances even taking over whole buildings. In many cases coordination exists so that the school board provides the teachers for classes in community agencies and workplaces. Generally, school board teachers must have some sort of ESL qualification if they teach credit courses, but not necessarily if they teach non-credit. Those who teach non-credit courses often have part-time, piece work jobs in ESL. Boards in high immigrant areas have ESL support departments that develop curriculum, coordinate programmes, and provide professional development for teachers.

Community colleges used to restrict their ESL teaching largely to the federally funded employment related programme and part-time classes for fee-paying students. However, they have in recent years branched out into cooperative arrangements with community agencies and the workplace. Standards of teacher qualifications vary from institution to institution. There has been at least one province-wide strike to protest, in part, college policies to keep ESL teachers and others on short-term contracts.

Universities offer ESL part-time mostly for high fees (Burnaby & Kidd, 1988). Some offer ESL placement and support to students registered in their degree programmes. Most concentrate on making profits from EFL for foreign students who come to Canada specially for short-term, full-time language training. (See Elson (1992) for a discussion of issues around language and admissions testing for Canadian post-secondary institutions.)

Non-governmental organisations (NGOs), serving immigrants from any background or focusing on single ethnic groups, have chosen to offer settlement services to immigrants for many decades. In the 1970s, federal funding was made available for NGOs to provide settlement services, especially to refugees, and new NGOs, many of them ethnic specific, were created while older ones expanded. The federal government and provinces, one since the 1960s and some more in the 1990s, facilitated the offering of settlement services and ESL classes in NGOs through grants that helped them maintain their infrastructures. Provinces have funded ESL classes in NGOs directly and, with the Settlement Language Program, federal money was available for that as well. In some areas, school boards supply the teachers for NGO programmes and in others the NGOs must hire their own. In the NGOs especially, but elsewhere as well, there is conflict between pressure for ESL teachers to have uniform qualifications and other pressures to hire people to teach ESL who may have other valuable qualities but little or no ESL training. The only province-wide survey of ESL provisions for adults in all types of delivery institutions was by Cumming (1991) of British Columbia.

Teacher training in ESL (as opposed to *anglais langue seconde* for Francophone students) is available in most universities from Montreal to British Columbia. Post-graduate degrees in ESL are not available but there are a number of applied linguistics graduate and diploma programmes that serve the needs of ESL teachers as well as those of teachers of English to Francophones and of heritage and modern language teachers. Ministries of education set standards for qualifications of teachers who will teach credit courses in school boards. Colleges often offer their own training.

Issues in ESL to 1990

Burnaby (1992a) provided an overview and analysis of ESL for immigrant adults while Ashworth (1992) did the same regarding immigrant children. The issues for children, as Ashworth saw them, clustered around the organisation of programmes and their administration; staff training and support; placement and monitoring of students; and communication among geographic regions, within school systems, between home and school, and generally between the school and the community.

Burnaby (1992a: 4) summarised the issues for adult ESL training under three main headings. The first concerned coordination in respect of funding and programmes at each and between all levels (federal, provincial, municipal and community) including ESL related initiatives other than training, through agencies related to health, transportation, etc.; of ESL and other kinds of training that immigrants need, from basic literacy to professional, in order for them to adjust to their new circumstances; and among immigrant settlement services of which ESL is one. The second heading related to problems in meeting specific needs: of immigrant students who live at a distance from the main centres; of immigrant settlement; of would-be learners experiencing barriers to ESL (internal, such as lack of confidence, and external, such as lack of childcare); and of immigrants who come with highly specialised training, but need specific language assistance to make it possible for them to use those skills in Canada, and particularly to qualify for Canadian credentials. The third heading addressed the lack of involvement in immigrant settlement and language development on the part of important stakeholders – the media, the political system, generic social services, business, and so on – in the positive outcomes of immigration.

The new federal ESL programmes – LINC and LMLT

In the new immigration plan announced by the federal government in 1990, language training and other settlement services were included as part of the package. Previously, language training had been linked to employment training strategies. It proposed to replace all previous federal language training with the new one. Immigration Canada (1993a) describes it as follows:

> The government is spending approximately $615 million for language training over the five years of the 1991–1995 Immigration Plan, exclusive of Quebec. This is an increase of about 60 per cent over funding previously available for language training.
>
> Employment and Immigration Canada (EIC) completed an extensive review of language training activities in 1991, leading to a new immigrant language training policy. Announced in January, 1992, this policy makes a range of flexible training options accessible to a greater number of immigrants, regardless of their labour market intentions.
>
> There are two new language training programs. Language Instruction for Newcomers to Canada (LINC) provides the basic communications skills which can help persons function in our society. Training options are matched to individual needs, to help participants achieve a basic level of language competence. Training is normally offered during an immigrant's first year in Canada, and includes an emphasis on orienting newcomers to Canadian society and to the rights and responsibilities inherent in membership in our society.
>
> This program accounts for about 80 per cent of the federal immigrant language training funds. All permanent residents, including refugees whose claims have been accepted, are eligible for this program regardless of their labour market intentions. Priorities are established in consultation with the provinces, training providers, and other partners so that funds will be directed to those most likely to experience barriers to integration.
>
> The other program, Labour Market Language Training (LMLT), provides specialized or advanced training oriented to labour market needs. It offers the training needed to acquire job skills, or to use existing skills which are in demand in the local labour market.
>
> This program accounts for about 20 per cent of federal immigrant language training funds. Flexible training options blend language training and occupational skills development. Special efforts are being made to help women, visible minorities and immigrants with disabilities achieve the language skills needed for full participation in the labour market.
>
> Both LINC and LMLT are flexible, allowing for a wide variety of training interventions, including classroom and/or workplace-based approaches. The new policy encourages community consultation and

participation by partners involved in immigrant integration. Under both programs it is possible to integrate language training with other training programs to meet individual client needs.

Funds are also provided abroad to basic language training and cultural orientation, for visa-ready immigrants awaiting final processing.[8] In 1991–92, this training was delivered through the International Organization for Migration in Rome, Vienna, Athens, Belgrade, Bangkok and Hong Kong. In 1992–93, the training was started in Ho Chi Minh City, Vietnam.

EIC is now working with partners from across Canada on the development of a set of progressive competency levels in language learning. This set of competencies will improve the administration of language training programs and will further facilitate access and equitable outcome for newcomers. (Immigration Canada, 1993a: 4–5)

The plan is to increase the proportion of newly arrived adult immigrants receiving language training from the 1990 level of about 28%, to about 45% in 1995 (Immigration Canada, 1991: 7). Among other things, EIC (now called Human Resources Canada) also plans to continue its long-standing Immigrant Settlement and Adaptation Program 'which funds non-profit organizations and educational institutions to help them deliver integration services to new-comers' (Immigration Canada, 1993a: 5); to expand its Host Program, which links newcomers with Canadian families, to include all classes of immigrants not just refugees; to fund the creation and distribution of multimedia kits and texts for use in orientation of immigrants to Canadian society; to admit immigrants to a number of employment related programmes (set up for Canadian citizens) in addition to the LMLT (including Canadian job search methods, employment counselling, literacy skills, high school equivalency and occupational skills)[9]; and to cooperate with the provinces on a Canadian Information Centre on International Credentials to help immigrants get their professional training accredited in Canada.[10]

At this time we are just beginning to see how LINC works. The programme is to work like the SLP in that individual NGOs, educational institutions, and private organisations can apply for funds to deliver a LINC programme through a one-year contract. It is not clear how a full range of programmes in any one area will be coordinated. No training allowances for students are available. Potential LINC students, who cannot be refugee claimants or Canadian citizens, are to be assessed at an A-LINC centre where their language skills will be tested and rated at one of five levels. They will be counselled about appropriate LINC programmes in their area if they score at Level 3 or below; if they score above that they may be eligible for LMLT. LINC graduates may also be eligible for LMLT. LINC curricula matching the levels are being developed cooperatively to fit with provincial standards. Also, a national committee is working to develop benchmarks. Child minding and transportation may be funded as well in LINC programmes. There has been some controversy over how much time a student will be allowed on the programme.

From this rather uncertain perspective of what LINC will develop into, one can still assess its potential to respond to criticisms of the programmes that it replaces. Regarding coordination of funding and programmes, at the federal level all the language training money will come as one programme from one department, indeed from one section (Settlement Branch of Immigration) of one department. It is hoped that LINC and LMLT will be well coordinated with other employment related training available to Canadian citizens. The latter training, federally, still comes out of the Employment side of Employment and Immigration. Publications about LINC have talked generally about cooperation with deliverers and provincial authorities, but specifics have not been given, so it is unclear how LINC might fit in with provincially funded programmes. Starkey (1993) gives an example of how stakeholders in a medium sized city have created a council to coordinate their efforts locally.

A major change is the attempt to standardise language training across the country through the use of the five levels and benchmarks. Teachers who believe in learner-centred curriculum are already worrying about how such standardisation will relate to their principles (Goldstein, 1993). Delivery agencies have their say in the type of programme they propose, but they must compete for funding decided on by federal officials. LINC Level 1 is supposed to address ESL literacy but it also includes all learners at the basic fluency level so that ESL literacy learners may be excluded again as they were before. LMLT has the potential to link better with professional training, but how that will be done remains to be seen. Coordination with other settlement services may well be improved if a good number of community agencies get LINC contracts and/or cooperate with educational institutions on LINC contracts (providing, of course, that they can stand the strain of competitively based funding that must be renewed annually).

In terms of LINC's ability to meet needs, presumably agencies in areas not well served now could be encouraged to apply for a contract provided that those administering the contracting have a clear plan of where they think training is needed. SLP showed that giving contracts to community agencies was inclined to improve access for non-confident learners and those who need special schedules, child minding, and transportation *if the quality of the programme was good*. LMLT has the potential to improve the quality of language training for the particular needs of professionals, but little information on how this programme will work is available.

LINC in itself does little to involve other stakeholders, such as social service deliverers, those involved in the political process, the media, etc. except for the fact that all immigrant settlement matters are now concentrated in one place federally and so might be easier to coordinate with other aspects of life in the country. Business may get more involved in that private companies can apply for a LINC grant.

Federal documents on LINC have generally been silent on how much training an individual learner can receive; however, Immigration Canada (1992c) suggests that no overall limit has been set other than that they cannot be in the programme for more than three years. It seems that the amount of training is to be determined by the people who do the initial assessment. This raises the issue of the adequacy of basic research much less the LINC assessment process to reasonably determine in advance the number of hours of instruction any learner will need.

Another concern expressed about LINC is the exclusion of refugee claimants and citizens. Immigration Canada (1993b: 9) indicates that 117,000 people claimed refugee status from 1989 to 1992. Although a streamlined refugee status adjudication system was put in place in 1989 to clear up the backlog of claimants, there are still thousands of them in the country. Also, immigrants who have become citizens have also been excluded from LINC. On the basis of 1986 Canadian census data, Pendakur (1992: 161) indicated:

> Roughly half the immigrants unable to speak English or French arrived in Canada prior to 1980; almost one third arrived prior to 1970. . . . It should be noted that the size of the group is likely to increase because while the number of persons unable to speak an official language remained relatively stable between 1981 and 1986, increasing immigration from non-English-French speaking countries will likely change this situation. This in turn will serve to increase the demand for federally and provincially funded language training programs.

According to Cumming (1991: 8–9): '. . . research has suggested that some immigrants to Canada, particularly women, only consider themselves able to pursue language studies after they have established a secure home life and economic position, a point which may be 3 to 10 years after their initial immigration' (Cumming & Gill, 1991; Seward & McDade, 1988). A high percentage of these people will have taken out Canadian citizenship. Clearly, the federal government is leaving responsibility for them to the provinces.

Canada's new ESL policy carefully avoids making promises to its citizens in general. Canada's higher immigration rate proportionate to the total population, relative to that of other countries, could justify a specific focus on immigrants. Provincial control over education and the negotiated character of federal/provincial relationships might account for the federal government's leaving all but initial language training in the hands of the provinces. Finally, provincial control over education has probably been the major reason why Canada federally has not created national level institutions on topics, such as ESL or literacy, related to training. On the other hand, federal powers in the area of economic development permit it to establish an institute concerned with the credentialling of immigrants.

Advances and challenges in Canadian ESL

Canadian ESL delivery has made slow but steady progress from practically nothing in the early 1960s to a large and complex undertaking. Most changes have been in the direction of greater volume, inclusion, flexibility, and sensitivity to holistic needs. Three trends in Canadian adult ESL are worth noting as achievements even if they are far from universal: (1) coordination of ESL programming across delivery and funding agencies; (2) community involvement through the use of NGOs; and (3) including native-born workers in adjustment of communications through multiculturalism in the workplace programmes.

These trends are three among many that underlie current ESL delivery in Canada. Not all trends have been positive and some have both positive and negative aspects. Several among the more negative ones include shortcomings in policy and implementation on ESL literacy, the exploitation of the knowledge and community trust of NGOs through short-term contracts, shifting and unsatisfactory conditions of teachers in ESL, and levels (volume) of ESL provision.

Finally, there is a constant, rather than a trend, that needs attention. Despite the fact that we never have adequate data to get the true picture, it is clearly the case that ESL provision in Canada is always substantially short of the needs. Not only do we need more direct ESL training for immigrants, we need accommodation by significant facets of Canadian society of the immigrant fact in our communities. A study of health and social services in Metropolitan Toronto (Doyle & Visano, 1987) showed that mainstream agencies like hospitals and social work deliverers had made virtually no moves to improve access to their services for immigrants and visible minorities. Also, it has been indicated (Cumming, 1989) that virtually no trade and professional organisations have considered the needs of immigrants in their credentialling systems. Before there is political will to change policies and apply more resources, the value of making adequate, appropriate ESL and social services available to those immigrants who want it will have to be impressed on those groups who see an economic, racist, or other advantage in keeping at least some immigrants silent (Rockhill & Tomic, 1992).

French as a second language for immigrants in Quebec

Mention must be made of the teaching of French as a second language (FSL) to immigrant children and adults in Quebec. 'Classes d'acceuil' were established even before Bill 101 (1977) to attract immigrant children to French schools. Children are placed in these classes for about 10 months to learn French and be introduced to school subjects and the school system; there may be additional time or follow-up services provided (d'Anglejan & De Koninck, 1992: 99). A Committee on Quebec Schools and Cultural Communities concluded that:

> . . . the measures [for immigrant students] provided for in the school system and implemented by school boards have made a first state of integration possible: mechanical integration. Focussing largely on language training, they have modernized teaching methods for dealing with linguistic adaptation, under-education and illiteracy. However, the various remedial measures that schools have implemented should be interpreted more as a response to the problems posed by students than as a desire on the part of schools to adapt themselves to the needs of these students. (Quoted in d'Anglejan & De Koninck, 1992: 100)

This view is in accord with the views of the authors quoted above about ESL school programmes in the other provinces. Some tension has built up in those schools in Quebec where school authorities have forbidden the use of languages other than French on school property.

FSL programmes for adult immigrants in Quebec follow much the same patterns as ESL adult programmes do in other provinces. Quebec has established nine Centres d'orientation et de formation des immigrants (COFI) where full-time programmes, usually longer than those in other provinces, are offered with training allowances to the categories of immigrants that would receive federal language training support in the rest of Canada. This is funded federally. The province also funds shorter full- and part-time programmes (some with training allowances) to immigrants who would not be eligible for the federally funded courses (as do several other provinces). Special classes have been developed in two COFI for immigrants with low levels of literacy in their first language. Childcare services are available for students with young children. Only one Quebec ministry is involved so coordination is good relative to that in provinces where several ministries or departments offer separate programmes (Canada Employment and Immigration Advisory Council, 1991: 35–44). Overall, immigrants in Quebec are served somewhat better with respect to language training than are immigrants in other provinces. Indeed, there is some resentment, in Ontario particularly, about the level of funding Quebec receives from the federal government per immigrant. Quebec has cut its immigration levels but continues to get the same amount of money while Ontario, the largest recipient of immigrants, gets the lowest amount of funding per immigrant of any of the provinces.

Recognition of non-official languages

In the discussion thus far, it is clear that Canada as a whole places a great deal of value in the official languages. English is a taken-for-granted powerful force in this continent where English speakers hold most of the economic and political power. French has made a political foothold, and the relationship between the two languages has become so important that the conflicts between them often threaten the stability of the country. Not only is political blood spilled and millions spent on creating equal services in both languages, but also individuals all across the country make an effort to learn a second official language and insist on such opportunities for their children. Most immigrants, too, buy into this value for the official languages at least to the extent of learning one of them as well as possible under the conditions in which they live. They and other Canadians continue to press for better opportunities for them to learn their first official language here. All levels of government put moderate amounts of money towards this end.

But what of the value of the languages that the immigrants bring to Canada with them? In the era of total Anglophone power before World War II, immigrants were expected to learn English, usually without help except from some charitable organisations. There was no accommodation for their needs in the schools (Ashworth, 1992). Before the rise of Francophone power in the 1960s, immigrants in Quebec tended to learn English rather than French. Their children went to English schools and immigrant parents were among the most vocal when French became the only medium of instruction for all except eligible Anglophones. Across Canada, languages other than English or French were viewed with suspicion and immigrants, especially children, were encouraged to forget their mother tongues. From the 19th century, a number of ethnic communities created non-official language classes for their children, organised and funded by the local community. Until the early part of this century when provincial Education Acts were changed to prevent them from getting public support, there were some bilingual schools (for example, Ukrainian and English on the prairies). Some religious groups (such as Mennonites and Doukhobors) struggled long into this century to run their own schools in their own languages (Ashworth, 1992: 40). Some ethnic groups have continued to fund private multilingual schools or evening or weekend classes in non-official languages.

When the French–English debate came on the scene, the question of the role of other languages inevitably came up. In the midst of what was largely taken to be a two-way struggle between English and French, the other languages had to be handled discretely. The Royal Commission on Bilingualism and Biculturalism's mandate (1967: 173) included 'taking into account the contribution made by the other ethnic groups to the cultural enrichment of Canada and the measures that should be taken to safeguard that contribution'. Note that culture but not language was mentioned. Book IV of the Commission's report was on the topic of the other cultural groups and endorsed linguistic diversity.

> The presence in Canada of many people whose language and culture are distinctive by reason of their birth or ancestry represents an inestimable enrichment that Canadians cannot afford to lose. The dominant culture can only profit from the influence of these other cultures. Linguistic variety is unquestionably an advantage and its beneficial effects on the country are priceless. (1970: 14)

The Official Languages Act of 1969 and its subsequent implementation created a climate of linguistic uncertainty, especially for speakers of non-official languages. To deal with objections to this strong focus on English and French only, the prime minister announced a new policy of multiculturalism in the House of Commons in 1971.

> We are of the belief that cultural pluralism is the very essence of the Canadian identity. To say that we have two official languages is not to say that we have two official cultures: no culture is in and of itself more 'official' than any other. (Quoted in Saouab, 1993: 4)

The only mention of language in the elaborated policy, which pledged to support cultural groups in their development and to overcome barriers to their participation in Canadian society, was for continued assistance to immigrants in learning at least one of the official languages. A Minister of State for Multiculturalism was appointed in 1972 and federal Multicultural grants and programs were established in 1973 (Saouab, 1993: 5).

Of most significance to this discussion is the establishment in 1977 of the federal Cultural Enrichment Program. It included support for the teaching of non-official languages primarily to children of communities where the target language is the mother tongue or ancestral language of the children. Such languages are called 'heritage' languages.

. . . support is provided [through this program] to ethno cultural communities for the teaching of heritage languages. Parallel support programs for community-operated heritage language programs and for heritage language bilingual programs in the public schools were already operating in the prairie provinces at the time the Cultural Enrichment Program was established, and in the same month the Ontario government announced the Ontario Heritage Languages program. By this time also, the provincial government in Quebec was supporting the teaching of heritage languages both in community-run schools and in regular school programs as part of their policy initiatives in the area of 'interculturalism', a construct intended to promote acceptance and communication between cultural groups without necessarily implying that all cultural groups are equal. (Cummins & Danesi, 1990: 26)

Further steps at the federal level include a provision in the 1982 Charter of Rights and Freedoms that the Charter 'shall be interpreted in a manner consistent with the preservation and enhancement of the multicultural heritage of Canadians', and in 1988 the Canadian Multiculturalism Act was proclaimed that led the way to the establishment of a Department of Multiculturalism and Citizenship but no further financial commitment to heritage languages. In fact, according to Ashworth (1992: 46), federal funds to heritage language classes were cut in 1990. Saouab (1993: 15) notes that a bill to establish a Canadian Heritage Languages Institute in Edmonton was passed in 1991 but that it had not been put in place.

Resistance to the establishment of heritage language classes at public expense has been extensive and vitriolic. Space precludes an elaboration of the incidents, but Fleras and Elliott (1992: 155–9), d'Anglejan and de Koninck (1992: 100–1), and especially Cummins and Danesi (1990: Ch. 3) outline a number of outbursts and the issues involved. For example, regular classroom teachers in Ontario objected strongly when the province attempted to force school boards to integrate heritage language classes into the normal school day.

In 1990, the Canadian Education Association (1991) conducted a survey of a sample of school boards about heritage language programmes. Their summary of the current situation is as follows:

Half of the provinces in Canada, that is, Quebec, Ontario, Manitoba, Saskatchewan and Alberta, support heritage language programs, some to a greater extent than others. Also noted is the fact that British Columbia is in the process of developing some policies and guidelines for similar programs. One or two areas of the country indicated that they are remaining open to community requests, and if sufficient demand arises, a program will be investigated. However the CEA survey also turned up other regions of the country where school administrators doubt that the interest for such programs will ever be found, given the unilingual nature of that community, whether it be French or English.

Corresponding involvement by school boards depends, to a large extent, on the underlying legislation, policies, programs and funding developed by the ministry or department of education in each province. Board programs range from the smallest (one class in one heritage language) to the large programs of over 10,000 students seen in Metropolitan Toronto.

Heritage language programs of instruction across the country appear to be a fairly recent phenomenon, in some cases arising in the 60s or 70s, and some are still developing in 1990. Virtually every language in the world is taught somewhere in Canada. The most common languages in the Prairie provinces are Ukrainian and German, while in Ontario and Quebec, Greek, Italian, Portuguese, Spanish and Chinese account for the majority of students.

Scheduling varies from province to province; some boards call heritage language programs a normal part of their school day, others use a bilingual format [up to 50 per cent of the school day], and still others restrict it to Continuing Education. Timetabling also runs the gamut from early morning, noon-hour, after school, weekends, and classes integrated into the regular school day. Total weekly time allotted to heritage language programs varies greatly, depending both on provincial legislation and school board policies. With few exceptions, the heritage language programs are offered only in the elementary grades. (1991: 47)

In sum, before the multiculturalism policy, heritage language classes (as opposed to modern or foreign languages as school subjects) were a private, community matter. Since then some have been associated with the schools in various ways and at least partially publicly funded, and new ones have been created in the schools (Ashworth, 1992; Toohey, 1992; d'Anglejan & De Koninck, 1992; Canadian Education Association, 1991). There was some money attached to the policy and provinces expanded heritage language programmes for the teaching of non-official languages in schools. Resistance was demonstrated in many areas to having heritage language classes as a regular part of the curriculum (Cummins & Danesi, 1990; Ashworth, 1992; d'Anglejan & De Koninck, 1992), and they remain largely as a non-academically recognised add-on in most jurisdictions (Ashworth, 1992; Toohey, 1992). Federal assistance through transfer payments to provinces for heritage language programmes was cut off in 1990, but many provinces continue to support them (Canadian Education Association, 1991). Although the multiculturalism policy and Act encouraged the learning of the official languages, they were never associated with *fiscal* support for official language training programmes.

Canadian heritage language programmes are not linked to issues of children being at risk concerning learning English (or French); their intention is to offer children the opportunity to learn a language that is present in the community. (See McAndrew, 1991 for a careful comparison between Quebec and Ontario classes.) The assumption is that most children in such classes will be learning their ancestral language, but other interested children are usually not excluded. Criticisms of the programmes include that they largely aim at the beginning level of learning the languages, do not capitalise on the non-official language skills that children bring with them from their homes, and are not coordinated with the goals and methods of ESL/FSL programmes focused on getting children to learn an official language (Toohey, 1992; Burnaby, 1987). Cummins and Danesi (1990: 113–4) summarise their conclusions about heritage language programmes in Canada as follows:

> . . . the issue [in Canada] is not whether linguistic and cultural diversity are desirable or not; they are an inevitable reality. The issue is rather whether our energies as a nation are better spent denying our emerging multilingual and multicultural identity or accepting the linguistic assets that minorities bring to Canada and promoting them as we would any other human resource. Despite our racist history and current manifestations of intolerance and discrimination, Canadian policies towards minorities are among the more enlightened in the western world. Yet far more could be done if we were to substitute imagination for pettiness by establishing alternative schools or programs where all Canadian students would have the opportunity to develop literacy and fluency in at least three languages. We have abundant research knowledge upon which to base such schools at the present time. We simply choose not to enrich our children.
>
> A major reason why we make this seemingly absurd choice is that to implement such trilingual schools would amount to an explicit valorization of multilingualism and the elevation of the status of minority groups whose languages would now be institutionalized within the mainstream educational system. In other words, such initiatives would alter the power relations between the dominant and subordinate groups within Canadian society.

Aboriginal Languages in Canada

Aboriginal peoples and their languages have been considered, until recently, as largely outside the kinds of debates outlined above. Since Confederation in 1867, Aboriginal people (that is, 'Indians' in the British North America Act of 1867 and 'Eskimos' by a court ruling in 1939) were constitutionally the responsibility of the federal government for all services. As noted, they were excluded by the Royal Commission on Bilingualism and Biculturalism on the grounds that their issues were more properly dealt with elsewhere. They have not been included, largely by their choice, in subsequent definitions of cultural minorities. As will be indicated below, they were administratively kept largely isolated from the rest of the population. Such separate treatment left open the possibility for special policies suited to their unique needs. Unfortunately, most of these opportunities have instead been used in racist and assimilative ways. One of the major factors in Aboriginal language development, relative to those of official or heritage languages, is that if North American indigenous languages are lost here, there is no reservoir of speakers elsewhere to draw on to renew that resource. In the following discussion, some background is provided on the Aboriginal population and its languages, policy development on language and education is outlined, and information on present language programmes is described.

Background information

At the time of first European contact in northern North America, it is estimated that there were almost as many Aboriginal people here as at present. Mistreatment, often brutal, and the effects of European diseases literally decimated their numbers in the 18th and 19th centuries, but these numbers have rebounded. There were about 470,000 people who identified themselves as of Aboriginal *single* origins on the 1991 census (Statistics Canada, 1993a: 1), or about 2% of the Canadian population. Also, more than 500,000 indicated Aboriginal plus other origins (Statistics Canada, 1991a: 8).

Linguists assume that Aboriginal peoples spoke about 450 languages and dialects in 11 language families before the Europeans came (Office of the Commissioner of Official Languages, 1992: xiii); now there are about 60 Aboriginal languages in Canada (depending on one's definition of language and dialect) in the same 11 language families. Some of these languages historically and at present (have) had large numbers of speakers while others have not. Various factors have acted to reduce the numbers of speakers of some languages more than others; indeed, some of these languages are no longer spoken.

Up to the 1980s, numbers of speakers of specific Aboriginal languages in North America were calculated by linguists' estimates (Chafe, 1965). Foster (1982) combined sets of estimates and projected a picture of the health of the Aboriginal languages of Canada based on the numbers of speakers, calling those with less than 100 speakers 'extremely endangered' and those with

more than 5000 speakers as having 'an excellent chance of survival' with several
categories in between. Only Inuktitut, Cree and Ojibwa had more than 5000
speakers according to his figures.

Until 1981, the Canadian census gathered information on Aboriginal
languages only under the two headings of Amerindian and Inuit. In 1981,
however, the census categorised Aboriginal languages by individual language.
Burnaby and Beaujot (1986) did an analysis of the language data and other
variables for the group of people who indicated Aboriginal ethnicity. The
most dramatic figures in the study came from a comparison of the proportions
of mother-tongue speakers of Aboriginal languages among the Aboriginal
population from the censuses of 1951 to 1981. In 1951, 87.4% of the Aboriginal
population had an Aboriginal language as a mother tongue, whereas in 1981
it was 29.3%. The Assembly of First Nations in 1990 published the results of
a survey of language use among Aboriginal people living on 593 reserves.
The results, estimates by band and educational leaders, show that 48% of
the sample were considered to be fluent speakers. These numbers were
compared with census figures for the relevant reserves, indicating that the
census figures were consistently lower than those of the survey (p. 29). Two
points are important here. One is that the Aboriginal languages, on any
measure, are in rapid decline (some much more than others). The other is
that various ways of enumerating the actual numbers of speakers produce
inconsistent results.

To the best of our knowledge, none of the Canadian Aboriginal languages
had a writing system (one which would enable a reader to recover exact
words from unknown text) before contact with Europeans. Since then, at
least one writing system for most languages has been devised but is not
necessarily in general use (Burnaby, 1985). At one time, only estimates and
anecdotal evidence were available about literacy levels in Aboriginal
languages. The Assembly of First Nations' 1990 survey asked band administrators to estimate Aboriginal language literacy as well as oral skills among
band members. Overall, the results worked out to 7% Aboriginal language
literates among the total number of people reported on (p. 21). In the survey,
70% of the communities said that they had access to a writing system; 7%
said that they did not know whether or not they did (p. 23). In 1991, Statistics
Canada conducted a special survey of people who reported Aboriginal identity
on the census. When asked if they could read or write an Aboriginal language,
13% of the adults (aged 15 or over) said they could read in one and 9% said
that they could write in one (Statistics Canada, 1993d: 10).

It seems to be a powerful Canadian myth that Aboriginal people and their
languages are 'up north and out west' but not 'here'. Aboriginal people are
remarkably evenly distributed across the country in urban and rural areas

and on reserves. Ontario has the highest numbers of Aboriginal people, followed by British Columbia; PEI has the lowest. In terms of percentages of Aboriginal people in the population, however, the Northwest Territories is the highest, followed by the Yukon. When the Northwest Territories are divided into Nunavut and Denendeh, Nunavut will have a very high proportion of Inuit people, the highest Aboriginal population density by far in the country. The prairie provinces, although much lower in percentages than the territories, are higher than any of the other provinces (Burnaby & Beaujot, 1987: 13).

With respect to Aboriginal language factors geographically, Burnaby and Beaujot (1987) found that high levels of Aboriginal language maintenance were most common among Aboriginal people who live in isolated, small communities and who tend not to change their place of residence. Historical length of contact with non-Aboriginal people as indicated by east–west or north–south location does not seem to be a strong factor; for example, Nova Scotia shows higher Aboriginal language maintenance levels than does the Yukon. Aboriginal language/English bilingualism is most common in the Atlantic provinces whereas Aboriginal language monolingualism is more common in northern areas (1987: 22–59). It is expected that future statistics will begin to show the effects of the extension of television into the north and of higher levels of schooling.

As Aboriginal students are scattered across the country, it is hard for political advocates of special provisions for Aboriginal education and for teachers of Aboriginal students to cooperate, especially those located in isolated communities and those who live in areas in which the Aboriginal population is low relative to other groups. Also, Aboriginal language maintenance varies greatly, making it difficult for advocates for and educators of Aboriginal education to develop comprehensive approaches to language in Aboriginal education.

Policy on Aboriginal education

There is very little policy on Aboriginal languages *per se*, so this part of the discussion on policy centres on education, where language treatment has been the most visible. According to the British North America Act (1867), responsibility for education was vested in the provinces but jurisdiction over Aboriginal peoples remained with the federal government. The first Indian Act (1876) initiated federal responsibility for education of Aboriginal peoples, among other things. Under this Act over time, most Amerindian people were designated as 'status Indians' and settled on 'reserves' of land; the Métis (half Amerindian/half French) were not included because they were promised another social role; a number of Amerindians were never included and some lost their status (now called non-status Indians); and the Inuit became a federal responsibility in 1939 following a court case, but were never included in the Act. From 1876 for the next eight decades or so, the main strategy of the federal government for education for status Indians was to contract with Christian groups to provide education for Aboriginal children. Such education was not normally the same as that for children in provincial schools. In a few cases, some of the special provisions in Aboriginal education recognised the first language of the Aboriginal students (examples in Toohey, 1982; Gresko, 1986). Most sources stress the assimilationist nature of Aboriginal education to the point of cruelty to the students and total prohibition of the use of Aboriginal languages in schools and residences (e.g. Tschantz, 1980). Much of this education required Aboriginal children to leave their homes at an early age to take education in a residential school. The more remote the Aboriginal group, the longer it took to provide educational opportunities for the children so that some groups were still not regularly served even into the 1950s. For example, among the Inuit, who tend to live in remote northern locations, 76% of those over 50 years old reported on the 1991 census that they had no formal education or less than grade 9 schooling (Statistics Canada, 1994: xlvi).

In the 1940s a parliamentary committee revised the Indian Act in such a way that strategies were put in place for the federal government to contract with the provincial governments to educate Aboriginal children in locations where this was possible, and for remote Aboriginal schools to adhere to appropriate provincial curricula and standards for teacher qualification. This policy was implemented to the extent that more than half of the Aboriginal elementary school population was attending provincial schools by the 1960s (Hawthorn, 1967). Hawthorn recommended that ESL methods be used with Aboriginal children who did not come to school speaking English, but into the late 1970s there was no great evidence of this recommendation being implemented (Burnaby et al., 1980). The integrative approach culminated in the Minister of Indian Affairs' White Paper in 1969 to Parliament which proposed an end to the Indian Act on the grounds that it was racist. Aboriginal reaction to the White Paper was swift in asserting that Aboriginal peoples did not want to give up their special relationship with the federal government; however, it also condemned past policies on residential schools and tuition agreements with provincial school boards, and called for fresh approaches with Aboriginal people in control. The most effective response to the White Paper was *Indian Control of Indian Education*, a policy document issued in 1972 by the National Indian Brotherhood, at that time the national body speaking for Aboriginal issues. This document insisted that Aboriginal parents have control over and responsibility for the education of their children, and that Aboriginal children should be educated in such a way as to enhance their self-esteem as Aboriginal people as well as to develop their ability to make a good living in Canadian society. It goes on to reinforce the need for Aboriginal children to get a good grounding in their ancestral language as a central factor in the development of their identity.

Much has happened since that pivotal time in Aboriginal education policy. With respect to language, federal, provincial and band controlled schools slowly began to offer Aboriginal languages as subject of instruction. Three jurisdictions have begun to offer the primary grades through the medium of the local Aboriginal language because the children speak it. In other areas, experiments in Aboriginal language immersion programmes for children who speak only English have been set up. Administratively, some Aboriginal groups have pulled out of tuition agreements with provincial schools (Hagey *et al.*, 1989: 7) but many others have stayed. Representation of Aboriginal community members on local provincial school boards has improved but is still an issue. The federal government has extended its day school programme into virtually all remote communities for elementary schooling at least. Most bands are in the process of taking over control of the education in their communities (Hagey *et al.*, 1989: 7). Education advisory committees, once just a rubber stamping agency, are gaining more control in at least some areas. It is still the case that federal/band schools often do not provide for high school education on reserves, so that children on remote reserves must leave home to attend high school in towns that are far from their home communities. Also, many Aboriginal children are attending provincial schools off reserves either because they are Métis or non-status or because their status Indian families are living away from their home reserves (Gerber, 1984). A federal–Quebec agreement and the Quebec Charter of the French Language exempts some Aboriginal school boards in Quebec from French language in education provisions. The essential characteristic of this picture is that the administration of Aboriginal education is so fragmented geographically and administratively that coordination and cooperation on policy is virtually impossible. See Paquette (1986) for a detailed description.

Hagey *et al.*, (1989: 6) note that: 'According to the 1986 Census, 28 percent of all status Indians have at least high school education, one-half the rate for all Canadians at 56 per cent.' While this represents a substantial improvement over the situation in the early 1970s, when status Indian people were completing high school at about one-quarter the national average (Indian Affairs and Northern Development, 1980: 49), the present situation is still deplorable. The problems facing children from isolated reserves coming out to high school in urban centres account for only a portion of the reasons that Aboriginal students complete high school at such a low rate relative to the rest of the population.

Political activity

To digress briefly from education, it is important to outline certain facets of the Aboriginal role in constitutional reform and official language policy before a final picture is drawn of current language programmes in Aboriginal education. When the White Paper on Indian Affairs was tabled in 1969, the main force opposing it came largely from status Indians through the relatively new national organisation, the National Indian Brotherhood. But, since the topic of the racist nature of the Indian Act had been raised, the other groups of people of Aboriginal ancestry, the non-status Indians, the Métis, and the Inuit, began to form political organisations and demand Aboriginal rights along with the status Indians. Therefore, there are now four national Aboriginal organisations representing these groups. The term 'Native' was adopted in the 1970s to refer to members of all of these groups. In the later 1980s, the term 'Aboriginal' began to replace Native with the same reference. As Aboriginal response to federal structures developed, a central point was that the English and French did not deserve the title of 'founding nations' that they had given themselves in the linguistic and cultural debates of the 1960s. Aboriginal people insisted that their governments and social structures, that existed before European contact, took precedence. Thus, they now frequently call themselves First Nations, the National Indian Brotherhood having evolved into the Assembly of First Nations.

The role of Aboriginal people in the constitutional reform activities since the late 1970s is too complex to do justice to here. Aboriginal leaders demanded and were refused official inclusion in the talks that preceded the signing of the Constitution Act of 1982, but their issues were included, by the prime minister and the nine signatory provincial premiers, in the Charter of Rights and Freedoms to the following extent:

> 25. The guarantee in this Charter of certain rights and freedoms shall not be construed so as to abrogate or derogate from any Aboriginal, treaty or other rights or freedoms that pertain to the Aboriginal peoples of Canada including:
> (a) any rights or freedoms that have been recognized by the Royal Proclamation of October 7, 1763; and
> (b) any rights or freedoms that may be acquired by the Aboriginal peoples of Canada by way of land claims settlement.
> 35. (1) The existing Aboriginal and treaty rights of the Aboriginal peoples of Canada are hereby recognized and affirmed.
> (2) In this Act, 'Aboriginal peoples of Canada' includes the Indian, Inuit, and Métis peoples of Canada.
> 37. (1) A constitutional conference composed of the Prime Minister of Canada and the first ministers of the provinces shall be convened by the

Prime Minister of Canada within one year after this Part comes into force.

(2) The conference convened under subsection (1) shall have included in its agenda an item respecting constitutional matters that directly affect the Aboriginal peoples of Canada, including the identification and definition of the rights of those peoples to be included in the Constitution of Canada, and the Prime Minister of Canada shall invite representatives of those peoples to participate in the discussions on that item.

(3) The Prime Minister of Canada shall invite elected representatives of the governments of the Yukon Territory and the Northwest Territories to participate in the discussions on any item on the agenda of the conference convened under subsection (1) that, in the opinion of the Prime Minister, directly affects the Yukon Territory and the Northwest Territories.

In fact, there were four such conferences in the 1980s, and although they served to develop and articulate positions among the Aboriginal groups, no agreement with the federal and provincial levels was reached. The last one was just over when the Meech Lake Accord (quoted above) was struck to get Quebec into the Constitution. The failure of the conferences and the at least temporary success of the Meech Lake Accord angered Aboriginal leaders who felt that their issues were not being taken seriously.

Indeed, it was more than symbolic that a key condition of the acceptance of the Meech Lake Accord failed to be met when the only Aboriginal member of the Manitoba legislature voted alone against it; thus Manitoba's support was lost (as was that of another province for its own reasons). In the next constitutional debate, over the Charlottetown Accord, which started in 1991, the federal government was obliged by the Charter to involve the Aboriginal peoples. It asked and funded the Assembly of First Nations to develop its positions. However, Quebec forced a deadline on negotiations before the AFN could complete its report. Nevertheless, a number of Aboriginal issues were addressed in the final accord, including one that mentioned language as an item to be included in the jurisdiction of any duly constituted legislative bodies of Aboriginal peoples.

Thus, at the present time, the Aboriginal peoples have gained considerable ground by getting a foothold on the federal agenda. However, very little of this ground has been consolidated in concrete legislation or programmes. With all this positioning going on at the federal level, it would appear that language issues were being totally submerged under the weight of constitutional and land-based matters. Nevertheless, there is one major example of language change affecting Aboriginal languages that can be reported here. Across the country, Aboriginal populations are so distributed that it has been possible to organise (if not gerrymander) electoral district in Canada so that Aboriginal people almost never have the majority in any. However, in the Northwest Territories, Aboriginal people have a bare majority in the total area and certainly in many of the districts. Therefore, it is not a surprise that a major policy breakthrough would occur there.

In 1982, the federal government, which has direct control over the territories that it does not have over the provinces, decided to amend the Northwest Territories Act and the Yukon Territory Act to make English and French the official languages of the territories. In the territories there was a strong negative reaction to this move since the local Francophone populations are quite small, especially relative to the size of the Aboriginal populations. The Dene Nation and Métis Association of the NWT, the political organisation representing the Dene groups, produced a paper entitled *Denendeh: Public Government for the People of the North* (1982). It proposed the establishment of a new state in the present day Dene area of the NWT with a constitution that would 'entrench native languages, along with English as official languages' (p. 9). A compromise was reached between the federal government and both territories in that they would accept French as an official language if the Aboriginal languages within their boundaries were also given official status. Thus, the official languages of the NWT now are English, French, Inuktitut, Dogrib, North and South Slavey, Chipewyan, Gwitch'in and Cree. The federal government would be responsible for costs of French services and provided $16 million to develop and promote Aboriginal languages (Task Force on Aboriginal Languages, 1986: 15).

Recent national studies on language in Aboriginal education

To return to Aboriginal education on the national level, two recent studies provide an overall picture of the numbers and characteristics of Aboriginal language programmes in schools in Canada. The most recent and the more comprehensive is a survey by the Canadian Education Association of all federal and band schools, and about 500 provincial schools (Kirkness & Bowman, 1992). Principals or other school officials completed a questionnaire on a range of topics related to Aboriginal education. In response to a question about mission statements or policy related to Aboriginal education, about 60% of the respondents said that they had one. Of these, 28.6% included the need for culturally relevant curricula and knowledge and 12.9% mentioned the need to teach the Aboriginal languages (Kirkness & Bowman, 1992: 30–2).

Questions on the survey about Aboriginal language programmes yielded data as follows:

Of the 458 schools in the sample, 158 (34.5%) reported that they taught a First Nations language. There were no differences across provinces.

As might be expected, band and federal schools taught such languages more often (. . . 86.9%); public schools taught First Nations languages less often (. . . 26.7%). (Kirkness & Bowman, 1992: 43–4)

In discussion of the findings of the survey, Kirkness and Bowman say of the Aboriginal languages data:

> . . . there seems to be a dearth of courses that use First Nations languages as the language of instruction, or which form part of an integrated system, fully responsive to the community's needs. An interesting exception to this statement was found in the schools of the Northwest Territories, in which a number of the respondents used Inuktitut as the language of instruction during the primary years. In these schools, English is gradually introduced as the instructional language as the students progress through the system. Generally speaking, schools enrolling higher percentages of First Nations students offered more programs, more courses and planned to develop these further. (Kirkness & Bowman, 1992: 56)

Although the sampling procedure and return rate of this survey certainly resulted in some existing Aboriginal language programmes not being represented in the figures, this material is the most complete and certainly the most recent. The Assembly of First Nations (1990) survey was directed at a rationalised sample of bands rather than at schools directly. However, valuable data on language programmes in schools were obtained. In line with Kirkness and Bowman's findings that schools with a high percentage of First Nations students had much higher numbers of language programmes, the AFN study data show proportionately more Aboriginal language programming available to the respondents.

In sum, there is a moderate amount of activity in Aboriginal language programming in schools for Aboriginal children, but the patterns of provision reinforce Churchill's (1986) findings that policies for indigenous groups are largely at the lower levels of his scale of policy development if most programmes are for the youngest children, only for a few years, inadequately funded, and if even the bilingual programmes are seen to be transitional to fluency in an official language. The great majority of programmes offer the Aboriginal languages as subject of instruction only. Divide and conquer has evidently been the strategy in majority efforts to force assimilation. Although there are many more programmes available now than there were in 1980, the current survey data would give the same impression as Clarke and MacKenzie got in their study of Aboriginal language programmes in 1980, namely that Aboriginal language programmes give only lip service to pluralist approaches and that they are actually assimilationist in intent. The status of Aboriginal peoples clearly is of central importance, but is all the denigration and racism going to be solved by decisions at the national level? In terms of language planning, virtually all the action has been at a corpus level (e.g. Burnaby, 1985) and very little at the status level. As for educational programmes for adults, literacy promotion, community language development, or the use of Aboriginal language in other spheres such as work or government, there is very little indeed. Although Aboriginal attention was strongly focused on education in the early 1970s and on Aboriginal languages in that context, the constitutional magnet in this country, among other things, has served to draw attention somewhat away from that currently.

Conclusions

A number of factors clearly influence the amount and kind of attention paid to various languages in Canada. One is voter strength. Francophone voters are a quarter of the federal voters and are mainly concentrated in one area. Immigrants who have not yet received Canadian citizenship cannot vote and those who speak little English or French are unlikely to vote. Those who do, tend to vote conservatively. The 'ethnic vote' has only recently been explicitly courted by political parties at the federal level. The federal government has justified some expenditures on language training for adult immigrants on the basis of a need for general citizenship training. What strength there might be in the Aboriginal vote is lost because they are in the majority in electoral areas in only a few places, especially the Northwest Territories. From this perspective, then, the Francophones are the only ones with a significant advantage.

A second factor is economics. Next to Ontario, Quebec is the most economically powerful province in the country. Quebec laws have gone a long way towards francisisation of the workplace although they have lost some large businesses to other provinces in the process; on the other hand, small and medium sized businesses have increased. The relative salaries of Francophones have improved considerably since the 1960s. With respect to immigrants, until 1991 the federal government has put its ESL/FSL money almost entirely into training for those explicitly recruited for their employment skills. Provinces have mostly funded those programmes with a more general intent. The economies of most Aboriginal communities are at Third World levels in a country with a First World national average. Supporting Aboriginal languages is not seen by many people as making much of a difference to these economic difficulties. It remains to be seen whether the Northwest Territories will be successful in making workplaces there more conducive to the use of Aboriginal languages.

A third factor is perception of need for language resources in the country. The focus on the French/English debate has drawn attention away from other languages in the country and their value. With national unity at stake, popular opinion tends to its old xenophobic view that people who speak languages other than English or French cannot be trusted in their commitment to this country. However, the new economy is much more international than before and resources in many languages are needed. Clearly, our language education and support policies are not in tune with this reality. Immigrant children are bombarded with official languages and subtly discouraged from maintaining and developing their first languages. Once these languages are subdued, the level of support in heritage language teaching is mainly insufficient to revive them to a workable level. We then use a lot of resources to teach 'modern' languages to a wide range of students. As for the Aboriginal languages, there is some public sympathy for them since they are unique to this country. Although the public is generally unaware of how endangered most of these languages are, it would be a matter of considerable international embarrassment for the country if these languages were permitted to disappear. However, it is a problem for Aboriginal peoples to decide where to put their energy and resources; their languages are at risk, but they also have drastic economic and social problems to deal with at the same time.

A fourth factor is people's sense of how to deal with language issues. Education and training are the most common solution. Meagre language classes in the first few grades of school are the best we have come up with for non-official and Aboriginal languages, and it is clear that these do not develop the hoped-for levels of fluency. Quebec, the federal government, and the immigrant experience have shown that adults and children can be persuaded to do a lot of second language learning, much of it at their own expense and on their own time, if it is expected that skills in that language will bring more economically and in terms of status. The question then is what can be done to create a climate more conducive to the fostering of other languages. The importance of legislation, programmes, and funding notwithstanding, real maintenance and development of French, immigrant languages, and Aboriginal languages will largely come about because of the valuing of and commitment to these languages on the part of individuals.

In the past 30 years, a great deal has been done in Canada in terms of language development and support. We have much to be proud of. However, in terms of racial and ethnic tolerance and its implications for language, the glass is still half empty at best.

Notes

1. Sincere thanks to Normand Labrie, Alister Cumming, Tom Ricento and Joan Speares for their careful reading of an earlier draft of this chapter. Any errors or omissions are entirely my own.

2. The census now permits respondents to report more than one ethnicity and more than one mother tongue.
3. These circumstances are substantially 'where numbers warrant' and where it is reasonable given the nature of the office.
4. Some would argue that the directions suggested by McManus in this quotation do not reflect entirely what happens in either of the countries in actual practice.
5. The succession of federal Acts has been the Technical Vocational Training Assistance Act of 1960, the Occupational Training for Adults Act of 1967, the National Training Act of 1982 and the Labour Force Development Strategy of 1989.
6. NGOs and school boards had been dealing with some of this through localised initiatives.
7. It is not clear on what basis this figure was arrived at.
8. Canada, unlike the US, has not conducted any significant amount of overseas language training and cultural orientation before this.
9. The federal government has recently reorganised its training programmes so that people on federal Unemployment Insurance and social assistance will no longer be barred from that training; indeed, they will be targeted as prime candidates.
10. This move was heralded by a major study conducted under Ontario government auspices (Ministry of Labour) on access to the trades and professions (Cumming, 1989). Considerable attention was paid to the role that language plays in creating barriers to professional accreditation.

References

ABBS, P. 1982, *English Within the Arts*. London: Hodder and Stoughton.

ADLAM, P.L. 1987, Language and identity: A sociolinguistic survey of the Indonesian speech community. MA thesis, Victoria University of Wellington.

African National Congress (ANC) 1992a, *African National Congress: Language Policy Considerations* (February 1992).

— 1992b, *African National Congress Policy Guidelines* (May 1992).

AGB/McNAIR 1992, *Survey of Demand for Bilingual and Immersion Education in Maori: A Report to the Ministry of Education*. Wellington.

ÀIPOLO, À. and HOLMES, J. 1990, The use of Tongan in New Zealand: Prospects for language maintenance. *Journal of Multilingual and Multicultural Development* 11 (6), 501–21.

ALEMAN, S.R. 1993, *Bilingual Education Act: Background and Reauthorization Issues*. Washington, DC: Congressional Research Service, The Library of Congress (25 January).

ALEXANDER, N. 1989, *Language Policy and National Unity in South Africa/Azania*. Cape Town: Buchu Books.

— 1991, The Nhlapo–Alexander proposal for the harmonisation of Nguni and Sotho languages in South Africa. *Language Projects Review* 5(4), 2–3.

ALLADINA, S. and EDWARDS, V. (eds) 1991, *Multilingualism in the British Isles*. Clevedon: Multilingual Matters.

Aotearoa Maori Tourism Federation, Inc. 1992, Notes supplied to Maori Language Commission concerning Kia Ora Campaign, May. Rotorua.

Argus, Angry words lead to S. Africa's own tower of Babel. *The Argus*, 20 September 1994.

ASHWORTH, M. 1988, *Blessed with Bilingual Brains: Education of Immigrant Children with English as a Second Language*. Vancouver: Pacific Educational Press.

— 1992, Views and visions. In B. BURNABY and A. CUMMING (eds) *Socio-political Aspects of ESL in Canada* (pp. 35–49). Toronto: OISE Press.

Assembly of First Nations 1990, *Towards Linguistic Justice for First Nations*. Ottawa: Education Secretariat, Assembly of First Nations.

ATKINS, J.D. 1992, Barbarous dialects should be blotted out. In J. CRAWFORD (ed.) *Language Loyalties: A Source Book on the Official English Controversy* (pp. 47–51). Chicago: The University of Chicago Press.

ATKINSON, A. 1992, *Non-English Speaking Background Students in New Zealand Schools*. Wellington: Data Management Section, Ministry of Education.

Australian Advisory Council on Languages and Multicultural Education (AACLAME) 1990, *The National Policy on Languages December 1987–March 1990*. Report to the Minister for Employment, Education and Training. Canberra: AACLAME.

Australian Institute of Multicultural Affairs (AIMA) 1980, *Review of Multicultural and Migrant Education*. Melbourne: AIMA.
— 1982, *Evaluation of Post-Arrival Education Programs and Services*. Melbourne: AIMA.
BAKER, C. 1985, *Aspects of Bilingualism in the British Isles*. Clevedon: Multilingual Matters.
— 1992, Bilingual education in Wales. In H. BAETENS BEARDSMORE (ed.) *European Models of Bilingual Education* (pp. 7–29). Clevedon: Multilingual Matters.
BAKER, K.E. and de KANTER, A.A. 1983, Federal policy and the effectiveness of bilingual education. In K.A. BAKER and A.A. de KANTER (eds) *Bilingual Education: A Reappraisal of Federal Policy* (pp. 33–86). Lexington, MA: Lexington.
BARNES, D. 1976, *From Communication to Curriculum*. Harmondsworth: Penguin.
BARRINGTON, J.M. and BEAGLEHOLE, T.H. 1974, *Maori Schools in a Changing Society*. Wellington: New Zealand Council for Educational Research.
BEATY, S. 1989, A new Official Languages Act for Canada – Its scope and implications. In P. PUPIER and J. WOEHRLING (eds) *Language and Law: Proceedings of the First Conference of the International Institute of Comparative Linguistic Law* (pp. 185–93). Montreal: Wilson and Lafleur.
BELFIORE, M.E. and HELLER, M. 1992, Cross-cultural interviews: Participation in decision-making. In B. BURNABY and A. CUMMING (eds) *Socio-political Aspects of ESL in Canada* (pp. 223–40). Toronto: OISE Press.
BENTON, N. 1981, *We Are All Mixed Up Now, Anyway: The Revitalization of Maori in a Small Community*. Paper given at SOL on the Horizon Symposium, University of California, Santa Cruz (8–11 July).
BENTON, R.A. 1979, *The Legal Status of the Maori Language: Current Reality and Future Prospects*. (Special report for the Minister of Maori Affairs). Wellington: Maori Research Unit, NZCER.
— 1981, *The Flight of the Amokura: Oceanic Languages and Formal Education in the South Pacific*. Wellington: NZCER.
— 1982, *Language Policy in New Zealand 1840–1982* (Te Wāhanga Māori Occasional Paper No. 9). Wellington: Te Wāhanga Māori, NZCER.
— 1984, Smoothing the pillow of a dying language: Official policy towards the Maori language in New Zealand since World War II. In A. GONZALEZ (ed.) *Panagani: Essays in Honour of Bonifacio P. Sibayan on his Sixty-Seventh Birthday* (pp. 24–39). Manila: Linguistic Society of the Philippines.
— 1991a, 'Tomorrow's Schools' and the revitalization of Maori: Stimulus or tranquilizer? In O. GARCIA (ed.) *Bilingual Education* (pp. 135–47). Amsterdam: John Benjamins.
— 1991b, *The Maori Language: Dying or Reviving?* (EWCA Working Paper 28). Honolulu: East West Center Association.
BLOOM, D. and GRENIER, G. 1992, Earnings of the French minority in Canada and the Spanish minority in the United States. In B. CHISWICK (ed.) *Immigration, Language, and Ethnicity: Canada and the United States* (pp. 373–410). Washington, DC: The AEI Press.
Board of Education, 1921, *The Teaching of English in England* (The Newbolt Report). London: HMSO.
BOLDT, M. 1993, *Surviving as Indians: The Challenge of Self-Government*. Toronto: The University of Toronto Press.

BOURDIEU, P. 1990, Artistic taste and cultural capital. In J.C. ALEXANDER and S. SEIDMAN (eds) *Culture and Society: Contemporary Debates* (pp. 205–15). Cambridge: Cambridge University Press.

BOURNE, J. 1990, *Moving into Mainstream*. London: NFER-Nelson.

BOYD, M. (1991) Gender, nativity, and literacy: Proficiency and training issues. In Statistics Canada, *Adult Literacy in Canada: Results of a National Study* (pp. 85–94). Ottawa: Minister of Industry, Science and Technology.

— (1992) Gender issues in immigration and language fluency. In B. CHISWICK (ed.) *Immigration, Language, and Ethnicity: Canada and the United States* (pp. 310–72). Washington, DC: The AEI Press.

BRITTON, J. 1970, *Language and Learning*. Harmondsworth: Penguin.

BROD, R. and HUBER, B.J. 1992, Foreign language enrollments in United States institutions of higher education. *ADFL Bulletin* 23 (3), (Fall 1990).

Bureau of the Census (US) 1990, *Census of Population, Social and Economic Characteristics, United States*. US Department of Commerce, Economics and Statistics Administration, CP-2-1.

— 1990, *Census of Population: General Population Characteristics, United States*. US Department of Commerce, Economics and Statistics Administration.

— 1993, *Statistical Abstract of the United States* (113th edition). US Department of Commerce, Economics and Statistics Administration.

BURNABY, B. (ed.) 1985, *Promoting Native Writing Systems in Canada*. Toronto: OISE Press.

— 1987, Language for native, ethnic, and recent immigrant groups: What's the difference? *TESL Canada Journal* 4 (2), 9–27.

— 1992a, Adult literacy issues in Canada. In R.B. KAPLAN (ed.) *Annual Review of Applied Linguistics* XII (pp. 156–71). Cambridge: Cambridge University Press.

— 1992b, Official language training for adult immigrants in Canada: Features and issues. In B. BURNABY and A. CUMMING (eds) *Socio-political Aspects of ESL in Canada* (pp. 3–34). Toronto: OISE Press.

— (forthcoming), ESL policy issues in Canada. To appear in T.K. RICENTO and B. BURNABY (eds) *Language and Politics in Canada and the U.S.: Myths and Realities*.

BURNABY, B. and BEAUJOT, R. 1986, *The Use of Aboriginal Languages in Canada: An Analysis of 1981 Census Data*. Ottawa: Social Trends Analysis Directorate and Native Citizens Directorate, Department of the Secretary of State.

BURNABY, B. and KIDD, R. 1988, *Inventory of English Language Training for Non-native Speakers of English at the Post-secondary Level in English-medium Institutions in Canada*. Toronto: TESL Canada Federation.

BURNABY, B., NICHOLS, J. and TOOHEY, K. 1980, *Northern Native Languages Project: Final Report*. Sioux Lookout: Northern Nishnawbe Education Council.

BURNABY, B., HOLT, M., STELTZER, N. and COLLINS, N. 1987, *The Settlement Language Training Program: An Assessment* (Report of behalf of the TESL Canada Federation). Ottawa: Employment and Immigration Canada.

CAIRNS, A. 1991, The Charter, interest groups, executive federalism, and constitutional reform. In D.E. SMITH, P. MacKINNON and J.C. COURTNEY (eds) *After Meech Lake: Lessons for the Future* (pp. 13–31). Saskatoon, Saskatchewan: Fifth House Publishers.

CAMPBELL, A.E. 1941, *Educating New Zealand*. Wellington: Department of Internal Affairs.

Canada Employment and Immigration Advisory Council 1991, *Immigrants and Language Training*. Ottawa: Canada Employment and Immigration.

Canadian Education Association 1991, *Heritage Language Programs in Canadian School Boards*. Toronto: Canadian Education Association.

— 1992, *French Immersion Today*, CEA Information Note. Toronto: Canadian Education Association.

CAZDEN, C. 1989, Richmond Road: A multilingual/multicultural primary school in Auckland, New Zealand. *Language and Education* 3, 143–66.

CHAFE, W. 1965, Corrected estimates regarding speakers of Indian languages. *International Journal of American Linguistics* 31, 345–6.

CHAMBERS, C. 1985, Practical suggestions for making Dene literacy functional. In B. BURNABY (ed.) *Promoting Native Writing Systems in Canada* (pp. 159–74). Toronto: OISE Press.

CHISMAN, F.P., WRIGLEY, H.S. and EWEN, D.T. 1993, *ESL and the American Dream*. Washington, DC: Southport Institute for Policy Analysis.

CHISWICK, B. and MILLER, P. 1992, Language in the immigrant labour market. In B. CHISWICK (ed.) *Immigration, Language, and Ethnicity: Canada and the United States* (pp. 229–96). Washington, DC: The AEI Press.

CHURCHILL, S. 1986, *The Education of Linguistic and Cultural Minorities in the OECD Countries*. Clevedon: Multilingual Matters.

CLARKE, S. and MacKENZIE, M. 1980, Education in the mother tongue: Tokenism versus cultural autonomy in Canadian Indian schools. *Canadian Journal of Anthropology* 1 (2), 205–17.

CLYNE, M. 1982, *Multilingual Australia: Resources – Needs – Policies*. Melbourne: River Seine Publications.

— 1991a, *Community Languages: The Australian Experience*. Melbourne: Cambridge University Press.

— 1991b, Australia's language policies: Are we going backwards? In A. LIDDICOAT (ed.) Language planning and language policy in Australia. *Australian Review of Applied Linguistics* Series S: 8, 3–22.

COBARRUBIAS, J. 1983, Ethical issues in status planning. In J. COBARRUBIAS and J.A. FISHMAN (eds) 1983, *Progress in Language Planning: International Perspectives* (pp. 41–85). Berlin: Mouton.

Commissioner of Official Languages (Canada) 1993, *Annual Report 1992*. Ottawa: Speaker of the House of Commons.

— 1994, *Annual Report 1993*. Ottawa: Office of the Commissioner of Official Languages.

CONKLIN, N.F. and LOURIE, M.A. 1983, *Host of Tongues: Language Communities in the United States*. New York: The Free Press.

COOPER, R.L. 1989, *Language Planning and Social Change*. New York: Cambridge University Press.

CORSON, D. 1990, *Language Policy Across the Curriculum*. Clevedon: Multilingual Matters.

— 1993, *Language, Minority Education and Gender: Linking Social Justice and Power*. Clevedon: Multilingual Matters and Toronto: Ontario Inst. for Studies in Education.

COUNCIL OF THE EUROPEAN COMMUNITY 1977, *The Education of the Children of Migrant Workers* (July 77/4861). Article 3.

CRANDALL, J. 1992, Adult literacy development. In W. GRABE (ed.) *Annual Review of Applied Linguistics* XII (pp. 86–104). New York: Cambridge University Press.

— 1993, Professionalism and professionalization of adult ESL literacy. *TESOL Quarterly* 27 (3), 497–515.

CRAWFORD, A. 1993, Tensions over translation. *Bua!* 8 (2), 18–20.

CRAWFORD, J. 1989, *Bilingual Education: History, Politics, Theory and Practice*. Trenton, NJ: Crane Publishing Co.

— 1992a, *Hold Your Tongue: Bilingualism and the Politics of 'English Only'*. Reading, MA: Addison-Wesley.

— (ed.) 1992b, *Language Loyalties: A Source Book on the Official English Controversy*. Chicago: The University of Chicago Press.

CROMBIE, W. and POUTNEY, C. 1994, Quality assurance and professional standards: Teaching English to speakers of other languages. Presentation to Annual Meeting of the Applied Linguistics Association of New Zealand, Victoria University of Wellington (May).

CUMMING, A. 1991, *Identification of Current Needs and Issues Related to the Delivery of Adult ESL Instruction in British Columbia*. Victoria, BC: British Columbia Ministry of International Business and Immigration.

CUMMING, A. and GIL, J. 1991, Learning ESL literacy among Indo-Canadian women. *Language, Culture and Curriculum* 4 (3), 181–200.

— 1992, Motivation or accessibility? Factors permitting Indo-Canadian women to pursue ESL literacy. In B. BURNABY and A. CUMMING (eds) *Socio-political Aspects of ESL in Canada* (pp. 241–52). Toronto: OISE Press.

CUMMING, A., HART, D., CORSON, D. and CUMMINS, J. 1993, *Provisions and Demands for ESL, ESD, and ALF Programs in Ontario Schools*. Toronto: Modern Language Centre, Ontario Institute for Studies in Education.

CUMMING, P.A. 1989, *Access!: Task Force on Access to Professions and Trades in Ontario*. Toronto: Ontario Ministry of Citizenship.

CUMMINS, J. and DANESI, M. 1990, *Heritage Languages: The Development and Denial of Canada's Linguistic Resources*. Toronto: Our Schools/Our Selves Education Foundation and Garamond Press.

CURTIS, L. 1993, Survey results. *Contact: Newsletter of the Association of Teachers of English as a Second Language of Ontario* 18 (2), 26–7.

D'ANGLEJAN, A. and DE KONINCK, Z. 1992, Educational policy for a culturally plural Quebec: An update. In B. BURNABY and A. CUMMING (eds) *Socio-political Aspects of ESL in Canada* (pp. 97–109). Toronto: OISE Press.

DASNOIS, A. 1994, Threat to peace if Afrikaans demoted. *The Argus*, 13 August 1994.

DEGENAAR, J. 1994, Taal is die psige se geluide: 'n gesprek met Johan Degenaar. *Die Suid-Afrikaan*, 48, 20.

Dene Nation and Métis Association of the NWT 1982, *Denendeh: Public Government for the People of the North*. Yellowknife: Dene Nation and Métis Association of the NWT.

Department of Education (NZ) 1988, *New Voices: Second Language Learning and Teaching*. Wellington.

Department of Education and Science (DES) 1975, *A Language for Life* (The Bullock Report). London: HMSO.

— 1984, *Mother Tongue Teaching in School and Community*. London: HMSO.

— 1985, *Education for All* (The Swann Report). London: HMSO.

— 1988, *Report of the Committee of Enquiry into the Teaching of English* (The Kingman Report). London: HMSO.

— 1990, *Modern Foreign Languages for Ages 11 to 16* (The Harris Report). London: HMSO.

Department of Employment, Education and Training (DEET) 1990, *The Language of Australia* ('Green Paper'), 2 Vols. Canberra: AGPS.
— 1991, *Australia's Language: The Australian Language and Literacy Policy*. 2 Vols. Canberra: AGPS.
Department of National Education 1994, *South Africa's New Language Policy: The Facts*. Pretoria: Department of National Education.
Department of Statistics (NZ) 1992, *1991 Census of Population and Dwellings: National Summary*. Wellington.
— 1993, *1991 Census of Population and Dwellings: New Zealand's Multicultural Society*. Wellington.
Department of the Secretary of State n.d., Official languages (a kit of information about official languages in the *Constitution Act* and the *Canadian Charter of Rights and Freedoms*). Ottawa: Department of the Secretary of State.
DES 1989, *English for Ages 5–16* (June, 1989). London: HMSO.
DESAI, Z. and TREW, R. 1992, Language rights in the draft Bill of Rights. Unpublished paper.
DEVINE, M. 1983, *Analysis of the Dene Language Information Review*. Yellowknife: Department of Information, Government of the Northwest Territories.
DOHERTY, N. 1992, Challenging systematic sexism in the National Language Training Program. In B. BURNABY and A. CUMMING (eds) *Socio-political Aspects of ESL in Canada* (pp. 67–76). Toronto: OISE Press.
DOYLE, J. 1994, High court lets English-only job rules stand. *San Francisco Chronicle*, 21 June.
DOYLE, R. and VISANO, L. 1987, *A Summary of Actions: A Summary Report of Report 1, 'A Time for Action' and Report 2 'A Program for Action'* (Access to health and social services for members of diverse cultural and racial groups.) Toronto: Social Planning Council of Metropolitan Toronto.
DRAPER, J.B. 1991, Foreign language enrollments in public secondary schools, fall 1989 and fall 1990. *American Council on the Teaching of Foreign Languages* (October).
DRAPER, J.B. and JIMENEZ, M. 1992, A chronology of the official English movement. In J. CRAWFORD (ed.) *Language Loyalties: A Source Book on the Official English Controversy* (pp. 89–94). Chicago: The University of Chicago Press.
EAGLETON, T. 1983, *Literary Theory – An Introduction*. Oxford: Blackwell.
Education Forum (NZ) 1994, *English in the New Zealand Curriculum: A Submission on the Draft*. Auckland.
Education Review Office (ERO) (NZ) 1993, *Annual Report 1 July 1992 to 30 June 1993*. Wellington: House of Representatives.
— 1994a, Students urged to become multilingual. Media release, 8 September. Wellington.
— 1994b, *Second Language Learning* (National Educational Evaluation Reports No. 6). Wellington.
— 1994c, *Annual Report 1 July 1992 to 30 June 1994*. Wellington: House of Representatives.
EDWARDS, J. 1993/94, Language policy and planning in Canada. *Annual Review of Applied Linguistics* 14, 126–36.
ELSON, N. 1992, The failure of tests: Language tests and post-secondary admissions of ESL students. In B. BURNABY and A. CUMMING (eds) *Socio-political Aspects of ESL in Canada* (pp. 110–21). Toronto: OISE Press.

Employment and Immigration Canada 1992, *Annual Report 1991–1992*. Ottawa: Minister of Supply and Services Canada.

— 1993a, *A New Immigration Program for the 1990s*. Ottawa: Minister of Supply and Services Canada.

— 1993b, *Language Instruction for Newcomers to Canada (LINC): Guide for Applicants*. Ottawa: Employment and Immigration Canada.

English Academy (SA) 1992, *Language Clauses in the Constitution: A Submission to Codesa by the English Academy of Southern Africa, 24 February 1992*. (Reissued with notes 16 June 1993). Johannesburg: English Academy of Southern Africa.

— 1994, *Analysis of Language Clauses in the Constitution: English Academy of Southern Africa*. Johannesburg: English Academy of Southern Africa.

EPSTEIN, N. 1977, *Language, Ethnicity, and the Schools: Policy Alternatives for Bilingual–Bicultural Education*. Washington, DC: Institute for Educational Leadership.

EUROPEAN COMMUNITY (EC) 1977, *The Education of the Children of Migrant Workers:* EEC Directive 77/4861. Brussels: EC.

EUROPEAN COMMUNITIES 1984, *Report on the Implementation of Directive 77/486/EEC on the Education of Children of Migrant Workers: COM (84) Final*. Brussels, 10 February.

FERNANDEZ, R.R. 1987, Legislation, regulation, and litigation: The origins and evolution of public policy on bilingual education in the United States. In W.A. VanHORNE (ed.) *Ethnicity and Language* (pp. 90–123). Milwaukee: The University of Wisconsin System, Institute on Race and Ethnicity.

FILLMORE, L.W. 1986, Teaching Bilingual Learners. In M. WITTROCK (ed.) *Handbook on Research in Teaching*. New York: Macillan.

— 1992, Against our best interest: The attempt to sabotage bilingual education. In J. CRAWFORD (ed.) *Language Loyalties: A Source Book on the Official English Controversy* (pp. 367–76). Chicago: The University of Chicago Press.

FISHER, J. 1990, The Queen v Blackie Hohua, 23–24 July, 1990. Oral Ruling of Fisher, J. The High Court of New Zealand, Rotorua Registry.

FISHMAN, J.A. 1971, The sociology of language: An interdisciplinary social science approach to language in society. In J. FISHMAN (ed.) *Advances in the Sociology of Language*. The Hague: Mouton.

— 1991, *Reversing Language Shift: Theoretical and Empirical Foundations of Assistance to Threatened Languages*. Clevedon: Multilingual Matters.

FISHMAN, J.A. *et al.* 1966, *Language Loyalty in the United States*. The Hague: Mouton Press.

FLAHERTY, L. and WOODS, D. 1992, Immigrant/refugee children in Canadian schools: Educational issues, political dilemmas. In B. BURNABY and A. CUMMING (eds) *Socio-political Aspects of ESL in Canada* (pp. 182–92). Toronto: OISE Press.

FLERAS, A. and ELLIOTT, J.L. 1992, *The Challenge of Diversity: Multiculturalism in Canada*. Scarborough, Ontario: Nelson Canada.

FOSTER, M. 1982, Canada's indigenous languages: Present and future. *Language and Society* 7, 7–16.

FOUCHER, P. 1985, *Constitutional Language Rights of Official-Language Minorities in Canada: A Study of the Legislation of the Provinces and Territories Respecting Education Rights of Official-Language Minorities and Compliance with Section 23 of the Canadian Charter of Rights and Freedoms*. Ottawa: Supply and Services Canada.

GERBER, L. 1984, Community characteristics and out-migration from Canadian Indian reserves: Path analyses. *Canadian Review of Sociology and Anthropology* 21 (2), 145–65.

GOLDSTEIN, T. 1993, Working with learners in LINC programs: Asking ourselves some questions. *Contact: Newsletter of the Association of Teachers of English as a Second Language of Ontario* 18 (2), 12–13.

GONZALES, R. 1972, *I am Joaquin: An Epic Poem.* New York: Bantam Books, Inc.

GRESKO, J. 1986, Creating little dominions within the Dominion: Early Catholic Indian schools in Saskatchewan and British Columbia. In J. BARMAN, Y. HÉRBERT and D. McCASKILL (eds) *Indian Education in Canada, Volume I: The Legacy* (pp. 88–109). Vancouver: University of British Columbia Press.

HAGEY, N.J., LAROCQUE, G. and McBRIDE, C. 1989, *Highlights of Aboriginal Conditions 1981–2001: Part III, Economic Conditions.* Qualitative Analysis and Socio-demographic Research Working Paper Series 89-3. Ottawa: Finance and Professional Services, Indian and Northern Affairs Canada.

HALEY, A. 1976, *Roots.* Garden City, NY: Doubleday.

HAWKINS, F. 1989, *Critical Years in Immigration: Canada and Australia Compared.* Kingston and Montreal: McGill-Queen's University Press.

HAWTHORN, H.B. (ed.) 1967, *A Survey of the Contemporary Indians of Canada: Economic Political and Educational Needs and Policies*, Volume II. Ottawa: Indian Affairs Branch.

HEATH, S.B. 1981, English in our language heritage. In C.A. FERGUSON and S.B. HEATH (eds) *Language in the U.S.A.* (pp. 6–20). Cambridge: Cambridge University Press.

HEUGH, K. 1993, Not so straight for English. *Bua!* 8 (2), 31.

HOLMES, E. 1911, *What Is and What Might Be.* London: Constable.

HOLMES, J., ROBERTS, M., VERIVAKI, M. and ÀIPOLO, À. 1993, Language maintenance and shift in three New Zealand speech communities. *Applied Linguistics* 14 (1), 1–23.

HORNBERGER, N. 1989, Continua of biliteracy. *Review of Educational Research* 9 (3), 271–96.

HOURD, M. 1949, *The Education of the Poetic Spirit.* London: Heinemann.

HOWARD, P. 1983, History of the use of Dene languages in education in the Northwest Territories. *Canadian Journal of Native Education* 10 (2), 1–18.

Immigration Canada 1991, *Annual Report to Parliament: Immigration Plan for 1991–1995: Year Two November 1991.* Ottawa: Minister of Supply and Services Canada.

— 1992a, *Annual Report to Parliament: Immigration Plan for 1991–1995: Year Three 1993.* Ottawa: Minister of Supply and Services Canada.

— 1992b, *New Immigrant Language Training Policy.* Ottawa: Employment and Immigration Canada.

— 1992c, *Questions and Answers of the New Immigrant Language Training Policy.* Ottawa: Employment and Immigration Canada.

— 1993a, *Immigration Consultations 1993: The Federal Immigrant Integration Strategy in 1993: A Progress Report.* Ottawa: Employment and Immigration Canada.

— 1993b, *A New Immigration Program for the 1990s: Background.* Ottawa: Employment and Immigration Canada.

Indian Afffairs and Northern Development 1980, *Indian Conditions: A Survey.* Ottawa: Indian Affairs and Northern Development.

INGRAM, D. 1977, Language teaching in the pluralist society – the challenge for teacher educators. *Babel* 13 (1), 9–18.

— 1979, The case for a national language policy in Australia. *Babel* 15 (1), 3–16.
— 1990, *The Teaching of Languages and Cultures in Queensland: Towards a Language in Education Policy for Queensland Schools*. Queensland Education Department, Centre for Applied Linguistics and Language, Griffiths University, Australia.
INMAN, J. 1994, The politics of English in the US. *TESOL Matters* 4 (1) 11.
JOHNSTONE, R. 1994, *The Impact of Current Developments to Support the Gaelic Language: Review of Research*. London: Centre for Information on Language Teaching and Research.
JONES, S. 1992, Literacy in a second language: Results from a survey of everyday life. In B. BURNABY and A. CUMMING (eds) *Socio-political Aspects of ESL in Canada* (pp. 203–20). Toronto: OISE Press.
KAPLAN, R.B. 1994. Language policy and planning in New Zealand. In W. GRABE (ed.) *Annual Review of Applied Linguistics* Vol. 14 (pp. 156–76). New York: Cambridge University Press.
KELLAS, B. 1994, Press statement on behalf of Omnichek Division. *Bua!* 9 (1), 2.
KIRKNESS, V. and BOWMAN, S.H. 1992, *First Nations and Schools: Triumphs and Struggles*. Toronto: Canadian Education Association/Association canadienne d'éducation.
KLASSEN, C. 1987, Language and literacy learning: The adult immigrant's account. Unpublished MA thesis. Toronto: University of Toronto.
KLASSEN, C. and BURNABY, B. 1993 'Those who know': Views on literacy among adult immigrants in Canada. *TESOL Quarterly* 27 (3), 377–98.
KLOSS, H. 1940, *Volksgruppenrecht in den Vereinigten Staaten,* Vol. 1, Essen.
— 1969, *Research Possibilities on Group Bilingualism: A Report*. Quebec, International Center for Research on Bilingualism, cited in J. COBARRUBIAS and J.A. FISHMAN (eds) 1983, *Progress in Language Planning: International Perspectives*. Berlin: Mouton.
— 1977, *The American Bilingual Tradition*. Rowley, MA: Newbury House.
KÖRNBLUM, H. and GARSHICK, F. 1992, *Directory of Professional Preparation Programs TESOL in the United States 1992–1994*. Washington, DC: TESOL.
KROON, S. and VALLEN, T. 1994, Multilingualism and education: An overview of the Dutch language and education policy towards ethnic minorities. *Current Issues in Language Society* 1 (2).
KUNTZE, M. 1993, Language rights for deaf children. *TESOL Matters* (3) 2, 15.
LABRIE, N. 1992, The role of pressure groups in the change of the status of French in Québec since 1960. In U. AMMON and M. HELLINGER (eds) *Status Change of Languages* (pp. 17–43). Berlin and New York: De Gruyter Verlag.
LAMBERT, W.E. and TUCKER, G.R. 1972, *Bilingual Education of Children: The St. Lambert Experiment*. Rowley, MA: Newbury House.
LANE, H. 1992, *The Mask of Benevolence: Disabling the Deaf Community*. New York: Alfred A. Knopf.
— 1993, *Looking Back: A Reader on the History of Deaf Communities and their Sign Languages*. Hamburg: Signum Press.
LEALAND, G. 1990, *Attitudes to Acceptable Standards of Language (Swearing and Blasphemy) on New Zealand Radio and Television*. Wellington: Broadcasting Standards Authority.
LEAP, W.L. 1981, American Indian languages. In C.A. FERGUSON and S.B. HEATH (eds) *Language in the U.S.A.* (pp. 116–44). Cambridge: Cambridge University Press.

LEIBOWITZ, A.H. 1969, English literacy: Legal sanction for discrimination. *Notre Dame Lawyer* 25 (1), 7–66.
— 1971, Educational policy and political acceptance: The imposition of English as the language of instruction in American schools. *ERIC* No. ED 047 321.
— 1974, *Language as a Means of Social Control*. Paper presented at the 6th World Congress of Sociology, University of Toronto, Toronto, Canada (August).
— 1982, *Federal Recognition of the Rights of Minority Language Groups*. Rosslyn, VA: InterAmerica Research Associates, Inc.
— 1984, The official character of language in the United States: Literacy requirements for citizenship, and entrance requirements into American life. *Aztlan* 15 (1), 25–70.
LINGUISTIC MINORITIES PROJECT 1985, *The Other Languages of England*. London: Routledge, Kegan & Paul.
LO BIANCO, J. 1987, *National Policy on Languages*. Commonwealth Department of Education, Canberra: AGPS.
— 1991, A review of some of the achievements of the National Policy on Languages. In A. LIDDICOAT (ed.) Language planning and language policy in Australia. *Australian Review of Applied Linguistics* Series S: 8.
LYONS, J.J. 1992, Secretary Bennett versus equal educational opportunity. In J. CRAWFORD (ed.) *Language Loyalties: A Source Book on the Official English Controversy* (pp. 363–6). Chicago: The University of Chicago Press.
MacDONALD, C. 1991, *The Threshold Project Report*. Pretoria: Human Sciences Research Council.
MACIAS, R. 1979, Language choice and human rights in the United States. In J.E. ALATIS and G.R. TUCKER (eds) *Language in Public Life* (pp. 86–101). Washington, DC: Georgetown University Press.
— 1982, U.S. language-in-education policy: Issues in the schooling of language minorities. In R.B. KAPLAN (ed.) *Annual Review of Applied Linguistics 1981* (pp. 144–60). Rowley, MA: Newbury House.
— 1990, Cauldron-boil & bubble: United States language policy towards indigenous language groups during the nineteenth century. Unpublished manuscript, University of Southern California.
MAKONI, S. 1993, The futility of being held captive by language policy issues in applied linguistics: An argument for implementation. *Per Linguam* 9 (2), 12–21.
MALAKOFF, M. and HAKUTA, K. 1990, History of language minority education in the United States. In A.M. PADILLA, H.H. FAIRCHILD and C.M. VALADEZ (eds) *Bilingual Education: Issues and Strategies* (pp. 27–43). Newbury Park: Sage Publications.
Maori Language Commission 1994a, Press release on *Evening Post* article of 26 May, issued 27 May. Wellington.
— 1994b, Blueprint for a languages policy: New Zealand Public Service (Document released by the Commission, May). Wellington.
Market Research Africa (MRA) 1994, *Critical Mass Survey*. Johannesburg: Market Research Africa.
MARTEL, A. 1991, *Official Language Minority Education Rights in Canada: From Instruction to Management*. Ottawa: Office of the Commissioner of Official Languages.
MAY, S. 1991, Making the difference for minority children: The development of an holistic language policy at Richmond Road School, Auckland, New Zealand. *Language, Culture and Curriculum* 4, 201–17.
— 1994a, *Making Multicultural Education Work*. Clevedon: Multilingual Matters.

— 1994b, School-based language policy reform: A New Zealand example. In A. BLACKLEDGE (ed.), *Teaching Bilingual Children* (pp. 19–41). Stoke-on-Trent: Trentham Books.

McANDREW, M. 1991, *L'enseignement des langues d'origines à l'école publique en Ontario et au Québec (1977–1980): Politiques et enjeux*. Les publications de la faculté des sciences de l'éducation, Université de Montréal.

McDONNELL, P.J. 1994, Prop. 187 turns up heat in U.S. immigration debate. *Los Angeles Times*, 10 August, A1.

McGECHAN, J. 1991, Judgement in the 'Broadcasting Assetts Case'. High Court of New Zealand, Wellington, May 1991.

McKAY, S.L. and WEINSTEIN-SHR, G. 1993, English literacy in the U.S.: National policies, personal consequences. *TESOL Quarterly* 27 (3), 399–419.

McKAY, S.L. and WONG, S.C. 1988, *Language Diversity: Problem or Resource*. Boston, MA: Heinle & Heinle.

McMANUS, W. 1992, Commentary on part three. In B. CHISWICK (ed.) *Immigration, Language, and Ethnicity: Canada and the United States* (pp. 299–302). Washington, DC: The AEI Press.

McNEILL, R. 1994, Damned if they do and damned if they don't. *Sunday Times*, 7 August 1994.

McPHERSON, J. 1994, *Making Changes: Action Research for Developing Maori Language Policies in Mainstream Schools*. Wellington: NZCER.

McPHERSON, J. and CORSON, D. 1989, *LPAC: Language Policy Across the Curriculum, Eight Case Studies of School-Based Policy Development*. Palmerston North: Department of Education, Massey University.

MEANGER, S. 1989, Adolescent Gujurati Indians in New Zealand: Their socialisation and education. MA thesis in education, Victoria University of Wellington.

MINER, S. (forthcoming), Legal implications of the official English declaration. To appear in T.K. RICENTO and B. BURNABY (eds), *Language and Politics in the U.S. and Canada: Myths and Realities*.

Ministry of Education (NZ) 1964–94, *Education Statistics of New Zealand*. Wellington.

— 1987, Maori Language Act. Wellington: Government Printer.

— 1990, Education Amendment Act. Wellington: Government Printer.

— 1992, *Draft Syllabus for Schools: English, Forms 6 and 7*. Wellington.

— 1993a, Conclusions drawn from analysis of submissions received in response to discussion document *Aotearea: Speaking for Ourselves*. Unpublished document issued by Merus Cochrane, Senior Manager, Learning and Evaluation Policy, to Dr Richard Benton in response to a request under the Official Information Act, 10 June.

— 1993b, *Nga Tikanga Tekau o Te Tatai mo te Akoranga Māori 1993/1994*. Wellington.

— 1993c, *Education for the Twenty-first Century*. Wellington: Learning Media.

— 1993d, *The New Zealand Curriculum Framework / Te Anga Matauranga o Aotearoa*. Wellington.

— 1994a, *Ngā Haeata Mātauranga* (Ministry of Education Annual Report 1993/4 and Strategic Direction for Maori Education 1994/5). Wellington: Ministry of Education.

— 1994b, *Blueprint for a languages policy: New Zealand Public Service*. (Document released by the Commission, May.) Wellington.

MOLESKY, J. 1988, Understanding the American linguistic mosaic: A historical overview of language maintenance and language shift. In S.L. McKAY and S.C. WONG (eds) *Language Diversity: Problem or Resource* (pp. 29–68). Boston, MA: Heinle & Heinle.

MULLARD, C. 1984, *Anti-Racist Education: The Three O's*. Coventry: NAME.

MURRAY, J. and MORRISON, C. 1984, *Bilingual Primary Education in the Western Isles Scotland*. Scotland: Acair.

National Education Policy Investigation (NEPI) 1992a, *Language*. Cape Town: Oxford University Press/National Education Coordination Committee.

— 1992b, *The Framework Report*. Cape Town: Oxford University Press/National Education Coordination Committee.

National Indian Brotherhood 1972, *Indian Control of Indian Education*. Ottawa: National Indian Brotherhood.

New Zealand 1974, *Maori Affairs Amendment Act*. Wellington: Government Printer.

New Zealand Qualifications Authority 1991, Minutes of the Maori Caucus Meeting held on Tuesday 7 May 1991. Wellington.

New Zealand Tourist Industry Federation, Inc. 1992, *Kia Ora: Welcome . . . the New Zealand Way*. (Notes for potential sponsors of the Kia Ora Campaign.) Wellington.

NOBLE, K.B. 1994. California immigration measure faces rocky legal path. *New York Times*, 11 November, A17.

Office de la langue française, Université du Québec à Chicoutimi 1994, *Les actes du colloque sur la problématique de l'aménagement linguistique*. Québec: Gouvernement du Québec.

Office of the Commissioner of Official Languages 1992, *Our Two Official Languages Over Time*, revised edn. Ottawa: Office of the Commissioner of Official Languages.

Ontario Council of Agencies Serving Immigrants 1993, *Report on the Findings of the OCASI LINC Questionnaire*. Toronto: Ontario Council of Agencies Serving Immigrants.

OZOLINS, U. 1993, *The Politics of Language in Australia*. New York: Cambridge University Press.

PADILLA, A.M. 1990, Bilingual education: Issues and perspectives. In A.M. PADILLA, H.H. FAIRCHILD and C.M. VALADEZ (eds) *Bilingual Education: Issues and Strategies* (pp. 15–26). Newbury Park: Sage Publications.

PAQUETTE, J. 1986, *Aboriginal Self-Government and Education in Canada*. Background Paper Number 10, Aboriginal Peoples and Constitutional Reform. Kingston, Ontario: Institute of Intergovernmental Relations, Queen's University.

PAULSTON, C.B. 1985, *Linguistic Consequences of Ethnicity and Nationalism in Multilingual Settings*. Paper delivered at the Conference on the Educational Policies and the Minority Social Groups' Experts Meeting, OECD Headquarters, Paris (16–18 January).

— 1988, *International Perspectives on Multilingualism and Language Policies*. Paper given at Conference on Language and Ethnicity, Baku, Azerbaijan (19–23 June).

— 1990, *Language Revival: The Case of Irish*. Paper given at the Conference on Ethnic and Linguistic Minorities and the State: Problems and Solutions, University of Limerick (4–7 June).

PEAT, MARWICK and PARTNERS and CHURCHILL, S. 1987, *Evaluation of the Official Languages in Education Program: Final Report*. Ottawa: Peat, Marwick and Partners.

PEDDIE, R.A. 1991, *One, Two, or Many?: The Development and Implementation of Languages Policy in New Zealand*. Auckland: University of Auckland.

— 1993, *From Policy to Practice: The Implementation of Languages Policies in Victoria, Australia, and New Zealand*. Auckland: Centre for Continuing Education, University of New Zealand.

PENDAKUR, R. 1992, Labour market segmentation theories and the place of immigrants speaking neither English nor French in Canada. In B. BURNABY and A. CUMMING (eds) *Socio-political Aspects of ESL in Canada* (pp. 160–81). Toronto: OISE Press.

PERROW, C. 1986, *Complex Organizations: A Critical Essay* (3rd edn). New York: Random House.

PLANLangPol Committee (Aust) 1983, *A National Language Policy for Australia.* Sydney: PLANLangPol Committee.

RAMIREZ, J.D., YUEN, S.D. and RAMEY, D.R. 1991, *Final Report: Longitudinal Study of Structured Immersion Strategy, Early-Exit, and Late-Exit Transitional Bilingual Education Programs for Language-Minority Children.* San Mateo, CA: Aguirre International.

REHYNER, J. 1992, Policies toward American Indian languages: A historical sketch. In J. CRAWFORD (ed.) *Language Loyalties: A Source Book on the Official English Controversy* (pp. 41–7). Chicago: The University of Chicago Press.

REICHMAN, A. 1993a, The invisible witness. Unpuplished paper presented at the Conference on *Teaching Translators and Interpreters: New Perspectives*, organised by the Department of Linguistics at the University of South Africa in March 1993.

— 1993b, Who is the witness? *Language Projects Review* 8 (1), 4–7.

REIMERS, D. and TROPER, H. 1992, Canadian and American immigration policy since 1945. In B. CHISWICK (ed.) *Immigration, Language, and Ethnicity: Canada and the United States* (pp. 15–54). Washington, DC: The AEI Press.

RESNICK, M.C. 1993, ESL and language planning in Puerto Rican education. *TESOL Quarterly* 27 (2), 259–73.

Review of Post-Arrival Programs and Services to Migrants 1978, *Migrant Services and Programs: Report of the Review of Post-Arrival Programs and Services for Migrants (The Galbally Report).* Canberra: AGPS.

RICENTO, T.K. 1988, The framers knew best. *TESOL Newsletter* 22 (2), 1–5.

— 1991, Sociopolitical concerns: Planning for action. *TESOL Matters* 1 (4), 6.

— (forthcoming), Partitioning by language: Whose rights are threatened? To appear in T.K. RICENTO and B. BURNABY (eds) *Language and Politics in the U.S. and Canada: Myths and Realities.*

RICHARDSON, J. 1979, Judgement of the Court of Appeal in the Case of Te Ringa Mangu Mihaka v. Police, 25 October. Wellington.

ROBERTS, M. 1990, Language maintenance and shift and issues of language maintenance education in a section of the Chinese community in Wellington. MA thesis, Victoria University of Wellington.

ROBERTS, S. 1993, *Who We Are.* New York: Random House.

ROCKHILL, K. and TOMIC, P. 1992, *Accessing ESL: An Exploration into the Effects of Institutionalized Racism and Sexism in Shaping the Lives of Latin American Immigrant and Refugee Women in Metropolitan Toronto.* Toronto: Department of Adult Education, Ontario Institute for Studies in Education.

Royal Commission on Bilingualism and Biculturalism 1967, *Report of the Royal Commission on Bilingualism and Biculturalism: General Introduction and Book I, The Official Languages.* Ottawa: The Queen's Printer.

Royal Commission on Education 1962, Report of the Commission on Education in New Zealand (Sir George Currie, Chairman). Wellington: Government Printer.

RUHLEN, M. 1987, Voices from the past. *Natural History* 96 (3), 6–11.

RUIZ, R. 1994, Language policy and planning in the United States. In W. GRABE (ed.) *Annual Review of Applied Linguistics* (pp. 111–25). New York: Cambridge University Press.

SAMPSON, G. 1921, *English for the English*. Cambridge: Cambridge University Press.

SAOUAB, A. 1993, *Canadian Multiculturalism*. Ottawa: Library of Parliament, Research Branch, Supply and Services Canada.

SCHLOSSMAN, S.L. 1983, Is there an American tradition of bilingual education? German in the public elementary schools, 1840–1919. *American Journal of Education* 91, 139–86 (February).

Senate Standing Committee on Education and the Arts (Aust) 1982–83, *Reference: The Development and Implementation of a Co-ordinated Language Policy for Australia, Evidence and Submissions*.

— 1984, *A National Language Policy* (ANLP). Canberra: AGPS.

SEWARD, S. and McDADE, K. 1988, *Immigrant Women in Canada: A Policy Perspective*. Ottawa: Canadian Advisory Council on the Status of Women.

SMITH, G.H. 1990, The politics of reforming Maori education: The transforming potential of Kura Kaupapa Maori. In H. LAUDER and C. WYLIE (eds) *Towards Successful Schools*. London: Falmer Press.

— 1992, *Tane-nui-a-Rangi's Legacy: Propping up the Sky*. Paper presented at Second AARE/NZARE Joint Conference, Deakin University, Geelong, Victoria (Nov.).

SMITH, L. 1993, eRhini Siyafunda. *Bua!* 8 (4), 10f.

SMITH, L. 1994a, State of the Nation's Education. (Address to Rotary Club of Wellington Central, 15 February.) Speech notes supplied by the Office of the Minister of Education. Wellington.

— 1994b. Speech notes for launch of draft Chinese and Spanish curriculum statements, 10 May. (Interoffice memorandum supplied by Office of the Minister of Education). Wellington.

South African Institute of Race Relations (SAIRR) 1992, *Race Relations Survey: 1991/92*. Johannesburg: South African Institute of Race Rations.

STARKEY, B. 1993, LINC in London. *Contact: Newsletter of the Association of Teachers of English as a Second Language of Ontario* 18 (2), 27–8.

State Board of Education: Ministerial Advisory Committee on Multicultural and Migrant Education 1985, *The Place of Language Other Than English in Victorian Schools*. Report to the Minister for Education, Melbourne.

Statistics Canada 1991a, *Adult Literacy in Canada: Results of a National Study*. Ottawa: Minister of Industry, Science and Technology.

— 1991b, *Canada's Aboriginal Population by Census Subdivisions and Census Metropolitan Areas*, Catalogue number 94-326. Ottawa: Statistics Canada.

— 1992a, *Mother Tongue: The Nation*, Catalogue number 93-313. Ottawa: Statistics Canada.

— 1992b, *Immigration and Citizenship: The Nation*, Catalogue number 93-316. Ottawa: Statistics Canada.

— 1993a, *Ethnic Origin: The Nation*, Catalogue number 93-316. Ottawa: Statistics Canada.

— 1993b, *Language Retention and Transfer: Dimensions*, Catalogue number 94-319. Ottawa: Statistics Canada.

— 1993c, *Population Estimates by First Official Language Spoken: Dimensions*, Catalogue number 94-320. Ottawa: Statistics Canada.

— 1993d, *Language, Tradition, Health, Lifestyle and Social Issues*, Catalogue number 89-533. Ottawa: Statistics Canada.

— 1994, *Schooling, Work and Related Activities, Income, Expenses and Mobility*, Catalogue number 89-534. Ottawa: Statistics Canada.

STEINBERG, C. 1992, Delivering the ABE goods. *Language Projects Review* 7 (4), 20–2.

STOFFEL, H.-P. 1982, Language maintenance and language shift of the Serbo-Croatian language in a New Zealand Dalmatian community. In R. SUSSEX (ed.) *The Slavic Languages in Emigré Communities* (pp. 121–39). Carbondale: Linguistic Research.

STREET, B. 1984, *Literacy in Theory and Practice*. Cambridge: Cambridge University Press.

SURUS, S. 1985, The Polish language in Auckland, New Zealand. PhD Thesis, University of Auckland.

TAMURA, E.H. 1993, The English-only effort, the anti-Japanese campaign, and language acquisition in the education of Japanese Americans in Hawaii, 1915–40. *History of Education Quarterly* 33 (1), 37–58.

Task Force on Aboriginal Languages (Canada) 1986, *The Report of the Task Force on Aboriginal Languages*. Yellowknife: Government of the Northwest Territories.

TAYLOR, M. and HEGARTY, S. 1985, *The Best of Both Worlds*. Windsor, NFER-Nelson.

THOMPSON, L. 1994, The Cleveland Study: A study of bilingual children in a nursery school. *Journal of Multilingual and Multicultural Development* 15 (2 & 3), 253–68.

— 1995a, Ecolinguistic biographies. In W. FASE, K. JASPAERT and S. KROON (eds) *The State of Minority Language: International Perspectives on Survival and Decline* (pp. 249–66). Lisse: Swets & Zeitlinger.

— 1995b, Bilingual children entering preschool education: An analysis of social and linguistic processes. PhD thesis, University of Durham, UK.

TITLESTAD, P.J.H. 1994a, The Pan-South African Language Board: Discussion paper for proposed conference: 27/28 May 1994. Unpublished paper.

— 1994b, The Language Clauses, Language Planning in South Africa and English. Unpublished paper delivered at the Association of University Teachers of English Conference (July 1994).

TOLLEFSON, J.E. 1991, *Planning Language: Planning Inequality: Language Policy in the Community*. Harlow: Longman.

— 1991, *Planning Language, Planning Inequality*. London: Longman.

TOOHEY, K. 1982, Northern Native Canadian Second Language Education: A Case Study of Fort Albany, Ontario. Unpublished doctoral dissertation. University of Toronto.

— 1992, We teach English as a second language to bilingual students. In B. BURNABY and A. CUMMING (eds) *Socio-political Aspects of ESL in Canada* (pp. 87–96). Toronto: OISE Press.

TREW, R. 1991, *Research Goals: Translation and Interpretation*. Johannesburg: NEPI.

TROYNA, B. 1991, Underachievers or underrated? The experience of pupils of South Asian origin in a secondary school. *British Educational Research Journal* 17, 361–76.

TSCHANTZ, L. 1980, *Native Languages and Government Policy: An Historical Examination*. London, Ontario: Centre for Research and Teaching of Canadian Native Languages, The University of Western Ontario.

TUCKER, G.R. 1994, TESOL and NAFTA: Challenges for the 21st century. *TESOL Matters* 4 (1).

US Department of Education 1992, *Conditions of Bilingual Education in the Nation*. Washington, DC: Tables C and E.

US Immigration and Naturalization Service 1991, *Statistical Yearbook*, 1991 Annual.

University of Auckland 1993, *Annual Review 1992–93*. Auckland: Information and Public Affairs Office, The University of Auckland.

VAILLANCOURT, F. 1992, An economic perspective on language and public policy in Canada and the United States. In B. CHISWICK (ed.) *Immigration, Language, and Ethnicity: Canada and the United States* (pp. 179–228). Washington, DC: The AEI Press.

WAGGONER, D. 1992, Indian nations task force calls for maintenance of languages and cultures. In D. WAGGONER (ed) *Numbers and Needs: Ethnic and Linguistic Minorities in the United States*. Vol. 2, no. 1 (p. 3). Washington, DC.

— 1993, Navajo dominant among Native American languages spoken by 331,600. In D. WAGGONER (ed) *Numbers and Needs: Ethnic and Linguistic Minorities in the United States*. Vol. 3, no. 5 (p. 2). Washington, DC.

Waitangi Tribunal 1986, *Finding of the Waitangi Tribunal Relating to Te Reo Māori and a Claim Lodged by Huirangi Waikerepuru and Nga Kaiwhakapumau i te Reo Incorporated Society*. Wellington: Government Printer.

WAITE, J. 1992a, *Aoteareo: Speaking for Ourselves Part A: The Overview*. Wellington: Learning Media.

— 1992b, *Aoteareo: Speaking for Ourselves Part B: The Issues*. Wellington: Learning Media.

WARDHAUGH, R. 1983, *Language and Nationhood: The Canadian Experience*. Vancouver: New Star Books.

WEBSTER, C. 1993, RAU moots opening up to more English speakers. *The Argus*, 11 December 1993.

WEINSTEIN, B. 1980, Language planning in francophone Africa. *Language Problems and Language Planning* 4 (1), 55–77.

WEST, N. 1994, Language row in regional govt. *Sunday Times Cape Metro*, 7 August 1994.

WILEY, T.G. 1990–91, Disembedding Chicano literacy. *School of Education Journal*, California State University, Stanislaus, 8 (1), 49–54.

— 1993, *Issues of Access, Participation and Transition in Adult ESL*. Working paper. Washington, DC: Southport Institute for Policy Analysis.

WILLIAMS, S.S. 1987, The politics of the black child's language: A study of attitudes in school and society. In W.A. VanHORNE (ed.) *Ethnicity and Language*, Vol. VI, Ethnicity and Public Policy Series (pp. 160–88). Milwaukee, WI: The University of Wisconsin System Institute on Race and Ethnicity.

WINN-BELL OLSEN, R.E. 1993, *Enrollment Statistics of Limited English Proficient Students in the United States (1985–1993)*. Washington, DC: TESOL.

WOODS, G. 1994, Needy pupils suffer from funding cuts. *The Evening Post* (Wellington), 5 October, p. 1.

WRIGLEY, H.S., CHISMAN, F.P. and EWEN, D.T. 1993, *Sparks of Excellence: Program Realities and Promising Practices in Adult ESL*. Washington, DC: Southport Institute for Policy Analysis.

Index

Languages